# Understanding Research in
# Second Language Learning

CAMBRIDGE LANGUAGE TEACHING LIBRARY
A series covering central issues in language teaching and learning, by authors
who have expert knowledge in their field.

# Understanding Research in Second Language Learning

## A teacher's guide to statistics and research design

### *James Dean Brown*

University of Hawaii at Manoa

Originally published in The New Directions
in Language Teaching Series, edited by
Howard B. Altman and Peter Strevens

**CAMBRIDGE**
UNIVERSITY PRESS

# CAMBRIDGE
UNIVERSITY PRESS

32 Avenue of the Americas, New York, NY 10013–2473, USA

Cambridge University Press is part of the University of Cambridge.

It furthers the University's mission by disseminating knowledge in the pursuit of education, learning and research at the highest international levels of excellence.

www.cambridge.org
Information on this title: www.cambridge.org/9780521315517

First published 1988
19th printing 2013

Printed in the United States of America

A catalog record for this publication is available from the British Library.

Library of Congress Cataloging in Publication Data

Brown, James Dean.
Understanding research in second language learning : a teacher's guide to statistics and research design / James Dean Brown.
p. cm – (New directions in language teaching)
Bibliography: p.
Includes index.
ISBN 978-0-521-31551-7(pbk.)
1. Second Language acquisition – Statistical methods. I. Title II. Series.
P118.2.B76                1988                87-35487
                                                CIP

418'.0021–dc19

ISBN 978-0-521-31551-7 paperback

# Contents

# Foreword

Since the early 1960s, as newly touted methodologies for second language teaching have waxed and waned, and as professional concerns have shifted from one area to another, the field of second language teaching has begun to develop a scientific basis. A discipline whose insights have historically been largely anecdotal and idiosyncratic, second language teaching has been shaped over the past two decades by attempts to validate statistically the claims of classroom practitioners and the postulates of ivory-tower theoreticians. This change in focus has yielded two results, one positive and one negative. On the positive side, the advent of research into language teaching and language learning processes has vastly increased our professional knowledge about "what works" in what settings under what conditions. But the flip side of the coin is that the "insights" yielded by a research study have become incomprehensible to many – perhaps most – classroom practitioners.

James Dean Brown's thesis is that research in second language teaching and learning *can* be made understandable to classroom practitioners; indeed, that second language teachers have a professional obligation to make sense of research results that have potential impact on the classroom. In order to evaluate research studies for their applicability, second language teachers need to be conversant with the language and procedures of statistical research.

Brown's book is designed to make the reader "research literate," and it achieves that aim skillfully. Second language teaching, like any other discipline, can progress only to the extent that the gap between theory and practice can be continually narrowed. The narrowing of this gap in second language teaching presupposes a common language and a common understanding between those who teach, at any level, and those who carry out research on teaching. That common language today is statistics.

Brown writes with warmth as well as understanding of the terror that statistical data can strike into the hearts of classroom practitioners. The illustrations he uses from actual research studies make the book extremely practical. In my view this book is "must reading" for second language teachers and researchers alike.

Howard B. Altman
*University of Louisville*
*Louisville, Kentucky*

# Preface

Why do so many language teachers draw back in terror when confronted with large doses of numbers, tables, and statistics? Why do other teachers accept at face value or reject without reason studies that contain numerical data? There may be some justification for these reactions by those of us who are in the humanities. We live in a world full of "statistics," wherein numbers come at us from all angles to cajole, convince, sell, and even fool us.

Certainly, statistics can be used to lie (see Huff and Geis 1954). But that they necessarily do lie is another thing entirely. Doubting statistics or even scoffing at them seems to be common among language teachers and may be due, in large part, to the natural human fear of the unknown. Once this fear is conquered, statistics become not a threat, but a useful tool – a tool that can help reduce the uncertainty in the world around us and help us to interpret otherwise bewildering events.

Lado (1961:4) felt that language among all human tools was "the most complex." It seems that he was right. Think of the many categories into which we subdivide language: vocabulary, structure, pronunciation, meaning, register, body language, and so forth. And think of the many subdisciplines that have sprung up: psycholinguistics, sociolinguistics, language acquisition, language testing, language teaching methodology, and so on.

It seems ambitious to attempt to study such a complex field as language. Yet study it we must. So we each choose some subdivision of language within some subdiscipline and use it or study it in our own way. Specialization, then, is one way of reducing the confusion that is caused by the magnitude of what we do not know about language and language teaching.

Increasingly, this confusion is also being attacked by members of the language fields through statistical studies. Such studies are used to describe and summarize the language behavior of individuals or groups. They explore trends and interactions among the many aspects of language learning and teaching and investigate relationships among various aspects of language learning or differences in the overall language behavior of groups. In short, although such studies are not the end-all answer to the problems of understanding language, they systematically reduce our confusion from bewildering to manageable proportions.

I am not suggesting that everyone should do statistical studies. That takes a considerable amount of time and effort to do well and requires a different approach from the one offered in this book. I am suggesting, however, that there is an increasing need to be able to *read and understand* statistical studies. As such, this book is oriented toward the consumer, rather than the producer, of statistical studies. Like all research, or all printed material, for that matter, statistical studies should be read critically with knowledge and understanding.

To help you critically interpret the increasing amount of statistical research in our field, this book has the following overall goals:

1. *To explain the basic terms of the statistics field.* Every field has its jargon, which makes that field inaccessible to "outsiders." To make you an "insider," this book clearly identifies and defines such terms in the text and lists them at the end of each chapter.
2. *To explain how tables, charts, and graphs work.* A great deal of information is often included in tables, charts, and graphs, which are, after all, powerful and visually attractive ways to present a lot of information in a small space. But many people skip right over them because they seem indecipherable. One purpose of this book is to make visual representations accessible to you. Visual representations can be an important aid to understanding both the strengths and weaknesses of a statistical study. For this reason, examples will be carefully explained.
3. *To explain the appropriate use of research designs.* Regardless of how powerful the statistics are in a study or how impressive the tables and graphs may be, a faulty research design can render a study meaningless. Every study must have a plan, called the research design. How will the people be selected to participate in the study? What tests or materials will be used? How will these be administered and scored? How will the results be analyzed? These are some of the questions addressed by a sound research design. Since such issues are important in understanding statistical research, they are stressed throughout the book.
4. *To explain the logic that underlies the use of statistics.* A clear overall logic governs the proper use of statistics. Like any form of logic, this one must proceed step by step without skipping over any of the building blocks of the argument. This is the topic of Chapter 9, and it is covered repeatedly in Chapters 10–12 so you can learn to detect errors, or steps that have been skipped, in the statistical logic for different types of studies.
5. *To explain an approach to critiquing and assessing statistical research.* It is safe to assume that *no* statistical study is perfect. Each study is carried out, after all, by human beings. The approaches

explained in Chapters 5 and 9 are designed to help you judge the relative merits of a given study. This probably does not mean that you will begin to accept or reject studies as you encounter them but, rather, that you will be able to judge their quality and, therefore, their relative value to you and your teaching situation.

In sum, not all teachers have enough time and interest to do statistical research. But I believe it is irresponsible to ignore such research just because you do not have the relatively simple tools for understanding it. The reading and interpretation of such studies is not only informative, but can even be useful in your teaching and career. So join me in exploring the notions that underlie statistical research on second language learning so that you can then better understand the insights such research has to offer.

James Dean Brown

# 1 What is research?

Many different approaches to studying the learning and teaching of language are currently being applied, all of which can be useful. The purpose of this chapter is not to argue that one approach, statistical research, is the only type of investigation that is worth doing or even the best type. Rather, this chapter explains how statistical research fits into the framework of different types of research and describes the characteristics of sound statistical research. By touching on these topics, I hope to clarify the value of statistical research within the larger framework of the various types of research.

## Types of research

For the purposes of discussion, I will categorize research into two arbitrary divisions: (1) secondary research and (2) primary research. Primary research, as defined here, differs from secondary research in that it is derived from the primary sources of information (e.g., a group of students who are learning a language), rather than from secondary sources (e.g., books about students who are learning a language). Of course, these categories are not mutually exclusive and, perhaps, not even all inclusive, but they help reduce the seeming confusion of different types of studies that are found in the literature.

### Secondary research

Secondary research, that is, research based on sources that are one step removed from the original information, is probably the type with which language teachers are most familiar. During our training at the undergraduate or graduate levels, most of us constantly use the library to search for the written wisdom of scholars in our chosen field. The requirement is usually that we synthesize ideas from these secondary sources into some coherent statement called a term paper. With a little luck, such a statement provides some useful ideas about the topic at hand. A number of people in the language teaching field continue this process in their professional lives and develop creative and productive insights into a given topic.

Such research may result from straightforward insights into how a language is learned. It may synthesize the life's work of a single important person or analyze aspects of theoretical movements. Some researchers may prefer to do historical studies, such as tracing the development of a language or exploring the evolution of methods of teaching languages. Still others may draw on a wider range of resources and experiences to do research. The name that immediately comes to mind in this context is Noam Chomsky. Chomsky undoubtedly drew on a wide range of experiences – including a background in mathematics and philosophy – and combined these experiences with his knowledge of linguistics. The result, generative-transformational grammar, created a new framework for understanding language. Regardless of whether you view this framework as "true," it has undoubtedly been controversial, productive, and useful for all language-related fields. The point is that insights can play an important part in research, either leading to useful syntheses of existing knowledge or resulting from such syntheses.

Clearly, then, secondary research can and does take many interesting and useful forms. Primary research, as we will see next, is another way of discerning patterns in the world around us.

## Primary research

Recall that primary research differs from secondary research in that it is derived from the primary source (e.g., students who are learning a language), rather than from secondary sources (e.g., books about students who are learning a language). Hence, it has the advantage of being closer to the primary source of information. Primary research itself seems to fall into two subdivisions: (a) case studies and (b) what I will call statistical studies.

### CASE STUDIES

Research that uses the *case study* approach centers on one or a few individuals. These studies are usually *longitudinal*, that is, they follow the individual or individuals over a relatively long period while tracing some aspect of language development. There are many examples of this approach in the literature, especially in relation to the acquisition of a second language. One example that immediately comes to mind is that of Leopold (summarized in Leopold 1978). Leopold watched and studied his child, Hildegard, over a long period. His comments and the insights he gained from this activity proved to be useful for research into how a second language is acquired. The case study approach, then, can be a helpful and productive one for the language teaching field.

## STATISTICAL STUDIES

Statistical studies deal with group phenomena as well as individual behavior. They are often *cross-sectional,* that is, they consider a group of people as a cross section of possible behaviors at a particular point or at several distinct points in time. In addition, statistical analyses are used in this approach to estimate the probability, or likelihood, that the results did not occur by chance alone. Statistical studies seem to fall into two additional subcategories: surveys and experimental studies.

Typically, *survey studies* focus on a group's attitudes, opinions, and/or characteristics. They often take the form of a questionnaire that is sent out to a group of people. Most of us have probably been involved in such research, perhaps in a course evaluation during our university training. The advantage of this type of research is that substantial amounts of information can be collected in a relatively short time. One disadvantage, however, is that the number of people who respond to a questionnaire, especially when it is mailed, is often low. A low response rate raises the question of how much the information obtained actually represents the attitudes, opinions, and characteristics of the group as a whole. Nevertheless, if carefully controlled, this approach can aid in discerning patterns in large amounts of information.

*Experimental studies* are defined here as a whole range of different possible studies that investigate the language behavior of groups under controlled conditions. For instance, a researcher might wish to study the effects of being male or female on students' performance on a language placement test. Such research might involve administering the test to the students, then separating their scores into two groups according to gender, and finally studying the similarities and differences in behavior between the two groups. Another type of experimental study might examine the relationship between students' scores on a language aptitude test and their actual performance in language classes, as measured by course grades. Experimental studies, then, can be varied in the types of questions being asked; they should, nonetheless, conform to the principles and strategies described in the remainder of this book.

# Characteristics of statistical research

Within the broad category of primary research, statistical research (including both survey and experimental studies) will be the focus of the rest of this book. So let's turn immediately to the essential characteristics of statistical research. Although these characteristics may overlap with those of other types of research, they seem to form a unique combination in statistical research. You should keep these characteristics in mind

3

when reading a statistical study because if one or more of these qualities is missing, an alarm bell should sound in your mind about the adequacy of that study. Statistical research, then, should be (1) systematic, (2) logical, (3) tangible, (4) replicable, and (5) reductive (Tuckman 1978, 10–12). Let's see how each of these works.

## Systematic research

A statistical study has a clear structure with definite procedural rules that must be followed. There are rules for designing a study, for controlling different problems that may adversely influence the study, and for choosing and applying statistics. It is these rules that make such studies systematic and that can help you read, interpret, and critique statistical studies. It is these rules that underlie the logic of statistical research. This is not to say that other types of research are not systematic but, rather, to emphasize the particular system underlying statistical studies.

## Logical research

The rules and procedures underlying these studies form a straightforward, logical pattern – a step-by-step progression of building blocks, each of which is necessary for the logic to succeed. If the procedures are violated, one or more building blocks may be missing and the logic will break down like any other logic. The overall procedures that are important to both the systematic and logical qualities of statistical research will be covered in much more depth in Chapter 9. The rules particular to each family of statistical study will be explained in Chapters 10 – 12.

## Tangible research

Statistical research is tangible in that it is based on the collection and manipulation of *data* from the real world. The set of data may take the form of test scores, students' ranks on course grades, the number of language learners who have certain characteristics, and so on. The types of data are numerous, but they are all similar in that they must be *quantifiable*, that is, each datum must be a number that represents some well-defined quantity, rank, or category. It is the manipulation, or processing, of these data that links the study to the real world. Again, this is not to argue that other types of research (e.g., studies based on qualitative data) are any less tangible but, rather, to point out the tangible nature of the particular form of primary research called statistical research.

### Replicable research

Statistical research should also be replicable. The researcher's proper presentation and explanation of the system, logic, data collection, and data manipulation in a study should make it possible for the reader to *replicate* the study (do it again under the same conditions). If the study is clearly explained and if you can understand it well enough to replicate it, then you probably have enough information to judge its quality. Perhaps then, you should consider replicability to be one of the first yardsticks when critiquing any such article.

### Reductive research

As I argued in the Preface, statistical research can reduce the confusion of facts that language and language teaching frequently present, sometimes on a daily basis. Through doing or reading such studies, you may discover new patterns in the facts. Or through these investigations and the eventual agreement among many researchers, general patterns and relationships may emerge that clarify the field as a whole. It is these qualities or potentialities that make statistical research (like other types of research) reductive.

## The value of statistical research

We have seen, then, that statistical research is neither the only kind of research in our field nor even necessarily the best type. It is, however, one type of research that is useful. Surveys and experimental studies can provide important information on individuals and groups that is not available in other types of research. Moreover, they are (1) systematically structured with definite procedural rules, (2) based on a step-by-step logical pattern, (3) based on tangible, quantifiable information, called data, (4) replicable in that it should be possible to do them again, and (5) reductive in that they can help form patterns in the seeming confusion of facts that surround us.

At this point, it should be clear that there are some distinct advantages to the characteristics of statistical research, especially when they are taken together. If so, it would seem logical that you should give such studies a chance, so you can judge their system and logic to determine whether their conclusions are relevant, warranted, and valuable to you and your teaching situation. After all, aside from a researcher's sense of responsibility, it is only through informed readers that the quality of such studies can be assured.

## Terms

| | | |
|---|---|---|
| case study | primary research | statistical studies |
| cross-sectional | quantifiable | survey studies |
| data | reductive | systematic |
| experimental studies | replicable | tangible |
| logical | replicate | |
| longitudinal | secondary research | |

## Review questions

1. How do secondary and primary research differ? How are they similar?
2. What are the differences between survey and experimental studies, as defined here?
3. What are some of the reasons for doing statistical research on the learning and teaching of languages?
4. Why is it important that a statistical study be replicable?
5. Is statistical research the only type of research that is tangible (based on reality)? Why or why not?

## Application

A. At this point, you might find it interesting to look through a few language teaching journals (such as the *Modern Language Journal*, *Language Learning*, and *TESOL Quarterly*). In glancing through the articles, try to decide what type of research each article represents. How many of the articles are statistical?
B. Find a statistical study in a language teaching journal. Look through the study. How much do you understand? Look for a section in the study headed Method or sometimes Subjects, Methods, and Procedures. Do you think, based on common sense, that there is enough information in the study to replicate it?

# 2 Variables

In this chapter, we will look at how variables fit into research, how they differ from constructs, how they are operationalized by researchers, how they are categorized in studies, how the categories relate to each other, and what you must consider in looking at the different types of variables. With an understanding of how clearly variables must be identified and thought out by the researcher, you should gain a healthy respect for the complexity of the research done within our field. But first, what are variables?

## How variables fit into research

### Variables

In the simplest terms, a *variable* is something that may vary, or differ. For instance, a person's proficiency in Spanish as a foreign language may differ over time as the person learns more and more Spanish. Likewise, we can expect individuals to vary in their respective levels of proficiency in Spanish at any given time. Thus, proficiency in Spanish can be considered a variable because it may change over time or differ among individuals. As a tentative definition for statistical research in our field, we will view variables as human characteristics or abilities that differ over time or among individuals. More on this in a few paragraphs.

Most variables that differ over time also vary among individuals, but the reverse is not necessarily true. Consider, for instance, sex (the state of being male or female) – a variable that is often considered in studies. Certainly, there are observable and interesting differences among individuals on this variable. Yet few people would expect to see numerous changes in this variable over time. Most individuals remain male or female throughout their lifetimes.

There are many other variables of interest in language studies – far too many to list here. However, a few examples might help. Some of the many variables that differ both over time and among individuals include language proficiency, motivation, self-esteem, and health. A few that typically vary only among individuals are sex, nationality, first-language background, intelligence, and language ability (although there is some controversy about whether the last two can vary over time as well). In some way, most statistical research in our field is concerned with identifying the variables that are important to language learning and discovering how these variables affect the teaching of languages.

## Variables versus constructs

It is important to distinguish variables from the underlying constructs that they represent. Both variables and constructs vary over time or among individuals. However, a *variable* is essentially what we can observe or quantify of the human characteristics or abilities involved, whereas a *construct* is the actual characteristic or ability that it represents in human beings. Proficiency in Spanish, for example, is something that goes on inside an individual's head. As such, it is difficult to observe and may be different from the indirect observations that a researcher makes (perhaps, scores on a Spanish proficiency test) to define this variable. The construct proficiency in Spanish (the actual human ability) could be represented by the variable test scores in Spanish proficiency (what we can observe and measure of the construct in question). However, it is important to remember that the scores are not the ability but a reflection of the ability. Like any reflection, it may be a blurred or distorted representation of the actual construct in question.

## Operationalization

The *operationalization* of variables is a researcher's chance to explain how each variable is being defined with respect to the construct in question. Such an *operational definition* should take a variable out of the realm of theory and plant it squarely in concrete reality. Basically, it must be a definition that is based on observable, testable, or quantifiable characteristics. Moreover, an operational definition must be unique, or exclusive; the definition must *not* also fit other possible constructs.

Let us return to the construct labeled language proficiency. This construct is hard to define, yet we all have a feel for what it is. Part of the problem is that it is an abstraction and is not directly observable because it has no tangible referent in reality. Of course, most researchers in language studies would probably limit the scope of this construct by using the compounding and adjectival processes that are so productive in English. Thus, we would probably encounter a much more narrowly labeled abstraction in any real study, such as a construct called "overall proficiency in English as a foreign language." One step, then, in looking at a researcher's operational definition of variables is to evaluate whether the construct has been labeled with adequate precision, both theoretically and practically.

Although the construct in this example may now seem narrower in scope, it should be clear to any language teacher that "overall proficiency in English as a foreign language" is still a broad abstraction. To bring this construct down to earth and form a variable, the investigator might choose to define it as follows: overall proficiency in English as a foreign language as measured by the *Test of English as a Foreign Language* (TOEFL). We now have an observable and quantifiable definition of what the researcher means by this construct. The author has described, in concrete terms, what is meant by the variable. This is an operational definition of the variable.

It is the reader's responsibility to make sure that the variable, as operationalized, makes sense – that it logically represents the construct involved. To this end, several questions might be posed:

1. Is the construct labeled with sufficient precision?
2. Does the operational definition of the variable adequately describe the characteristics of the construct in question? (Is the TOEFL an adequate test of overall proficiency in English as a foreign language?)
3. Could the definition describe any other constructs? (Does the TOEFL test other things?)

The importance of thinking about a study at this level should not be underestimated. The results of a study cannot be logical if the variables are defined poorly or erroneously. The variables are, after all, the focus and center of any study.

## Different types of variables

In addition to knowing how constructs are operationalized as variables, it is important to understand how such variables are classified and, indeed, manipulated by researchers in their quest to improve our understanding of what goes on in the language classroom. To that end, let us turn to the five different classifications of variables within statistical language studies: dependent, independent, moderator, control, and intervening variables. These five types of variables are distinguished primarily by the relationships that the researcher hypothesizes to exist among them. Hence, a variable that functions as a dependent variable in one study may be an independent variable in another. And you should keep in mind that a variable is an observed or quantified representation of a construct, which is the actual underlying human characteristic or ability in question.

## Dependent variables

A *dependent variable* is observed to determine what effect, if any, the other types of variables may have on it. In other words, it is the variable of focus – the central variable – on which other variables will act if there is any relationship. Thus, a dependent variable cannot be identified in isolation. It makes sense only in the context of the other variables in the study. Perhaps an example will help clarify what all of this means.

Let's assume that a researcher, Dr. Moreno, has a test called the Spanish Language Proficiency (SLAP) test, which she is using to operationalize the construct, proficiency in Spanish, in her students. Let's further assume that Dr. Moreno wants to find out what effect studying Spanish for one year has on the SLAP scores of the students in her program. The SLAP test is administered at the beginning of the year before any Spanish is studied. After the students study Spanish for one year, the test is administered again. What is the variable of focus or dependent variable in this case? Is it the number of students? The number of test administrations? The length of time Spanish was studied? Or is it the students' scores on the SLAP test?

All these items are potential variables. But the key to figuring out which is the dependent variable is to ask which variable is being measured to determine the effect of other variables on it. In this case, proficiency in Spanish is being measured with the SLAP test to determine the effect of one year of instruction on students' scores. What is being measured to determine how instruction affects it? Proficiency in Spanish. What is the dependent variable? Proficiency in Spanish.

One other point should be made clear. A researcher may use more than one dependent variable in a given study. In the example, the investigator might also be interested in determining the effect, if any, that one year of studying Spanish has on the students' overall aptitude for languages. If a test of overall language aptitude – let us call it the OLA battery – were administered along with the SLAP test, there would be two variables of focus, and the study would be investigating the effect of one year of Spanish study on two dependent variables.

## Independent variables

*Independent variables* are variables selected by the researcher to determine their effect on or relationship with the dependent variable. In the foregoing example, Dr. Moreno selected one year of Spanish study as the independent variable. Do you see how this is a variable? When the SLAP test was first administered, the students had completed no Spanish study. The second SLAP test was administered to the same students after they had completed one year of study. Thus, the investigator systematically varied, or manipulated, the independent variable (whether the students had studied one year of Spanish) to determine its effect on the dependent variable (proficiency in Spanish).

In short, an independent variable is one that is selected and systematically manipulated by the researcher to determine whether, or the degree to which, it has any effect on the dependent variable. As with dependent variables, the researcher may include more than one independent variable in a given study.

## Moderator variables

A *moderator variable* is a special type of independent variable that the investigator has chosen to determine how, if at all, the relationship between the independent and dependent variables is affected, or modified, by the moderator variable. For instance, Dr. Moreno might have decided to study the degree to which the relationship between one year of Spanish study (the independent variable) and proficiency in Spanish (the dependent variable) differed for males and females (the moderator variable). Although it may turn out that there are no differences between the sexes in terms of the relationship between the length of Spanish study and proficiency, the fact that the researcher included sex as a possible moderator makes it a moderator variable. Thus, the essential difference between independent and moderator variables lies in how the researcher views each in the study. For independent variables, the concern is with their direct relationship to the dependent variable, whereas for moderator variables, the concern is with their effect on that relationship.

## Control variables

It is virtually impossible to include all the potential variables in each study. As a result, the researcher must attempt to control, or neutralize, all other extraneous variables that are likely to have an effect on the relationship between the independent, dependent, and moderator variables. *Control variables*, then, are those that the investigator has chosen to keep constant, neutralize, or otherwise eliminate so that they will not have an effect on the study. As will be discussed in Chapter 4, there are numerous ways to deal with variables that are extraneous to a given study.

The simplest method is to eliminate a given variable and thereby control for it. For instance, Dr. Moreno would probably want to control for any effect due to previous background in Spanish. After all, if there is a relationship between the length of Spanish study (the independent variable) and proficiency in Spanish (the dependent variable), which may or may not be different for the two sexes (the moderator variable), this

11

issue would only be muddied by having students with two years of high school Spanish lumped together with some who had spent time in Mexico and others who had no previous background in the language. The researcher must decide how to control for such variables. One simple approach would be to interview all the subjects, find out about their background in Spanish, and eliminate those with any such background from the study. In this way, Dr. Moreno would neutralize, or eliminate, any extraneous effects (caused by the previous study of Spanish) on the relationship under investigation.

### Intervening variables

Perhaps the most difficult type of variable to understand is the intervening variable. Intervening variables are hard to grasp because they are abstract, theoretical labels applied to the relationship or process that links the independent and dependent variables. They are constructs that may explain the relationship between independent and dependent variables but are not directly observable themselves. In the example, Dr. Moreno is basically interested in how one year of Spanish study is related to proficiency in Spanish. But what is she really interested in conceptually? It seems that the real question is whether the language is being learned. The sticky problem is that language learning is a process that goes on inside the students' heads and is not directly observable. Nevertheless, it is a conceptual link between one year of Spanish study (the independent variable) and proficiency in Spanish (the dependent variable) in this example. Thus, an *intervening variable* is an abstract, theoretical label that can be applied to the relationship or process that links the independent and dependent variables. *Language learning* is one possible way of stating or labeling the intervening variable in this example. But perhaps there are other ways of labeling the relationship as well (e.g., "exposure to language" or "teacher effectiveness"). Thus, we must always be careful of intervening variables because they are only labels – applied from the researcher's point of view – and they may artificially color the way we interpret the results of a study.

## The relationship among variables

To understand the different types of variables better, let's turn first to how variables interrelate in general terms and then look at a few examples.

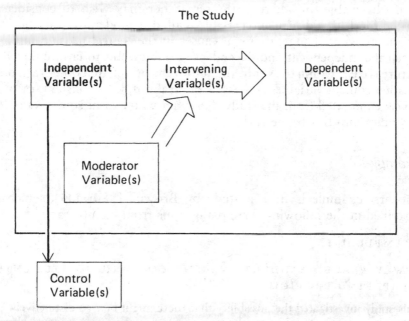

The Study

*Figure 2.1 Relationship among variables*

## General interrelationship

One attempt to express the relationship between the various types of variables is found in the model shown in Figure 2.1. In looking at this figure, recall that there are five types of variables (dependent, independent, moderator, control, and intervening) and that the researcher determines which variables fall into each category when designing the study. Note also that all five types may not be included in all studies and that there may be more than one variable of each type that is included.

In Figure 2.1, you will notice that the central relationship within the study is between the independent variable chosen by the researcher and the dependent one. The arrows are meant to indicate the direction of focus in the researcher's thinking and design of the study, rather than any causal or temporal relationship. Thus, they indicate that the variable of overall focus is the dependent variable. A study is initially designed to determine the effect of the independent variable on the dependent variable. The intervening variable serves to label the relationship or process that links the independent and dependent variables but is not

13

itself observable. In addition, the researcher may wish to consider a special kind of independent variable, called a moderator variable, to determine what change, if any, it causes in the central relationship between the independent and dependent variables. But to ensure that the picture is clear within the study, the author may think that other variables – called control variables – must be neutralized, kept constant, or otherwise eliminated from the study. Now, let us try to fit some examples of studies into this framework.

## Examples

The first example is from a study by Brown (1980: 111), which is described in the following three paragraphs from the abstract:

EXAMPLE I.I

NEWLY PLACED STUDENTS VERSUS CONTINUING STUDENTS: COMPARING PROFICIENCY

This study investigated the possibility that there might be two distinctively different student populations within some ESL classrooms: 1) students placed directly into a course (Placed Ss) and 2) those who are continuing from lower-level courses (Continuing Ss). During three successive quarters (Fall, Winter and Spring 1978) at UCLA, proficiency data were gathered on Placed and Continuing Ss in English 33C (advanced ESL).

The 33C level was chosen because it was suspected that any differences in proficiency would be greatest at the advanced levels. The Placed Ss ($N = 201$) had been placed in English 33C by the UCLA ESL Placement Examination (ESLPE). The Continuing Ss ($N = 118$) had needed and successfully completed at least one prerequisite ESL course before entering English 33C.

Three measures of proficiency were used to compare the two types of student: the students' course grades, their scores on the departmental final examination and their acceptable-answer scores on a 50 item cloze test.

Notice that the answers have been supplied in Figure 2.2. Let's start with the dependent variables. Figure 2.2 indicates that there were three dependent variables: course grades, results of the final examination, and scores on the cloze test. These dependent variables were observed so that the effect of the chosen independent variable (whether students were placed directly into the course or came from the previous level) on those measures could be determined. The intervening variable could be labeled *placement differences* (or numerous other labels). Notice, however, that this label is not applied in the abstract (or in the study itself). Often the intervening variable will not be labeled in a study. Thus, you are free to think about and label the relationship in any way logical to you.

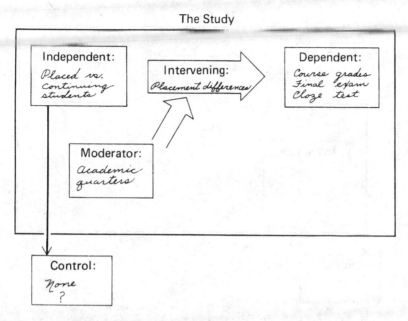

The Study

Independent:
*Placed vs.
continuing
students*

Intervening:
*Placement differences*

Dependent:
*Course grades
Final exam
Cloze test*

Moderator:
*Academic
quarters*

Control:
*None
?*

*Figure 2.2   Variables in Brown's study*

Having successfully identified the dependent, independent, and intervening variables, let us turn to the moderator variable. In this case, the researcher chose to investigate each quarter (Fall, Winter, and Spring 1978) separately. He was checking to see if the relationship between the independent variable and the dependent variables was moderated by different academic quarters. It turns out that it was not, but it was worth checking.

What about control variables? I have put none in the diagram because there were none in the study. Nevertheless, some variables should perhaps have been controlled. Consider variables like sex, the academic status (graduate or undergraduate) of the students, and the students' native language backgrounds. Do you think that these potential variables might have made a difference in the relationship between the independent and dependent variables? In fact, these variables were described in the Subjects section of the study, which is a common practice in language studies. But is that description enough? Should these variables have been controlled in the study? And is the fact that they were not a serious flaw in the research? These are all important questions to ask when reading such a study.

The Study

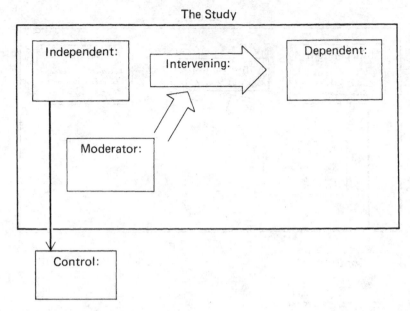

*Figure 2.3    Variables in Braun's study*

EXAMPLE I.2

In this example, you will be left to your own devices:

Hans Braun wanted to find out whether there was any link between intelligence and proficiency in German as a foreign language. So he set up a study that included a nonverbal IQ test and a German proficiency test. He administered both on the same day to the 200 third-year students of German at his college. He also wanted to discover whether sex and age had any effect on the relationship between intelligence and proficiency in German. Furthermore, he was deeply concerned that any effect of the students' previous travel in Germany should not interfere with the interpretation of the results.

Please fill in the boxes in Figure 2.3 before reading further.

Let's compare answers. It is difficult to decide here whether intelligence or proficiency in German is the dependent variable. In such a case, the author's intent or focus can help you determine which is the dependent variable and which is the independent one. In this study, the researcher's primary interest would probably be German proficiency. After all, it is his German students who are under investigation. So the dependent variable is the German proficiency test. Furthermore, Braun is interested in the relationship between intelligence scores and scores on the German proficiency test. Because of the researcher's focus, then, intelligence scores must be the independent variable.

The intervening variable is also problematic in this example because it is not labeled in the abstract. Again, you are free to think of it in any logical way you choose. Could it be labeled the language/intelligence factor or, perhaps, the unitary learning factor? Or maybe we should wait to concern ourselves with it until we have much more theoretical information about any existing link.

Next we must determine Braun's moderator and control variables. Sex and age seem to be his moderator variables because he wants to know if they have any effect on the relationship between intelligence and German proficiency. At the same time, he is concerned that previous travel in Germany should not interfere with the results. He must be planning to eliminate students who have previously traveled in Germany. So previous travel in Germany would be a control variable. Remember that the role of these variables is determined or assigned by the researcher. Since they are not clearly categorized in the abstract, we are just guessing, but our guesses seem logical.

## Important caveats

You should now have a good sense of how the five types of variables are defined, how they interrelate, and how to identify them in a study. But is it clear why they are important?

Remember that the way variables are assigned and the way they interrelate are mostly in the hands of the researcher. That, along with the basic fallibility of researchers as human beings, places great responsibility on you as the reader of a study. First, it is your responsibility to try to ferret out the variables in a study. Are they clearly identified? If so, do they make sense in the categories in which they are placed? Are they clearly thought out? Do they logically represent the underlying constructs of interest? Second, you should evaluate the investigator's use of labels for the variables involved. Are they appropriate? Are they sensible? Are they too broad? Third, the relationships between variables must make sense. Is it possible to distinguish which type is which? Do the variables fit together properly in these relationships? And do you agree with the relationships that the author has chosen to set up? Finally, you should ask yourself whether the author has included all the variables that are important to the investigation involved and none that are extraneous. Are there any variables representing constructs of importance that you think are missing from the study (particularly moderator or control variables)? Are there any unnecessary variables that add nothing to the study and just confuse the issue?

Thinking about the variables in a study will help you not only to read and understand the article but perhaps to understand the relationships between the myriad variables in our complicated and demanding field.

## Terms

| | |
|---|---|
| construct | moderator variable |
| control variable | operational definition |
| dependent variable | operationalize |
| independent variable | variable |
| intervening variable | |

## Review questions

1. What is a variable? Can you name some?
2. How are variables different from constructs? Can you think of an example of a construct in language learning that can be operationalized as a variable for a study?
3. Why is identification of the different types of variables important? Why is it important to understanding a given study?
4. How can you identify the dependent variable or variables in a study?
5. How can you identify the independent variable or variables?
6. How do the dependent and independent variables interrelate?
7. What is the variable called that labels the relationship between the independent and dependent variables?
8. What is the essential difference between independent and moderator variables?
9. What is the purpose of control variables?
10. Why is the identification and study of variables important to language teaching as a profession?

## Application

A. Consider the following example and then fill in the boxes in Figure 2.4:

Jas Menbrow noticed that people do not all perform in their native languages with equal ability. It occurred to him that there might be some relationship between the native language ability of his American students and their proficiency in French after three years of high school study. To investigate this possibility, he administered the verbal subtest of the

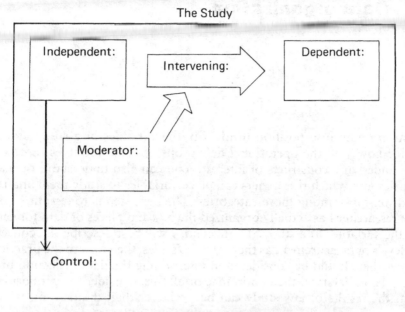

The Study

Independent:

Intervening:

Dependent:

Moderator:

Control:

*Figure 2.4   Variables in Menbrow's study*

Scholastic Aptitude Test (to measure proficiency in native English) and his school district's French Proficiency Test to all 132 students who were finishing their third year of study. He was concerned that differences between the sexes should not interfere with the results, so he eliminated all males from his analysis. Thus 89 female students were left. In addition, he wanted to determine what differences there might be between the women in the college-bound track (44 students) and those in the accelerated track (45 students). So he considered the two groups separately on this basis.

B. On the basis of the example, answer the following questions:

1. Are the variables clearly identified? Do they make sense as variables?
2. Do the investigator's labels or names for the variables make sense?
3. How has the investigator operationally defined the construct "native language ability"?
4. Do you agree with the way the investigator has chosen to set up the relationships among the variables?
5. Are there any variables that the investigator should have included, but did not? Are any unnecessary variables mentioned?
6. What value, if any, might a study like this have for you and your teaching situation?

# 3 Data organization

You are now in a position to identify the variables in a study and to judge how well the operational definitions of these variables represent the underlying constructs of interest. You can also understand the categories into which researchers can place variables to study them and the relationships among those categories. The next step is to examine how the researcher has actually organized the bits and pieces of data for each of the variables in a study. To this end, I will first describe the concept of levels of measurement as they relate to scales, then turn to the practical issues that should be considered in interpreting the data collection process. To understand the importance of all this, consider the proposition that the results of any study can be no better than the data on which they are based.

## Levels of measurement

By definition, all quantifiable data are observable in some way. The problem is that data may be observed or measured in different ways. For example, the variable proficiency in English as a second language can be measured on a test that will produce a set of different scores for a group of students. Variables like sex or nationality, however, usually are determined by asking the students themselves for the information. Of course, this procedure produces a set of categories with certain numbers of people in each, rather than a set of scores. Do you see the difference between how the data must be organized for the variables language proficiency and nationality? Language proficiency is observed as a set of test scores and nationality is observed as a set of categories.

This distinction is accounted for by the different kinds of scales used in statistical studies. *Scales*, then, are names for the different ways of observing, organizing, and assigning numbers to data, which makes them important for understanding the entire data collection process. In addition, the different types of scales can be said to measure with varying degrees of precision. As you will see, the four types of scales differ markedly and can be arranged hierarchically from least precise to most precise; that is why they are often termed *levels of measurement*. The four types of scales are the nominal, ordinal, interval, and ratio scales. Let's look at each in turn.

## Four types of scales

### Nominal scales

Nominal scales are used for naming and categorizing data in a variable – usually in the form of identifying groups into which people fall. Membership in such groups may occur either naturally (as in the sex or nationality groupings just discussed) or artificially (as in a study that assigns students to different experimental and control groups). On a particular nominal scale, each observation usually falls into only one category. The next observation may fall into a different category, but it, too, will fall only into one such category. Examples of variables that group people naturally include sex, nationality, native language, social and economic status, level of study in a language and a specific like or dislike (e.g., whether the subjects like studying grammar rules). Artificially occurring variables might include membership in an experimental or control group and membership in a particular class or language program. So the essence of the nominal scale is that it names categories into which people fall, naturally or artificially. One source of confusion with this type of scale is that it is variously labeled a *discrete, discontinuous, categorical,* or even *dichotomous* scale (in the special case of only two categories). In this book, I will always call this type of scale nominal.

### Ordinal scales

Unlike a nominal scale, an ordinal scale is used to order, or rank, data. For instance, if you were interested in ranking your students from best to worst on the basis of their final examination scores (with 1 representing the best; 2, the next best; and 30 being the worst), you would be dealing with an ordinal scale. In our field, numerous rankings may be of concern, including ranking students in a class, ranking teachers in a center, or even ranking grammatical structures in a language (e.g., in French tenses, *subjonctif* is more difficult than the *passé composé*, which is more difficult than the *present*). In an ordinal scale, then, each point on the scale is ranked as "more than" and "less than" the other points on the scale. The points are then lined up and numbered first, second, third, and so on.

## Interval scales

Interval scales also represent the ordering of things. In addition, they reflect the interval, or distance, between points in the ranking. When you look at the final examination scores in one of your courses, you are dealing with an interval scale. For instance, if Jim scored 90 out of 100, Jack scored 80, and Jill scored 78, you could rank these three students first, second, and third; that would be an ordinal scale. But the scores themselves give you more information than that. They also tell you the interval, or distance, between the performances on the examination: Jim scored 10 points higher than Jack, but Jack only scored 2 points higher than Jill. Thus, an interval scale gives more information than does an ordinal scale.

An interval scale gives you the ordering and the distances between points on that ranking. Examples of interval scales include most of the variables measured with tests like language placement, language aptitude, language proficiency, and so on. But some interval scales are measured in different ways, such as age, number of years of schooling, and years of language study.

It is important to note that an interval scale assumes that the intervals between points are equal. Hence, on a 100-point test, the distance between the scores 12 and 14 (2 points) is assumed to be equal to the distance between 98 and 100 (also 2 points). The problem is that some items on a language test may be much more difficult (particularly those that make a difference on high scores like 98 and 100) than are others, so the distances between intervals do not seem equal. Nevertheless, this assumption is one with which most researchers can live — at least until knowledge in the field of language teaching becomes exact enough to provide ratio scales.

## Ratio scales

The discussion of ratio scales will be short because such scales are not generally applied to the behavioral sciences, for two reasons: (1) a *ratio scale* has a zero value and (2) it can be said that points on the scale are precise multiples of other points on the scale. For example, you can have zero electricity in your house. But if you have a 50-watt bulb burning and then you turn on an additional 100-watt bulb, you can say that you are now using three times as much electricity. Can you, however, say that a person knows no (zero) Spanish? I think not. Even a person who has never studied Spanish will bring certain lexical, phonological, and syntactic information from the native language to bear on the task. It is also a shaky proposition to state that a person who scores 120 on a Spanish placement test knows three times as much Spanish as does one

TABLE 3.1. INFORMATION PROVIDED BY DIFFERENT SCALES

| | *Type of information provided* | | | |
|---|---|---|---|---|
| *Scale* | *Category (Name)* | *Order (Rank)* | *Interval (Distance)* | *Zero and can multiply (Not used)* |
| Nominal | X | | | |
| Ordinal | X | X | | |
| Interval | X | X | X | |
| Ratio | X | X | X | X |

who scores 40. So for now, ratio scales are best left in the hands of physical scientists.

## Scales can be slippery

One way to look at the four types of scales is to realize that they are related and build one on the other, as shown in Table 3.1. Nominal scales name and categorize only. Ordinal scales are concerned with categories as well, but they provide the ordering, or ranking, of those categories. Similarly, interval scales tell about the ordering within categories, but they provide additional information about the distances between points in that ordering. And, finally, ratio scales give the intervals between points in the ordering of certain categories but with considerably more information because there is an interpretable zero and multiples of points along the scale make sense. Remember, however, that ratio scales are seldom applicable to language studies.

It is also important to recognize that scales can be slippery, that is, they can change forms in the hands of a researcher. If an investigator wishes, for logical reasons, to convert a set of observations from one scale to another, it is possible, but it is a unidirectional process. Any of the three types of scales that are of interest here can be changed into the scale or scales above it in Table 3.1. For example, let's consider a set of scores on an interval scale for a German achievement test. These scores could easily be changed into an ordinal scale by going through the scores and ranking the students first, second, third, and so on. Likewise, either the interval scale scores or the ordinal scale ranks could be changed into a nominal scale by grouping the scores into "high achievers" (the top 50 percent of the students) and "low achievers" (the bottom 50 percent). The result would be a nominal scale, with all students falling into one of the two groups.

However, once established, a scale cannot be changed into the scale or scales below it in Table 3.1. Let's consider a set of data recorded on a nominal scale. Perhaps a researcher has collected a set of data that classifies American students who are studying Chinese into three groups – "high," "middle," and "low" achievers – on the basis of their grade-point average in Chinese 101. It would be impossible to convert that nominal scale to an ordinal scale on the basis of this set of nominal-scale data, because the information about the ordering of students within the three categories is not present. Likewise, it would be impossible to convert this nominal scale to an interval scale, not only because the information about ordering is not available but, what is more important for an interval scale, there is no information about the distances between the levels of the individual students' achievement. In short, the information necessary to convert to an ordinal or interval scale is not contained in the nominal scale. The researcher could, of course, retrieve the original grade-point averages and establish an interval scale or convert that interval scale into an ordinal scale, but that would mean starting afresh by establishing a new scale – not converting a nominal scale to an ordinal or interval scale.

Along with the potential flexibility to change scales (at least in one direction) comes certain responsibilities. The researcher and reader must both realize that changing scales, as was just described, will have two effects on the variables involved: (1) valuable information may be lost in the process and (2) the assumptions about the nature of the underlying variable may change. For example, by changing your students' test scores on a final examination from an interval scale to an ordinal scale, you retain the information about how the scores are ordered, or ranked, but lose the information about the intervals, or distances, between those scores. Likewise, you are now viewing the variable (final examination), as reflected by the rankings, in a different way. The important aspect of this variable is now how it ranks the students, rather than how it ranks them *and* the intervals between their performances. It is therefore important to carefully consider the types of scales used in a study and how well they represent the variables and underlying constructs in question.

## Practical considerations

You might reasonably ask how the information in this and the previous chapter applies, in a practical sense, to the studies you are encountering. You certainly have two new things to think about when evaluating a study: the definitions of variables and scales. Basically, you should ask yourself three questions about each when you read a study: (1) Is it present? (2) Is it adequate? and (3) Is it appropriate? Let's look at each of these questions in turn.

For the definitions of variables, you should essentially be concerned with whether the researcher has shown enough clarity in the definitions to reflect clear thinking about the variables themselves. To that end, your first question might be whether all important constructs have clear theoretical definitions and whether all variables, which are meant to represent those constructs, are operationally defined. Once these definitions are identified, the next logical question is whether they are adequate. You can establish their adequacy by asking yourself if you understand exactly what the researcher means by each construct and the variables set up to operationalize them. If you are satisfied with the precision of labeling and definition for each construct and variable, you should finish by asking yourself whether these constructs and variables are the appropriate ones for the study involved. Are there any extraneous ones or others that should have been included, but are not? Here, of course, you must rely on your own experience, knowledge, and judgment – all of which should improve as you apply these questions to more and more studies.

For scales, the questions are essentially the same, but you must remember that scales can be changed from interval to ordinal to nominal, depending on how the researcher is viewing them. Changing them is not a matter of trickery but, rather, a useful property of scales that makes it possible to look at the same variable in different ways. Nevertheless, the choice of scales is in the hands of the researcher; thus, it is your responsibility as a reader to watch for possible problems. First, you should ask yourself whether the study clearly identifies which kinds of scales represent each variable. This information may be found either in the operational definitions or elsewhere in the study. Second, because the scales most often are not labeled as nominal, ordinal, or interval, you should ask yourself if enough information is provided to determine what kinds of scales have been used for each variable. Finally, you must make your own judgment about the appropriateness of each scale. In short, you must determine whether the researcher has clearly and adequately explained the manipulation of the scales so that you can judge whether they are appropriate. Remember, no study can logically be any better than the data on which it is based.

## Terms

| | |
|---|---|
| interval scale | ordinal scale |
| levels of measurement | ratio scale |
| nominal scale | scales |

## Review questions

1. What is a scale?
2. How are nominal, ordinal, and interval scales similar and different?
3. Why is the ratio scale not used in language studies?
4. How would you change the scores on a final examination in a course from the existing interval scale to an ordinal scale or to a nominal scale?
5. What kind of scale would most likely be used for each of the following variables: sex, class rank, IQ, language placement, high/low achievers, native language background, and years of studying Urdu? Can you change some of your answers to another type of scale?
6. Is the fact that scales can be manipulated from one type to another by a researcher a detrimental or beneficial quality? Why or why not?
7. What kind of scale is represented by the question, On a scale of 1 to 10, how are you doing today?

## Application

A. In his enthusiasm for data collection, Jas Menbrow has a great deal of information on each of his third-year French students. For each of the potential variables listed below, please fill in the most likely type of scale it would represent:

| *Potential variables* | *Most likely type of scale* |
| --- | --- |
| 1. Sex | ................................................ |
| 2. Age | ................................................ |
| 3. Class rank | ................................................ |
| 4. Nationality | ................................................ |
| 5. Native language | ................................................ |
| 6. Test scores on proficiency in French | ................................................ |
| 7. Scores on the verbal subtest of the Stanford Achievement Test | ................................................ |
| 8. Rank on the department's final examination | ................................................ |
| 9. Amount of time spent studying a foreign language | ................................................ |

10. Whether students had been to
    France ...............................................

B. Consider the types of scales that you have identified above and answer
   the following questions:
   1. For age, what would be the most appropriate intervals for the
      scale: days, months, years, or decades?
   2. For amount of time spent studying a foreign language, how might
      Menbrow increase the precision of the variable by rewording it?
      What would be the most appropriate intervals for this scale?

C. Menbrow discovered that many of his students had been studying
   Spanish while they were studying three years of French in his program.
   He decided to investigate whether the simultaneous study of another
   Latin-based language, Spanish, had any effect on achievement in
   French, as measured by the average of students' grades in their French
   courses. There were several variables that he did not want to cloud
   his results, so he looked only at data from 17-year-old female students
   whose native language was English. From this group, he randomly
   selected 30 who had simultaneously studied Spanish and 30 who had
   not. He then compared the average grades in French of these two
   groups. He was also interested in any effect that intelligence, as measured by a nonverbal IQ test, would have on the relationship between
   the study of Spanish and the students' grades in French. Can you fill
   in the following blanks?

| Type of variable | Label for variable | Type of scale |
|---|---|---|
| ...................... | ...................... | ...................... |
| ...................... | ...................... | ...................... |
| ...................... | ...................... | ...................... |
| ...................... | ...................... | ...................... |
| ...................... | ...................... | ...................... |
| ...................... | ...................... | ...................... |
| ...................... | ...................... | ...................... |

D. What might be a fatal flaw in the logic of the second study? What if
   Mr. Menbrow finds that students who simultaneously study Spanish
   also get much higher grades, on average, than do those who are not
   studying Spanish? Should he recommend that all students be required
   to take Spanish with their French to perform better in French? Of
   course not, but why not? Can he say that the simultaneous study of

Spanish and French causes students to do better in French? Or is it possible that there are other variables that should have been controlled? Consider the possibility that students who, at the outset, take two or more languages might be more highly motivated toward language study and have a greater aptitude for languages in general than do students who take only one language. Now what do you think of Menbrow's potential results?

# 4 Controlling extraneous variables

The central issues in thinking about any type of research hinge on whether the research is logical and meaningful. In statistical studies, a number of problems can arise, both within and outside a study, that may create major flaws in its *validity* – the degree to which a study and its results correctly lead to, or support, exactly what is claimed. The problems themselves result from extraneous variables that are relevant to a study but are not noticed or controlled. Since they may dramatically affect the results, it is your responsibility to determine whether the researcher has considered and controlled for all such relevant variables. Only then can you determine whether the study is logical and meaningful to you and your teaching situation. This discussion of the validity of a study will be approached from four perspectives: (1) environmental issues, (2) grouping issues, (3) people issues, and (4) measurement issues. It will be followed by an explanation of how extraneous variables are typically controlled and how such controls can affect the meaningfulness of a study for you.

## Environmental issues

It is possible, then, that a number of variables may influence a study without the researcher being aware of them. Such extraneous variables may occur naturally in a study and remain undetected, or they may simply be due to the artificiality of the conditions set up for the study.

### Naturally occurring variables

*Naturally occurring variables* often become a problem when the researcher is comparing the language performance, perhaps on a proficiency test (the dependent variable), of several groups of subjects (the independent variable). In such a case, the researcher would certainly want only the dependent, the independent, and any moderator variables to vary and would control for all other relevant variables. But what if variables in the environment have influenced the study without being noticed? Could they critically affect the results and, therefore, the whole study?

Take for instance a problem that arose while I was doing research in the People's Republic of China. Part of the study involved a listening comprehension test that was administered to one group during the class hour just before lunch when it was reasonably quiet outside, even with the windows open. However, when a second comparison group was tested several hours later, workers were using diesel tractors to haul building materials up from the river. Even with the windows closed (with a subsequent rise in temperature), it was clear that any comparison of the listening comprehension performances of these two groups would not only have serious problems with validity but would also be absurd.

Although this is an extreme example, it points up how variables that must not be overlooked can occur in the environment. If they are not noticed, such variables can dramatically affect the results. Primary among the environmental variables that may be encountered in studies of language teaching are noise, temperature, adequacy of light, time of day, and seating arrangements. Of course, all such potential environmental variables should be considered by the researcher, as well as by the reader.

### Artificiality

Another environmental issue that may surreptitiously alter the intentions of a study is the artificiality of the arrangements within the study. This issue is analogous to the issue of whether experimental mice will perform the same way in a laboratory, in which the conditions are artificial, as they would in the real world. For example, numerous researchers are trying to investigate the communicative language competence, or at least the communicative performance, of students. In a broad sense, this research involves collecting data on the students' actual ability to use language in authentic situations. Is it realistic to require subjects in a study to come to the researcher's office and communicate "naturally," or are these conditions too artificial? Perhaps it would be better to videotape the students in authentic communicative situations with a hidden camera. In such a case, are the results affected if the subjects notice the camera? And what about the ethics of using a hidden camera? These are questions that center on the problem of *artificiality*. Artificiality may or may not be a problem in a given study, but the researcher should certainly consider it to make sure it is not.

## Grouping issues

Other extraneous variables may crop up because of the initial composition of the groups involved or changes in the composition over time.

Three such issues will be referred to here: self-selection, mortality, and maturation.

## Self-selection

*Self-selection* generally refers to the practice of letting the subjects decide which group to join. There are certain dangers inherent in this practice. Let's say that two groups of third-year students of Russian are to be compared. One group might be made up of students who had volunteered (self-selected) to spend one extra hour per day in the language laboratory while the other group consisted of students who followed the regular syllabus. If the volunteers scored much higher than the regular students on a Russian proficiency test at the end of the course, would the researcher be justified in saying that an extra hour a day of language laboratory is beneficial to the students? No!

There is a definite danger in such an interpretation. Volunteers may be different at the outset from nonvolunteers. Therefore, any differences in the performances of the groups may be accounted for by the possibility that volunteers, by nature, are higher in motivation, ambition, aptitude for the task, or other possible variables that make the two groups different, regardless of visits to the language laboratory. So the problem is that the researcher has no way of knowing whether differences between the groups were due to extra time in the language laboratory or to other extraneous differences between the two groups.

Volunteering is just one way that self-selection may occur. Another not-so-obvious form of self-selection may happen when two existing classes are compared. Like volunteer and nonvolunteer groups, two classes may be different; for a wide variety of reasons, students may flock together and thereby create unequal groups. A researcher would generally like the groups to be the same on all relevant variables – at least at the beginning of a study, but self-selection generally defeats this intention. So you should be alert to this potential problem.

## Mortality

The issue of *mortality*, also called *attrition* or *dropout*, is not nearly as morbid as it sounds. It is simply a variant of the problem just discussed. However, instead of referring to students who select themselves into one group or another, mortality refers to students who self-select themselves *out* of a group by dropping out of the study for any number of reasons, including transfer to another institution, serious illness or dropping out of school. Again, the researcher would like the groups to be equivalent on all relevant variables other than those that are the focus of the study. But students who drop out have certain characteristics. If the characteristics of dropouts were to be uniform across the groups in a study, this form of attrition would not be as big a problem. At least the groups could still be compared, although it would be difficult to interpret the results. When the characteristics of the dropouts in one group are different from those who drop out of another group, serious problems arise because the pattern of mortality itself may be a variable that causes one or both groups to change in unpredictable and uncontrolled ways. Such changes will, of course, affect the interpretation of the results in much the same way as does self-selection. Since it is difficult to determine whether students who drop out of one group are the same on all relevant variables as those who leave another group, mortality can seriously undermine the validity of a study.

## Maturation

*Maturation* is a third way in which the characteristics of groups may diverge, particularly in studies that are conducted over a long period of time. Even though two groups of people may be similar at the beginning of a study, different individuals can have different experiences that cause them to mature or change over time. Such experiences might include other simultaneous learning; a family catastrophe; or psychological, emotional, and physical changes. Like self-selection and mortality, such changes may result in differential maturation that, in turn, may cause the characteristics of the groups to diverge and hence may interfere with the interpretation of the results by introducing extraneous variables.

# People issues

Variables may also be introduced by the attitudes that the people involved have toward the study. After all, people are people. They may relate to experiences in a study with different and unpredictable emotions and attitudes that may, in turn, introduce uncontrolled variables. These uncontrolled variables may take the form of what is called the Hawthorne effect, may engender a halo effect, or may be based on the subjects' or researchers' expectations.

## Hawthorne effect

It is possible for subjects to be so pleased at being included in a study that the results of the investigation are more closely related to this pleasure than to anything that actually occurs in the research. This situation is called the *Hawthorne effect*. The Hawthorne effect was first noted by Mayo, Roethlisberger, and Dickson in their study at the Hawthorne branch (Chicago) of the Western Electric Company (as reported in Brown 1954). The researchers observed that when they were present, the production of workers increased, regardless of the conditions that were imposed. The workers were apparently reacting to their inclusion in the study in addition to any effect of the conditions that were being studied.

Consider, for instance, a hypothetical study of the effectiveness of a much-publicized Spanish-English bilingual-immersion program in the elementary schools. One group of Spanish speakers might be chosen to participate in the program, while another, equivalent, group would stay in their monolingual English-speaking schools. If the study found that the subjects in the bilingual setting far outperformed those in the mono-lingual settings, the results might be due to the greater effectiveness of the bilingual program or to the pleasure or superiority that the one group of subjects felt because they were selected to participate in the special program. The researchers would be unable to separate these two variables as they are described here and thus would have a problem owing to the Hawthorne effect.

## Halo effect

Another variable that is related to the subjects' attitudes is called the *halo effect*. This effect is due to the tendency among human beings to respond positively to a person they like. Such positive feelings could be reflected on all scales related to that person. The results on the scales could be more highly related to these positive feelings than to the actual characteristics of the person in question. For example, let's say that a study of the effectiveness of teachers was being conducted in an ESL program for Vietnamese refugees. A questionnaire in Vietnamese might be administered asking the students to rate their teachers on a number of characteristics. In such a case, it is possible that the results would show that a popular teacher (e.g., one who had a lot of parties for the students) was punctual, hardworking, and firm in discipline (when, in fact, he was often late, ill prepared, and lax), simply because the students liked him. Pity any other teacher who was truly punctual, hardworking, and firm but was not the life of the party! In short, then, subjects' attitudes toward people, whether based on conscious personal prefer-ences or cultural biases, can affect the results of a study. Thus, the halo effect should be controlled whenever it is likely to occur.

## Subject expectancy

Related to the halo effect is the natural tendency of people to want to please. One possible result of this tendency is *subject expectancy*, which

33

occurs when the subjects think they have figured out what a study is about and try to "help" the researcher to achieve the apparent aims. This problem arose when I was trying to investigate the effectiveness of teaching English reduced forms (e.g., "I wanna gedouda here" for "I want to get out of here"). Two equivalent groups of foreign students took a test on reduced forms at the beginning of the study. Then, one group was explicitly taught reduced forms while the other was not. At the end of the study, both groups were again tested on reduced forms. It was not surprising to find that the group who had been taught them did much better on the second test. Along with many other problems, I was concerned that there would be no effect resulting from subject expectancy. After all, it was possible that the subjects would guess from a reduced-forms test at the beginning of the study that an investigation was afoot on this new and unusual element in their curriculum. The problem was that by guessing this fact, they might form expectancies about the results of the investigation and try to help me achieve those results by performing poorly on the pretest and well on the posttest. They would, thereby, introduce a new variable into my study, and knowing this bound me to control for such subject expectancy.

## Researcher expectancy

Like subjects, researchers have expectations that may color the results of a study. As Rosenthal (1966) showed, *researcher expectancy* can be a problem in behavioral research. For example, if subjects are divided into two groups – high language aptitude and low language aptitude – the researcher, who knows which group is which, may affect the performance of the groups in subtle and uncontrolled ways. Thus, any differences that are later found in the language learning or performance of these groups might be due to actual differences between the two types of students or to the effects of researcher expectancy. The proportion of these two variables to each other would remain indeterminable and, therefore, would make the results difficult to interpret.

In medical research, this effect is often controlled for with the *double-blind technique*, wherein a placebo (e.g., a sugar tablet) is given to half the subjects and a real drug is given to the other half. The important point in this technique is not just that the subjects do not know which pill they are getting but, at the time, neither do the researchers. So the researchers' expectancies presumably have no effect on the outcome. Because the treatment in language learning experiments is much more complicated than in such medical experiments, it is difficult to set up a double-blind experiment. Thus, researcher expectancy should always be considered as a potential problem in interpreting the results of language-related studies.

## Measurement issues

Another set of potential problems centers on the measures that are used: tests, questionnaires, observations, interview procedures, or any other means of quantifying language behavior. Since the results of a study are only as good as the data (reflected in measures) on which they are based, it is essential to make sure that the measures themselves are not introducing extraneous variables into the study. Three problems that the researcher should particularly watch for are the practice effect, the reactivity effect, and the instability of the measures or of the results.

### Practice effect

The *practice effect* essentially involves the potential influence of the measures on each other. Its strongest form occurs when the same test is given repeatedly in a study to determine if there are changes in performance. For instance, a study might be conducted to determine whether students are making gains in grammar during three weeks of intensive Spanish study. By giving the same grammar test before and after such learning, the researcher might attempt to determine how much the students improved during this period. The problem is that students often learn from their mistakes. So, formally or informally, they may have cleared up any problems they had with the first test at the time of the second test, especially if subject expectancy was involved. Thus, any apparent gains in the scores on the second test may reflect the students' actual growth in general proficiency in grammar or their learning the items on the particular test in question. If the practice effect is not controlled, it will obviously be impossible to separate these two variables. Thus, the results will be ambiguous and difficult to interpret.

### Reactivity effect

In some language studies, a *reactivity effect* may occur when the measures themselves are causing a change in the subjects. One example of this effect might be an attitude questionnaire, in which the subjects actually form or solidify attitudes that they did not have before filling out the questionnaire. In this instance, the questionnaire becomes the catalyst for the very attitudes that are being studied. This effect would obviously influence, to an unpredictable degree, the results and the interpretation of the results.

### Instability of measures and results

The *instability of a measure* of any kind refers to the degree to which the results on the measure are consistent. Would those results be the same if the measure was administered repeatedly while the effect of testing was controlled? Likewise, the *instability of the results* of a study refers to the degree to which the results would be likely to recur if the study was replicated. Although it is not possible to control both types of instability absolutely, statistical procedures provide the researcher with tools to determine the degree to which measures are stable, or consistent (see Chapter 8), and to estimate the probability that the results of a study are stable, or will recur in replication (see Chapters 9–12). The instability of measures and results are both potential sources of problems within a study, but since their influence will be the subject of over half this book, further discussion of them must be deferred for the moment.

## Controlling for validity

At the beginning of this chapter, it was stated that the central questions to ask about any study are whether it is logical and meaningful. In this section, I will explore how extraneous variables are typically controlled and how certain of these variables affect the logic of a study (internal validity) while others affect its meaningfulness (external validity).

### Control of extraneous variables

Until now, I have painted a bleak picture of the many ways in which variables can covertly enter a study. Actually, such variables do not sneak into studies; they are simply present and must be considered and controlled. So the picture is far from hopeless. A researcher can take a number of steps to minimize, if not eliminate, the effects of these potential problems. If you sense that any of them may have occurred in a study, you should immediately check to see that the researcher has taken appropriate steps to control for them. These steps will be discussed here from the same four perspectives used earlier: environmental issues, grouping issues, people issues, and measurement issues.

ENVIRONMENTAL ISSUES

Recall that the environment can present two types of problems by introducing natural variables (noise, temperature, bad lighting, and so forth) or by being so artificial that it bears no resemblance to reality. You should look for indications that the researcher has carefully prearranged the conditions (so there were no "natural" surprises) and that the researcher describes those conditions. It may also be wise to make your own estimation of how natural the conditions were. Phrases like "the experiment was conducted in a quiet, well-lit classroom for all groups" would be comforting in this regard. Even then, you would want to ask yourself if the "classroom" is the appropriate and natural setting for the type of study involved.

## GROUPING ISSUES

The ways in which the subjects are grouped can present the potential problems of self-selection, mortality, and maturation. The moment you encounter the word *volunteer*, you should suspect the possibility of self-selection. More positive indications would be that the subjects were selected and assigned to groups randomly or by stratified random sampling (discussed in more depth in Chapter 9). The important point is to check that the researcher took standard steps to assure that the groups were representative and equivalent on all potentially related variables except those under investigation. In addition, studies of short duration are less likely to include the potential problems of mortality and maturation. When mortality is encountered, however, it might be wise to check that dropouts are not logically too numerous and that they have been identified and accounted for in some way – that is, the reasons for their dropping out have been described and explained. When potential problems of maturation are found, the researcher should indicate that substantial efforts were made to monitor and control the experiences of the subjects that were extraneous to the study, even to the point of including these experiences as moderator or control variables in the study.

## PEOPLE ISSUES

The attitudes of the people involved in a study toward each other and toward the study can cause four major problems: the Hawthorne effect, the halo effect, subject expectancy, or researcher expectancy. Whenever you suspect a Hawthorne effect or influence from researcher expectancy, you should look for the double-blind technique. Remember, when it is used, neither the researchers nor the subjects know which groups are which until after the data are collected. If you encounter a possible problem with subject expectancy, you would want to search for indications that the researcher has attempted to minimize the obviousness of the aims of the study by including elements (e.g., test questions or even whole tests) that have no actual purpose other than to distract the subjects from the real aims of the study. When you find a halo effect, you should check to see if "general attitude" (positive or negative) has been included as a moderator or control variable to counter any halo that attitude may be creating over the more specific evaluations found in the study.

37

MEASUREMENT ISSUES

Remember that measurement can cause three sorts of problems through practice effect, reactivity effect, or instability in the measures and study results. A potential practice effect is usually countered in one of two ways. One approach is to allow sufficient time between tests to avoid the practice effect. The assumption is that students will forget what was on the test if enough time passes before they take it again. This is not a satisfactory approach because that assumption has not been shown to be true, nor has the amount of time necessary for such "forgetting" been established.

Another approach is called *counterbalancing*. The purpose of this procedure is to see that no individual takes the same test twice. To achieve this goal, two different but equivalent tests (say, forms A and B) might be given to random halves of each group at the beginning of the study. Then the opposite forms would be given to these halves at the end of the study. The result would be that no subject had taken the same test twice. Once averaged, however, the results provide comparative data for estimating any changes that occurred between the two administrations.

The reactivity effect, that is, when the measures are causing a change in the subjects, can best be controlled by thoughtful study of the measures themselves. The measures can be studied by carefully questioning the subjects after the test to find out what thought processes they were using while they were taking the test or filling out the questionnaire, or by conducting a well-planned pilot test and review of the literature on the topic. In all cases, controlling for this effect will involve a thorough understanding of the measures involved in a study.

The instability of measures and of results are other sources of trouble in any statistical research. Since the stability of measures is rarely perfect, you should look for statistical estimates of the consistency of all measures and the probabilities involved in the results. (I will discuss these concepts in greater detail later.) Table 4.1 summarizes the potential problems and some of the typical ways that language researchers control them.

## Control versus generalizability

In addition to understanding each of the potentially troublesome sources of extraneous variables, it is important to realize that these variables can interact with each other if two or more are present simultaneously in a study. This means that the picture may be considerably more clouded if two or more uncontrolled and extraneous variables are also influencing each other. For instance, researcher expectancy could cause behavior

TABLE 4.1. CONTROLLING EXTRANEOUS VARIABLES

| Four perspectives | Potential problems | Steps toward control |
|---|---|---|
| A. Environment | 1. Natural variables | Prearrangement of conditions (no surprises). |
| | 2. Artificiality | Approximation of "natural" conditions. |
| B. Grouping | 1. Self-selection | Random, matched-pair, or stratified assignment. |
| | 2. Mortality | Short duration; track down missing subjects. |
| | 3. Maturation | Short duration or built-in moderator or control variables. |
| C. People | 1. Hawthorne effect | Double-blind technique. |
| | 2. Halo effect | Built-in general attitude as moderator or control variable. |
| | 3. Subject expectancy | Minimize obviousness of aims. Distraction from aims provided. |
| | 4. Researcher expectancy | Double-blind technique. |
| D. Measurement | 1. Practice effect | Counterbalancing. |
| | 2. Reactivity | Careful study of measures. |
| | 3. Instability of measures and results | Statistical estimates of stability and probability (see Chapters 10–14). |

that triggers subject expectancy, which, in turn, could magnify a practice effect.

Moreover, each of these sources of problem variables may have different effects on a study. A clear distinction can be made in the way that different extraneous variables may alter the validity of a study internally or externally (Campbell and Stanley 1963).

On the one hand, *internal validity* refers to whether the results of a study are due solely to those variables being identified and compared within the study. If other unnoticed or uncontrolled variables are affecting the results, a threat to internal validity arises, and the study is no longer logical because the results have been altered by factors that are internal to the study. On the other hand, *external validity* refers to factors that affect the generalizability of the findings to the real world. A study can be well designed, controlled, and internally valid but lack external validity. The problem is that controls, when introduced, may make the study artificial and thus limit the external validity. In a statistically ideal and unethical world, researchers would be able to put subjects in laboratory cages and control all the variables that might influence their language learning (except, of course, any effects that were due to the cages themselves). Such a procedure would allow the nearly complete control of internal validity. However, external validity would be lacking because any results thus obtained would not be meaningful since one could not generalize them to real-world situations.

To sum up, then, this chapter started by asserting that "the central issues in thinking about any type of research hinge on whether the research is logical and meaningful." For a study to be logical, it must have sound internal validity. The meaningfulness to you and your teaching situation will depend on external validity. To obtain the one, a researcher may have to sacrifice a bit of the other. This tradeoff is sometimes necessary and requires you, as the reader, to judge whether it was necessary and appropriate as described in a given study.

## Terms

| | |
|---|---|
| artificiality | instability of the results |
| counterbalancing | internal validity |
| double-blind technique | maturation |
| external validity | mortality |
| generalizability | naturally occurring variable |
| halo effect | practice effect |
| Hawthorne effect | reactivity effect |
| instability of a measure | researcher expectancy |

self-selection                    validity (of a study)
subject expectancy

## Review questions

1. What are some of the naturally occurring extraneous variables that might be found in the environment in which a study is conducted? How might they affect the results?
2. What effect might artificiality have on a study? Would it have more effect on the internal validity or the external validity?
3. Why are self-selection, mortality, and maturation potential problems?
4. How are the Hawthorne effect and researcher expectancy similar? How are they different?
5. How are the halo effect and subject expectancy similar? How are they different?
6. How does counterbalancing relate to the testing effect? And how is it done?
7. Can instability in the measures and results of a study be controlled absolutely? What should you look for in a study for each of these problems?
8. If you cover column 3 of Table 4.1, can you suggest the ways in which researchers should control for the potential problems listed in column 2?
9. How are internal validity and external validity related? How do they differ?
10. Why is a tradeoff between internal validity (control) and external validity (generalizability) sometimes necessary? How do these concepts relate to the logic and meaningfulness of a study?

*The Application follows on the next page.*

## Application

Focusing on the Method section of any study of interest to you, answer the following questions:

1. Do you perceive any problems or potential problems with the study in terms of environment, grouping, people, or measurement issues? List the problems below in the appropriate blanks.

   A. Environment   1. ......................................................................

                                2. ......................................................................

   B. Grouping   1. ......................................................................

                                2. ......................................................................

                                3. ......................................................................

   C. People   1. ......................................................................

                                2. ......................................................................

                                3. ......................................................................

                                4. ......................................................................

   D. Measurement   1. ......................................................................

                                2. ......................................................................

2. Did the researcher recognize the problems you found, or were they overlooked?
3. Were these potential problems controlled, explained away, or ignored?
4. How would you suggest that the researcher should have controlled for the potential problems?
5. If they were controlled, were the procedures followed adequately? How would you improve the controls?
6. Is the study internally valid? Externally valid?
7. On the basis of your answers to Questions 1–6, do you think the study is interesting and generalizable to your teaching situation?

# 5  Critiquing statistical studies

Reading and interpreting statistical research in language learning and teaching is, or should be, a creative and critical exercise. It is creative in the sense that you must actively participate with the original researcher. You should attempt to re-create the process of doing the research in your own mind. For this reason, the quality of *replicability*, or the degree to which a study could be performed again on the basis of the information provided by the author, is important to the structure of a study and is perhaps the single most important yardstick to hold up against any study. Ask yourself if you could do the study again at your institution from the information given by the author.

It is also important to remember that the word *criticism* has both a positive and negative connotation. If the author does something well, make a note of it in your mind. If something seems weak or wrong, keep track of that as well. In my experience, it is the balance of positive and negative elements that must be weighed to judge a study intelligently. But this is not a simple tally. Certain errors clearly are more disastrous than are others. On the one hand, if the basic research design or the primary statistical tests are faulty, the results may be meaningless. On the other hand, if a study fails to mention a related study that you think is pertinent, this is a far less drastic fault. Here, of course, is where judgment is necessary.

Indeed, when you make such judgments about statistical studies, you are contributing to the field as a whole. So please start actively critiquing statistical studies. A sophisticated and critical audience can only help to improve statistical research in our field. And, of course, there is always room for improvement.

The remainder of this chapter will look at the typical organization of research articles. A number of issues will be raised that you should consider, section by section, as you read through a study. These issues should automatically guide you into thinking about what the author did, how it was done, and how you should interpret the results. The concepts are summarized in a checklist near the end of the chapter. Try to understand why the author of a study should be providing you with such information and why the information is important to the replicability of the study. Remember, if you are not given enough information to replicate a study, the author has *not* explained it adequately.

A sample study is also provided. The study used here was my first effort (Brown 1980). In evaluating the study you should focus on the flaws but also look at the good points, reading in a critical manner.

Research articles typically provide hierarchical headings with three different levels. These headings will help you follow the organization of an article. The presentation of these headings differs from journal to journal but will usually be found in some form. One standard three-level format is that of the American Psychological Association (APA, 1983:66–67), which is as follows:

## CENTERED MAIN HEADINGS

*Flush Left Side Headings*
  *Indented paragraph headings.*

This three-level format for headings corresponds directly to the following outline hierarchy:

I. Centered main headings
  A. Flush left side headings
    1. Indented paragraph headings

If the headings are well done, the organization of topics in the article should be easy to follow. It should also be noted that the APA provides ways of handling four and five levels of headings, so the pattern shown here must be viewed as one possible way to handle headings, although the policies regarding the use of more than three levels vary from journal to journal in our field. Regardless of the format, the headings should help the reader follow the overall organization of the sections in a study.

These sections are fairly standard from article to article. In the APA heading format, the sections of a typical research report will be as in Table 5.1. Of course, there will be text between the headings. Notice that the headings form an outline, which can be especially helpful if you know the kind of information to look for in each section. So let's consider each section in turn.

## Abstract

The purpose of an abstract is to summarize the article. The abstract appears first and usually contains 100–300 words, depending on the journal. It provides considerable information in a short space, so it must be tightly written. An abstract should contain at least the following information: (1) a clear statement of the topic and purpose of the article, (2) a brief description of the participants and materials used in the study, (3) an explanation of the procedures followed and the statistical analyses

TABLE 5.1. TYPICAL RESEARCH HEADINGS

ABSTRACT

INTRODUCTION

METHOD

*Subjects*
  *French speakers.*
  *English speakers.*
*Materials*

*Procedures*

*Analyses*

RESULTS

DISCUSSION/CONCLUSION

REFERENCES

APPENDIXES

used, and (4) a summary of the results and their implications for the field. This information should provide you with a good idea of what you will find in the article and of whether you are interested in reading it. Now, read Example 5.1 critically. I will reserve my judgments of this study until Chapter 13.

EXAMPLE 5.1 ABSTRACT

# *Newly Placed Students Versus Continuing Students: Comparing Proficiency*

James Dean Brown

University of California, Los Angeles

This study investigated the possibility that there might be two distinctively different student populations within some ESL classrooms: 1) students placed directly into a course (Placed Ss) and 2) those who are continuing from lower-level courses (Continuing Ss). During three successive quarters (Fall, Winter and Spring 1978) at UCLA, proficiency data were gathered on Placed and Continuing Ss in English 33C (advanced ESL).

The 33C level was chosen because it was suspected that any differences in proficiency would be greatest at the advanced levels. The Placed Ss (N=201) had been placed in English 33C by the *UCLA ESL Placement Examination*

(ESLPE). The Continuing Ss (N=118) had needed and successfully completed at least one prerequisite ESL course before entering English 33C.

Three measures of proficiency were used to compare the two types of student: the students' course grades, their scores on the departmental final examination and their acceptable-answer scores on a 50 item cloze test.

Multivariate and discriminant analyses of the three measures indicated that the Placed Ss did significantly better ($p < .05$) than the Continuing Ss on all three measures in all three quarters. Probable causes of this phenomenon are discussed, as well as a possible relationship between this "new" variable and previous discouraging learning-gain (pretest/posttest) findings.

# Introduction

The introduction (usually without a heading) serves the overall purpose of putting the study in perspective. Generally, it tells you which area of the field is involved and then narrows to the specific specialization and topic that was investigated. This goal is normally accomplished through a review of the relevant literature and a statement of the purpose of the study.

## Review of the literature

This section (usually untitled) should be a discussion of the previous research that is relevant to the study. Such a discussion should, at a minimum, provide (1) the background or rationale for the study, (2) a demonstration of how previous research is related to the study, and (3) a framework for viewing the study. However, an author who is broaching an unexplored area of research cannot cite previous works. In this case, the author should at least explain the route by which this new area was reached. In either case, the author must give you enough information so that you can tell where the study fits into the field (see Example 5.2).

EXAMPLE 5.2 INTRODUCTION

Language placement testing has generated a great deal of interest in the ESL field. Two general schools of thought are presently dominant: one which supports the "discrete-point" approach to language testing, and another which advocates the "integrative" approach. In addition, numerous studies have been conducted on the reliability and validity of various types of tests. Yet, in this plethora of theoretical activity, the student himself often seems to be forgotten.

This is not to say that the theoretical endeavors are not worthwhile. There just seems to be a general lack of follow-up on what actually happens to a student after we have affected his life by placing him at one level or another in our ESL classes. What does happen to him, one or two quarters/ semesters later, when he has moved through our classes to a higher level?

The purpose of this study is to investigate possible differences in proficiency between students who are continuing through our system of classes and the students around him who have been placed directly into the same class. This problem first surfaced during a meeting of the UCLA Service Course Committee. One of the instructors said that students who progress through our courses do not do as well as those who are placed directly into the same level. After that meeting, an informal poll of the teaching staff of our service courses showed that 16 out of 19 teachers believed that there was a difference between these two types of students.

This study, then, focused on the question: do students who have progressed through our system of service courses (Continuing Ss) perform differently at the end of the course on various measures of proficiency than those who have been placed directly into the same course (Placed Ss)? This question merits investigation for two reasons: 1) if the Placed Ss are, in fact, performing significantly better than the Continuing Ss, it would indicate a serious mismatch between the placement test and the material being learned in the service courses; 2) if such a mismatch exists at UCLA, the same problem may be widespread at institutions that use norm-referenced ESL placement examinations.

## Statement of purpose

This section (usually untitled) follows the literature review and further narrows the introduction to the exact topic under consideration. It does so by (1) stating the purpose in such a way that you know precisely what the author was looking for in the study, (2) presenting precise research questions that clarify what was being investigated, or (3) including specific research hypotheses that are stated in such a way that you know exactly what was being tested or studied. Any or all of these approaches are found in language studies. But, obviously, if all are used, the maximum amount of information is provided. This section, then, should give you enough information so you know exactly where the author was heading in the study (see Example 5.2).

Example 5.2 illustrates a situation in which the author thought that there was no previous literature relevant to the study because the area of research had not previously been explored. Nevertheless, the first three paragraphs explain where the study fits into the general area of language research, as well as how the particular study came about. The last paragraph indicates the central research question and gives a rationale for its importance. Does the sample study provide enough information for you to understand where the study fits into the field of language teaching and what the researcher was attempting to do?

EXAMPLE 5.3 METHOD

**Method**

The study was conducted by comparing the means of Continuing Ss and Placed Ss at the English 33C level on three measures of proficiency. The English 33C level was chosen because, if there was any difference in performance, it could reasonably be expected to be greatest at the most advanced level in the series of courses (see Table 1).

TABLE 1
UCLA ESL Service Courses

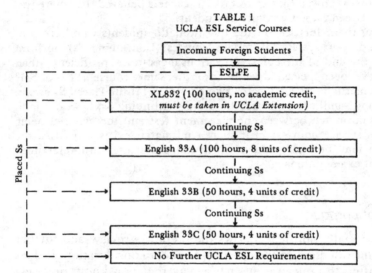

(Adapted from Bailey, 1977)

## Method

The purpose of this section is to describe what happened in the study (see Example 5.3). It is here that you should look for the information that is necessary to decide whether you could replicate the study. Hence, this section should answer most of the Wh-questions. More specifically, this section should tell you (1) who participated in the study, including when and where (*subjects*), (2) what type of materials were used (*materials*), (3) what the participants were asked to do (*procedures*), and (4) how the analyses were performed (*analyses*) (see Examples 5.3–5.6).

### Subjects

Each person, or participant, in the study is considered a subject. The subjects should be described in this section. How many were there? Who were they? When and where were they investigated? Other characteristics of the subjects that it might be important to describe here include age, sex, school level, native language background, level of proficiency in a second/foreign language, nationality, and socioeconomic status.

It is also important that the author explain how the subjects were selected. Were they randomly chosen from a larger population of possible subjects? Were they volunteers? Or were any special criteria used for choosing them? The characteristics and selection methods are important in determining how the results apply to your situation or how the results can be generalized to the field at large (see Example 5.4).

EXAMPLE 5.4 SUBJECTS

*Subjects.* In the Fall 1977 pilot study (n = 164), all of the students enrolled in seven sections of UCLA's English 33C were included. The study was replicated during Winter 1978 (n = 82) using all four sections of 33C and again during Spring 1978 (n = 73) with all three sections. In these three experiments (N = 319), the Placed Ss and Continuing Ss seem to be similarly distributed in terms of language background (Table 2), sex (Table 3) and academic status (Table 4).

TABLE 2
Language Distribution

| Language | Fall 77 | | Winter 78 | | Spring 78 | |
|---|---|---|---|---|---|---|
| | Placed | Contin. | Placed | Contin. | Placed | Contin. |
| Chinese | 28 | 4 | 9 | 12 | 8 | 7 |
| Korean | 27 | 11 | 4 | 15 | 6 | 8 |
| Persian | 14 | 8 | 4 | 8 | 6 | 6 |
| Vietnamese | 12 | 1 | 1 | 1 | 4 | 2 |
| Spanish | 11 | 2 | 2 | 3 | 3 | – |
| Japanese | 8 | – | – | 3 | 5 | 4 |
| French | 5 | – | 2 | 1 | 2 | – |
| Thai | 4 | – | – | 1 | – | – |
| Arabic | 3 | 1 | – | 2 | 1 | 2 |
| Armenian | 2 | – | – | – | – | – |
| Indonesian | 2 | – | 1 | 1 | – | – |
| Italian | 2 | – | – | 1 | – | – |
| Portuguese | – | – | – | 2 | 2 | – |
| Russian | – | – | – | 1 | 2 | – |
| Other (one each) | 15 | 4 | 4 | 4 | 2 | 3 |
| TOTAL | 133 | 31 | 27 | 55 | 41 | 32 |

TABLE 3
Sex Distribution

| Sex | Fall 77 | | Winter 78 | | Spring 78 | |
|---|---|---|---|---|---|---|
| | Placed | Contin. | Placed | Contin. | Placed | Contin. |
| Male | 56% | 61% | 48% | 62% | 68% | 56% |
| Female | 44% | 39% | 52% | 38% | 32% | 44% |

TABLE 4
Academic Status

| Status | Fall 77 | | Winter 78 | | Spring 78 | |
|---|---|---|---|---|---|---|
| | Placed | Contin. | Placed | Contin. | Placed | Contin. |
| Undergraduate | 70% | 74% | 63% | 64% | 72% | 68% |
| Graduate | 30% | 26% | 37% | 36% | 28% | 32% |

Notice that Example 5.3 introduces the section on methods by describing the context of the study in terms of the courses at UCLA (University of California at Los Angeles). This description is then logically followed by a section that details the number, language background, sex, and academic status of the groups involved in the study (see Example 5.4). The selection process is also covertly described in the phrase "all of the students enrolled...." Is this sufficient information for you to decide how the results might apply to your situation?

## Materials

This section gives the author the opportunity to describe any materials that were used in the study. These materials are also sometimes included in appendixes. Teaching materials, questionnaires, rating scales, tests, and so forth should be described in detail unless they are well known. Any other pertinent information, such as the range of possible scores, scoring methods used, types of questions, and types of scales, should also be included. The reliability and validity (see Chapter 8) of any tests or scales should appear in this section as well (see Example 5.5).

EXAMPLE 5.5 MATERIALS

*Measures of Proficiency.* The Placed and Continuing Ss were separated into two groups on the basis of departmental records. Then, three measures of proficiency were used to compare the groups: the students' course grades, their scores on the departmental 33C final examination, and their scores on an open-ended cloze test.

The course grade was given by teachers to reflect the students' performance in the course. It was given on the basis of a point system which had been agreed upon by all teachers at the beginning of Fall quarter. This grade was dependent on the department 33C final examination in so far as the students had to pass the final in order to pass the course and the final amounted to 20% of the point total for the grade.

The final examination was first developed during the Spring quarter of 1977 by a committee of English 33C teachers and has since been refined.

It was a criterion-referenced test designed to assess the main course objectives: reading, note-taking from lectures, and composition.

The cloze test was developed by this investigator (Brown, 1978). It was adapted from a passage in the intermediate ESL reader, *Man and His World: a Structured Reader* (Kurilecz, 1969). It was a 399 word passage on "Man and His Progress," a topic of general interest. The deletion pattern was every 7th word for a total of 50 blanks.

The cloze procedure is thought by many to be an integrative measure of overall language proficiency (Darnell, 1968; Oller, 1972). This cloze passage seemed valid for this purpose because it was reliable (K-R 20 = .95) and correlated at r = .90 with the ESLPE at UCLA as a criterion-related validity measure (Brown, 1978). The cloze test was scored by the acceptable-answer method being native-speaker responses collected on a pretest (n = 77) as the acceptable answers.

Any special equipment involved in the experiment, such as slides or reading machines, should also be described. How many slides were used? At what intervals were they shown? Or what kind of reading machine was used and how? Sometimes, information about equipment is included in a separate section called Equipment or Apparatus. In either case, all information that is necessary for the reader to understand exactly what materials and equipment were used should be fully documented.

One thought to keep in mind when reading through this section is that sometimes you may encounter misplaced accuracy, for instance, a detailed description of the technical specifications of a tape player, including frequency response and signal/noise ratio, but no indication of how many items were on the test or how reliable it was. There is obviously a limit to the amount of detail that can be provided. Therefore, it seems important for the author to find the correct level of detail so that nothing important is left out and yet the section is not cluttered with extraneous details.

In Example 5.5, no special equipment was used, but the three measures of proficiency in the study are described under a matching heading. Do you find the information provided about the measures, their development, and the scoring procedures sufficient to take the results based on them seriously? Is too much detail provided? Perhaps, more important, are the variables represented by the measures adequate operational definitions of the underlying constructs involved?

## Procedures

This section should tell you exactly how the materials and equipment were used. What did the subjects do in the study, or what was done to them? In detail, how were the materials prepared, administered, and scored? What were the environmental conditions like during the experiment? Were they the same for all the subjects involved? How long did the process take? Did any of the subjects drop out? The answers to these and many other potential questions should make it possible for the reader to understand exactly how the study was conducted. You should note here that there is no clearly defined procedures section in the sample study. Do you find answers to these questions anywhere else in the study?

## Analyses

Sometimes, this section is also headed Data Analysis, Statistical Procedures, or Design. Its basic purpose is to describe how the data were arranged and analyzed in the study. Since most studies compare two or more groups of subjects (or other types of data), it is important for the reader to understand exactly how the data were arranged or grouped for analysis. In addition, statistical analyses have many variants, and choosing one variant over another can dramatically affect the results. So it should be clear to you exactly which analyses were used and in what order. In other words, the analyses should be explained just as they were planned, step by step.

Usually, such analyses also have certain *assumptions*, or preconditions, that must be met for the mathematical calculations to be accurate and appropriate. These assumptions differ in importance, depending on the form of analysis and the particular assumption involved. Nevertheless, any research report should make clear to the reader that the assumptions were checked and met (see Example 5.6).

EXAMPLE 5.6 ANALYSES

*Analyses.* In this posttest only design, mean comparisons were first calculated by multivariate analysis for each experiment. The Mahalanobis $D^2$ statistic was converted to an F ratio to determine whether or not there were significant overall differences between the Placed and Continuing Ss. Then, discriminant analysis was performed. An approximate F ratio was calculated from Wilks' lambda to estimate differences on the individual variables: grade, final and cloze (*BMDP*, 1977).

There was no previous empirical evidence for differences in these means or for directionality. Consequently, null hypotheses of no difference between group means were adopted and the significance level was set at $\alpha < .05$, nondirectional.

Various types of analyses, including their assumptions, are the topics of Chapters 9–12. So, with a bit of patience, you will be able to read and understand this seemingly impenetrable but important section of a research paper as well as the other sections.

## The sections so far: a review

Now that you have looked at everything up to and including the Method section, you should stop and review by asking yourself the following general questions:

1. Did the author successfully summarize the study in the abstract?
2. Did the introduction provide an adequate framework for viewing the study?
   a. Did the literature review show where the study fits into the field?
   b. Was the author's purpose made clear through a precise statement of the purpose, the research questions, or the research hypotheses?
3. Do you now have enough information to replicate the study if you want to do so?
   a. Is there enough detail about the subjects to determine to whom the results may safely be generalized?
   b. Is it clear what teaching materials, questionnaires, and tests were used in the study? Are the instruments reliable and valid?
   c. Do you understand exactly how the materials were administered to the subjects?
   d. Does the author clearly state how the data were organized and analyzed?
4. At this point, you should also think back over the issues raised in Chapters 2–4.
   a. What types of variables were involved? Which were the dependent and independent variables? the intervening variable(s)? the moderator and control variables? Were they properly labeled? Do they make sense considered together?
   b. Were all the key concepts and variables operationally defined? Were these definitions adequate and appropriate?
   c. What types of scales were involved: nominal, ordinal, or interval? Do the scales that were used make sense in the context of the study?
   d. Are there any extraneous variables that were not accounted for in the study, in relation to the environment, the groupings, the people involved, or the measures themselves? Has the author successfully controlled them or were they unnoticed? What would you have done to eliminate these problem variables?

Only after you review all these questions will you be ready to look at the results to determine whether they are logical and meaningful for you, your teaching situation, and our field as a whole.

## Results

The purpose of the results section is to summarize the grouped data and the results of the analyses. For the sake of economy, this technical summary is often done through the use of tables or figures. Tables usually take the form of labeled columns of numbers, while figures are usually graphs or diagrams. Since the interpretation of these various forms of visual summary is important to understanding research, it will be an integral part of Chapters 6–12.

EXAMPLE 5.7 RESULTS

**Results**

&#x25B9;The descriptive statistics (Table 5) indicate that, in all three experiments, there was a consistent difference in the mean performance of the Placed and Continuing Ss on all three measures. These differences are all significant at well below the .05 probability level set for this study. The probability, then, is less than 5% that these differences occurred by chance alone. Therefore, all null hypotheses of no difference between means are rejected.

In addition to being significant, the differences are meaningful because they are large. During the entire school year 1977-1978, the Placed Ss had a mean of .69 grade points higher than the Continuing Ss. The Placed Ss also scored 9.82 points higher on the final examination and 6.71 points higher on the cloze test than the Continuing Ss.

TABLE 5
Descriptive Statistics and Significance of Differences in Proficiency

| Measure | Group | Fall 77 (n=164) | Winter 78 (n=82) | Spring 78 (n=73) | Total N=319) |
|---|---|---|---|---|---|
| | | Mean (SD) | Mean (SD) | Mean (SD) | Mean |
| Course | Placed | 2.99 ( .62) | 3.21 ( .50) | 3.35 ( .50) | 3.13 |
| Grade | Contin. | 2.04 (1.04) | 2.88 ( .51) | 2.83 ( .27) | 2.44 |
| | (Diff.) | .95* | .33* | .52* | .69 |
| Final | Placed | 67.83 (7.89) | 78.33 (8.33) | 78.15 (7.03) | 72.89 |
| Exam | Contin. | 55.31 (9.66) | 73.36 (7.01) | 68.97 (6.01) | 63.07 |
| | (Diff.) | 12.52* | 4.97** | 9.18* | 9.82 |
| Cloze | Placed | 22.97 (4.56) | 24.22 (4.26) | 23.12 (4.72) | 23.32 |
| | Contin. | 15.87 (4.57) | 18.56 (4.92) | 16.09 (5.91) | 16.61 |
| | (Diff.) | 7.10* | 5.66* | 7.03* | 6.71 |

\* $p < .01$
\*\* $p < .05$

The first topic of the results section is usually a summary or description of the grouped data (see Example 5.7). Such information as the number of subjects, the subjects' average scores or ratings, some indication of how the scores varied among the different groups and within each group is often included. Another topic that is normally covered is the actual results of any statistical procedures applied in the study. For example, if the average scores of two groups on the same test were different, were they different because of chance or because of real differences between the groups? This section may momentarily seem confusing. However, the rest of the book is designed to make such concepts accessible to you.

## Discussion/conclusions

Although the results section is a technical report of what happened in the study, the discussion (sometimes headed Discussion, sometimes Conclusion, and sometimes both) section usually reflects on these results in nontechnical terms (see Examples 5.8 and 5.9). Remember that the author should have clarified the purpose or research questions in the introduction. It is in the discussion section that you should expect to find direct answers to those original issues.

EXAMPLE 5.8 DISCUSSION
**Discussion**

Clearly then, there were differences in the performances of the Continuing and Placed Ss. However, to adequately address the issue, the results must first be considered individually.

*Course Grade.* The average Placed S in all three experiments received 3.13 grade points or slightly higher than a "B" for the course. The average Continuing S, on the other hand, received 2.44 grade points or about a "C+." The .69 grade points difference amounts to more than two-thirds of a grade average difference between the two groups. In addition, 8.5 percent of the Continuing Ss did not pass the course (D+ or below), as opposed to only 1.5 percent of the Placed Ss. So it seems clear that, based on a standard point system, the teachers rated the performance of the Placed Ss significantly higher than that of the Continuing Ss.

*Final Examination.* Again on the course departmental final examination, the average Continuing S was considerably lower. The Placed Ss averaged 72.89 points on this measure, while the Continuing Ss had a mean of only 63.07, a difference of 9.82 points. The test was designed to tap three main course objectives: 1) the ability to read college level texts; 2) the ability to understand and take notes on a college level lecture; and 3) the ability to write a college level composition. The nearly 10 point difference between the means of the two groups indicates that the Placed Ss were significantly better than the Continuing Ss at mastering one or more of these course objectives.

*Cloze Procedure*. As mentioned above, the cloze procedure seems to be a good integrative test of overall ESL proficiency. Therefore, the data indicate that the Placed Ss were considerably higher in general ESL proficiency than the Continuing Ss. The mean score in the Placed group was 23.32; in the Continuing group, it was 16.61. The difference of 6.71 points is more than one standard deviation lower—a considerable difference in overall ESL proficiency.

EXAMPLE 5.9 CONCLUSIONS

**Conclusions**

The differences in proficiency found in this study seem to indicate a mismatch between the norm-referenced placement test (ESLPE) and the amount being learned in the courses. In other words, students in lower-level courses do not appear to be learning enough in those courses to make up the number of points which separate levels on the ESLPE and might not be placed in the next level if they had to take that test again. This observation is not meant, by any means, to be an attack on the UCLA placement test and service courses in particular. In fact, this mismatch may be widespread at institutions which use norm-referenced placement tests.

*Possible Causes*. Possible explanations for the differences between groups may be found by considering the following three variables: 1) the amount of instructional time devoted to the Ss' ESL study, 2) the amount and nature of the Ss' previous EFL study, and 3) the amount of time that has passed since that previous EFL study.

First, the amount of instructional time devoted to each level in the UCLA ESL service courses is limited (see Table 1). For instance, English 33B and 33C provide only fifty hours of instruction each. Previous studies indicate that fifty hours of instructional time is not enough to make any significant difference in overall English language proficiency.

For instance, at the University of Hawaii, Mason (1971) found that there was no signficant difference in proficiency between an experimental group that was artifically exempted from ESL requirements and a matched-pair control group that completed 180 hours of ESL course work in twelve weeks.

Mosback (1977) found similarly discouraging results in two studies at the University of Addis Ababa in Ethiopia. In the first study (1971-2), he reported an average decline in proficiency of .05 percent at the intermediate level and a decline of 2.4 percent at the advanced level. These results were obtained in a pretest-posttest study after 36 hours of instruction. In a second study (1972-3), he found a mean overall improvement of only 0.9 percent after 36 hours of instruction. Mosback concluded on the basis of these studies that "general 'back-up' courses in service English are largely a waste of resources" (p. 318).

Not all studies have been discouraging. At the University of California, San Diego, Newmark (1971) found that measureable gains could be achieved by narrowly defining the course objectives. He found that after thirty weeks with 12 hours of instruction per week (360 hours total), 37 percent of the Ss had achieved the intended goals. In forty weeks (480 hours), 50 percent had achieved the course objectives; in fifty weeks (600 hours), 80 percent; and in 60 weeks (720 hours), 98 percent had reached the intended goals. Though Newmark reports success in this study, 720 hours of instruction over a two year period is not always possible. For instance, a student who completes all four of the UCLA service courses has received a total of only 300 hours of instruction.

In light of these studies, how can we expect students with only 50-100 hours of instruction to gain enough in overall language proficiency to make up the difference in points which separates levels on the ESLPE? If the Continuing Ss have not made this point gain at the English 33B level, they will then be competing with more proficient Placed Ss at the English 33C level. This effect may be further magnified for those Continuing Ss who were originally placed into English XL832, then took English 33A, 33B and 33C. They would probably fall further behind the Placed Ss at each level.

Second, the amount and nature of previous EFL study may be factors contributing to the observed differences. If we view the ESLPE as a measure of achievement for an S's previous EFL study, those who score low either did not do well in their previous study or had little, if any, instruction in English. If they did not do well in EFL study at home, there is no reason for us to expect them to do much better in the United States. If they had little or no previous instruction, we are being overly optimistic to expect them to learn enough English in 250 hours of instruction to be competitive at the English 33C level with Placed Ss who may have studied English for many years at home. In either case, Continuing Ss who had low scores on the ESLPE are eventually promoted into the advanced English 33C course where they *must* compete with Placed Ss.

Third, the amount of time that has passed since studying English may be another factor which explains the observed differences. Some or all of the Placed Ss may have studied a great deal of English at home; however, because of the amount of time that has elapsed since that study, they may have become "rusty." Consequently, their ESLPE scores reflect only what they remember at the time. Later, when they are doing the course work for English 33C, they may simply be relearning what they already knew and do so much faster than those Continuing Ss who are learning the material for the first time.

These three "time" variables are all possible explanations for the repeatedly observed differences between the Placed Ss and Continuing Ss, but they are only conjecture. There is clearly a need for further research in this area.

You should also look for some exploration of why the results turned out as they did and their implications. This may appear in a separate section headed Conclusion or be part of the Discussion section. Such an exploration may relate the results to previous research or may be pure speculation or both. Although there is nothing inherently wrong with speculation, the author should make it abundantly clear that it is speculation. In either case, you should judge the logic of the arguments in the context of the study and of what you know about language teaching.

In the course of doing the study or pondering the results, the researcher often discovers that more questions have been raised than resolved. This is a natural and creative part of statistical research. So suggestions for further research are also often included in the last part of the discussion or conclusions section (see Example 5.10).

EXAMPLE 5.10 FURTHER RESEARCH

*Further Research.* The mismatch found in this study between the placement and the learning that is going on in the service courses at UCLA begs answers to the following questions:

1) Will the same results be obtained by replicating this study at other institutions?

2) What is the relationship between the above three "time" variables and differences in performance between Placed and Continuing Ss?

3) Are there other variables which may account for the observed differences in performance?

4) Would a pretest-posttest research design help to explain the apparent differences between Placed and Continuing Ss?

5) Would a criterion-referenced placement test, based on clear-cut, realistic and measurable course objectives (see Popham, 1978), more accurately match the courses than a norm-referenced test?

6) Would learning gains in ESL surface more clearly if they were measured by objectives-based criterion-referenced tests rather than norm-referenced tests (see Mehrens and Ebel, 1979)?

7) Should students be "automatically" promoted in the next level without first demonstrating that they have gained enough to compete at that higher level?

## References

The reference section takes various forms, depending on the format used by a particular journal. It may consist of an alphabetical (by author's last name) list of the articles and books cited in the article, or it may be entitled Notes, and take the more traditional form of numerically noted and listed notes and references, or footnotes. In either case, the purpose is to tell the reader where each citation or bit of secondary information was found. It should include all and only those references cited in the text of the article. The reader is, of course, free to check such references or may wish to follow up a citation with further reading from a particular reference. Therefore, references are a necessary and useful part of any research paper (see Example 5.11).

EXAMPLE 5.11 REFERENCES

## REFERENCES

Bailey, K. M. 1977. The ESL service courses at UCLA: a progress report. *Workpapers in Teaching English as a Second Language. 11*, 1-16.

*BMDP Biomedical Computer Programs*, Berkley: University of California Press, 1977.

Brown, J.D. 1978. A correlational study of four methods of scoring cloze tests. M. A. Thesis, University of California, Los Angeles.

Darnell, D. K. 1968. The development of an English language proficiency test of foreign students using a clozentropy procedure. Boulder, Colorado: University of Colorado. (ERIC Document Reproduction No. ED 024 039).

Kurilecz, M. 1969. *Man and His World: a Structured Reader.* New York: Crowell, 58-59.

Mason, C. 1971. The relevance of intensive training in English as a second language for university students. *Language Learning, 21*, (2), 197-203.

Mehrens, W. A. and R. L. Ebel. 1979. Some comments on criterion-referenced and norm-referenced achievement tests. *NCME Measurement in Education, 10*, (1), 3-4.

Mosback, G. F. 1977. Service courses in ESL at university level—How effective are they? *Modern Language Journal, 60*, (3), 313-18.

Newmark, L. D. 1971. A minimal language teaching program. In *The Psychology of Second Language Learning.* (ed.) P. Pimsleur and T. Quinn, Cambridge University Press, 11-18.

Oller, J. W., Jr., 1972. Scoring methods and difficulty levels for cloze tests of proficiency in English as a second language. *Modern Language Journal.* 1972, *56* (3), 151-57.

Popham, W. J. 1978. *Criterion-Referenced Measurement.* Englewood Cliffs, N.J.: Prentice-Hall.

# Appendixes

This section is sometimes used to present information that would not properly fit into the text. The information provided should be necessary and complete. It might include copies of the scales or measures used in the study, examples of the subjects' performance (e.g., representative writing samples), other examples of data as they were collected, and so on. Though they may seem like an afterthought, appendixes often clarify what the study was all about. Note, however, that the editorial policy of some journals precludes the use of appendixes (for reasons of length). There were none in the sample study.

# Overall merits of a study

Before deciding the overall merits of a study, you should probably review the various sections that we have looked at. The following checklist may be helpful in this regard. Try it with the sample study.

*Checklist for critiquing a statistical study*

I. *Abstract* (optional heading). Has the author correctly summarized the article? Are the following items included?

A. Statement of the topic and purpose
B. Description of the participants and materials and procedures
C. Explanation of the statistical analyses
D. Summary of results and implications

II. *Introduction* (optional heading). Is the framework for the study clear?
    A. *Literature Review* (optional heading). Can you tell where the study fits in?
        1. Is the background or rationale provided?
        2. Is the relationship to previous research clear?
    B. *Statement of Purpose* (optional heading). Can you tell where the study is heading? Are any of the following included?
        1. Purpose
        2. Research questions
        3. Research hypotheses

III. *Method.* Is the study replicable?
    A. *Subjects*
        1. Is the description of participants adequate?
        2. Is the method of selection clear?
    B. *Materials*
        1. Is there a description of tests, questionnaires, rating scales, and so forth?
        2. Do the variables represent reasonable operational definitions of the underlying constructs or characteristics involved?
        3. Is there a description of any equipment (when applicable)?
    C. *Procedures*
        1. Is there a description of the preparation of materials, administration, scoring, and so on?
        2. Is there a description of the conditions during the study?
    D. *Analyses*
        1. Is there a description of the arrangement and grouping of the data?
        2. Are the statistical tests listed in order of use?

IV. *Results*
    A. Are all the statistical tests previously listed represented as results?
    B. Is there a prose explanation (optional)?

V. *Discussion/Conclusion*
    A. Is the original research question, or questions, answered?
    B. Is there an explanation of why the results were as they were?
        1. If the conclusion is based on previous research, is it well supported and reasoned?

2. If the conclusion is speculative, is it qualified as such and well reasoned?

C. Are suggestions for further research provided?

VI. *References, Notes, or Footnotes*

A. Are all the references cited in the text included?

B. Are any pertinent references missing?

VII. *Appendixes*

A. Are they necessary?

B. Are they complete?

Once you have reviewed the study section by section, you should probably step back from it a bit and consider a few more global questions to help you evaluate the study as a whole. Do the sections taken together make sense, or are there contradictions and inconsistencies? Are any sections missing or flawed? If so, is this a serious problem in interpreting the results or in thinking about how meaningful the results are to you and your teaching?

The most important question, however, may be, "So what?" Is the study interesting or even important to you or to the language teaching field? And, if so, how is it important? In short, you are justified, as a member of our profession, to make judgments about the studies you encounter. It has also been my experience that virtually no study is completely without value. In most cases, at least somebody in our profession liked it or it would not have been published. Even if you have given up on a study as a whole, you may want to ask yourself if any interesting ideas or approaches were presented that might help you as a language teacher. And, in the worst of all possible cases, remember that even a horrendous study can serve as a bad example.

If, at this point, you are interested in another person's viewpoint on the sample study presented in this chapter, you will find my critique of it in Chapter 13.

## Terms

| | |
|---|---|
| assumptions | replicability |
| criticism | subject |
| figures | tables |

## Review questions

1. The sample study in this chapter seems to have major implications for placement and overall curriculum design in ESL programs and

possibly for other language programs. Do you agree with the specific implications suggested or that, in general, the study has useful implications?

2. Now that you have read the study, how did you rate the introduction section? Why was there no review of the literature? Was the approach satisfactory in the sense that you could tell where the study fit into the field? Was the purpose of the study clear?

3. Did the methods section give you enough information about the subjects, materials, procedures, and analyses to replicate the study (aside from doing the actual statistics)?

4. How would you replicate the study in your teaching situation?

5. Are the results clear enough that you can at least understand what the author found?

6. Do the discussion and conclusions sections give a nontechnical explanation of the results as they relate to the original purpose of the study? Is some interpretation given of why the results turned out as they did? Are there any suggestions for further research? Are the suggestions reasonable?

7. Are the references complete? Are there any unnecessary ones?

8. As a whole, how would you rate the study? Are there any serious flaws in its operationalization, in the scaling, in the definition and manipulation of variables, in the control of extraneous variables, or in logic that would cause you to doubt the results of the study?

9. Does this study have any value to you and your teaching? To your program? To your field? Why or why not?

## Application

Using all the tools you now have as a reader of research, read any statistical study of interest to you and critique it.

# 6 The group and the individuals

In the long run, a study should help you picture how the subjects behaved or performed on each measure, either through graphic representations of the performances or through descriptive statistics that indicate the central tendency and dispersion of the scores. To begin with, then, it is useful to understand how data can be visually represented.

## Frequency

If I were to ask you how frequently you brush your teeth, you would probably answer something like two times per day. Likewise, if I were to ask you how frequent a score of 67 was in Table 6.1, the obvious answer would be "three people received 67." *Frequency* is just this commonsense idea. It indicates how many people did the same thing or performed a certain task in the same way. When you figured out how many people received a score of 67, you counted up, or tallied, the number of people at 67. To calculate the frequency at each score level, then, the researcher simply tallies them up and records the result, as shown in Table 6.1. But why would anyone bother to do this? Fre-

TABLE 6.1. TALLYING FREQUENCIES

| Students | Score | Tally | Frequency |
|----------|-------|-------|-----------|
| Robert | 65 | / | 1 |
| Randy | 67 | /// | 3 |
| Henk | 67 | | |
| Shenan | 67 | | |
| Jeanne | 69 | //// | 4 |
| Corky | 69 | | |
| Millie | 69 | | |
| Archie | 69 | | |
| Dean | 70 | // | 2 |
| Elisabeth | 70 | | |
| Monique | 72 | / | 1 |
| Iliana | 73 | / | 1 |
| Bill | 74 | / | 1 |

TABLE 6.2. FREQUENCY DISTRIBUTION

| Score value | Frequency |
|:-----------:|:---------:|
| 65 | 1 |
| 66 | 0 |
| 67 | 3 |
| 68 | 0 |
| 69 | 4 |
| 70 | 2 |
| 71 | 0 |
| 72 | 1 |
| 73 | 1 |

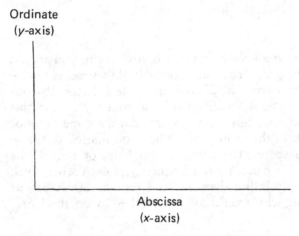

*Figure 6.1  Abscissa and ordinate*

quencies are useful because they can be used to collapse, or summarize, information about scores received by a group, as shown in Table 6.2. This arrangement of score values from high to low and the frequency of each score value in a table is called a *frequency distribution*.

## Graphic representation of frequencies

There are, however, more appealing ways to show the frequency distribution. You will generally encounter such graphic representations in one of three forms: a histogram, a bar graph, or a frequency polygon. All three are drawn on two axes: a horizontal line (also called the *abscissa*, or *x*-axis) and a vertical line (*ordinate*, or *y*-axis). These are shown in Figure 6.1.

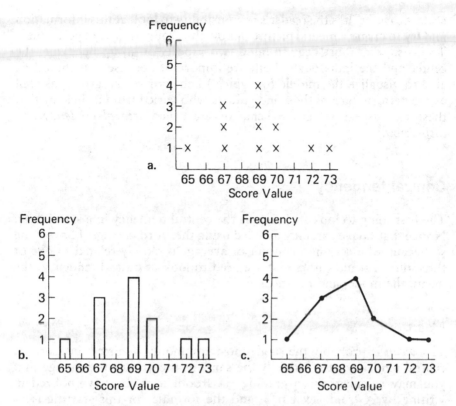

*Figure 6.2 Graphic representation of frequency distributions. a: Histogram. b: Bar graph. c: Frequency polygon.*

A *histogram* of a frequency distribution is usually created by assigning score values to the horizontal line, putting potential frequency values on the vertical line, and marking an asterisk or "X" to represent each student who received each score, as shown in Figure 6.2a. If bars are used instead of asterisks to represent the same information, you are looking at a *bar graph*, as shown in Figure 6.2b. When dots are placed where the top asterisk would be at each score value and the dots are connected by lines, you have a *frequency polygon,* as shown in Figure 6.2c. All three types of graphs are important in reading statistical studies because they represent information that you should have about the way the groups performed. Another excellent reason for getting a good grip on these concepts is that they are sometimes used to misrepresent or distort information graphically (see Huff and Geis 1954).

Studies in our field often omit these useful forms of graphs. However, they usually provide some form of *descriptive statistics,* that is, numerical representations of exactly how each group performed on the interval scale measures. It is the reader's responsibility to look at this information and try to create a mental picture of how the group or groups performed. To do so, you must keep in mind two aspects of group behavior: the center and the individuals. Both are important because you should be able to visualize the middle (or typical) behavior of the group, as well as the performance of those individuals who varied from it. In statistics, these two aspects of group behavior are called *central tendency* and *dispersion*.

## Central tendency

The first thing to look for, then, is the central tendency in a set of data. Notice that I have carefully avoided using the word *average*. I have done so because the common concept of average is closely related to *one* of three different indicators that are used to look at central tendency: the mean, the mode, and the median.

### Mean

The *mean* is probably the single most commonly reported indicator of central tendency. It is virtually the same as the arithmetic average that you may calculate when grading classroom tests. It is symbolized in writing by $\overline{X}$ (said "ex bar"), and the formula for this statistic is as follows:

$$\overline{X} = \frac{\Sigma X}{N}$$

where $\overline{X}$ = mean, $X$ = scores, $N$ = number of scores, $\Sigma$ = sum (or add).

For future reference, let's take a brief look at this formula. It simply says, to get the mean ($\overline{X}$), you add up ($\Sigma$) the scores ($X$) and divide by the number ($N$) of scores that you have. This formula is shown more graphically in Table 6.3. To find this mean in the example, you (1) add up the scores, (2) find the number of scores, and (3) divide the totaled scores by that number. So the mean in the example would be 70.

Even though the focus of this book is on reading and interpreting statistics, rather than doing them, it is often necessary to understand the symbols and how they work. Hence, a little exposure to this simple formula will not hurt. In addition, some of the concepts explained in this book will be easier to introduce with formulas. Of course, the concepts will always be explained in "real" language and examples will be provided. In any case, the formula for the mean was not so difficult.

TABLE 6.3. CALCULATING THE MEAN

| Students (Group J) | Scores (X) | Calculations |
|---|---|---|
| Jan | 40 | 1 $\Sigma X$ = sum of scores = 40 + 67 + 67 + |
| Jakob | 67 | 70 + 76 + 80 + 90 = 490 |
| Jaime | 67 | 2 $N$ = number of scores = 7 |
| Jimmy | 70 | 3 $\overline{X} = \dfrac{\Sigma X}{N} = \dfrac{490}{7} = 70$ |
| Juanita | 76 | |
| Jean | 80 | |
| Jacques | 90 | |

It is just another way of saying something you already know how to do – much in the same way that we use *syntax* and *phonology* when others use the terms *grammar* and *pronunciation*. Try to view these simple mathematics as part of learning to understand statistics.

## Mode

The *mode* is the score that occurs most frequently in a set of scores. In Table 6.3, what would be the mode? The mode would be 67, the only score received by two students. To keep the mode straight in my mind, I associate the term with its more common meaning of fashionable (as in à la mode). Thus, the mode is the score that is most fashionable, or is received by the most students. There is no statistical formula for this straightforward idea. It should be noted, however, that, in some cases, there may be two or more modes in a set of scores. Such a distribution of scores would be termed *bimodal, trimodal,* and so on.

## Median

The *median* is defined as the middle point in a distribution, or that point below which 50 percent of the scores fall and, logically, above which 50 percent fall. In Table 6.3, you will see that Jimmy's score of 70 has three scores below it (40, 67, and 67) and three scores above it (76, 80, and 90). So the median in this example is 70. What, then, is the median for the following set of scores: 10, 25, 30, 40, 52, 60, 76? It should be clear to you that it is 40.

There are cases, however, when the median is not so clear. For example, what is the median for these scores: 8, 10, 13, 14, 16, 25? When there is an even number of scores, as in this example, the median is taken to be midway between the two middle scores. In this example, the two middle scores are 13 and 14, so the median is 13.5. Does that make sense? If so, what is the median for these scores: 10, 25, 37, 40,

50, 62, 71, 98? Your answer should have been 45, because that is the midpoint between the two middle scores, 40 and 50.

There are other cases in which there may be more than one score at the median, such as in the following: 45, 47, 48, 50, 50, 50, 67, 74, 87. Here, the midpoint is clearly 50, because there is an odd number of like scores at the median separating equal numbers of scores on either side.

Still other situations arise in which fractions other than .5 occur in the median, but the important thing to remember is that the median is the point that divides the scores 50/50, much like the median in a highway divides the road into two equal parts. In statistics, however, the median may turn out to be a fraction.

To review briefly, in Table 6.3, the mean, or arithmetic average, was 70; the mode, or most-often-received score, was 67; and the median, the score that divided the scores 50/50, was 70. These are all indicators of central tendency, and each has its strengths and weaknesses. None is necessarily better than the others, although the mean is most commonly reported. The measures simply serve different purposes and are appropriate in different situations.

## Dispersion

Now that you understand how to interpret the typical behavior of a group in the form of central tendency, let's look at how the performance of individuals may vary from that typical behavior. There are two commonly reported indicators of the dispersion of a set of scores: the range and the standard deviation.

### Range

You may already be familiar with the notion of range from correcting your classroom tests. *Range* is defined here as the number of points between the highest score on a measure and the lowest score plus one (plus one because it is viewed as including the scores at both ends). Thus, in Table 6.3, where the highest score is 90 and the lowest score is 40, the range is 51 points (90 − 40 + 1 = 51). The range provides some idea of how individuals vary from the central tendency. But it represents only the outer edges of that variation and, as a result, is strongly affected by behavior that may not be truly representative of the group as a whole. For instance, if Jan in Table 6.3 had already decided to drop the course involved and, therefore, had just guessed on the test, the range of 51 would not really represent the behavior of the group, because that behavior was strongly affected by something (Jan's personal problem) extraneous to the students' performances on the measure itself. Nevertheless, the range is often reported as one indicator of the dispersion and should be interpreted as just what it is – the number of points between the high and low scores, including both of them.

## Standard deviation

The *standard deviation* provides a sort of average of the differences of all scores from the mean. To understand what this means, let's look again at the formula. Recall that $\overline{X}$ was the symbol for the mean, that $X$ symbolized the scores, that $\Sigma$ indicated that something should be added up, and that $N$ was the number of subjects. The formula for the standard deviation ($SD$) is

$$\sqrt{\frac{\Sigma\ (X\ -\ \overline{X})^2}{N}}$$

Starting from the inside and working outward, you can see that the formula first requires you to subtract the mean, already calculated, from each score $(X\ -\ \overline{X})$; square each of these values $(X\ -\ \overline{X})^2$; and add them up $\Sigma_2\ (X\ -\ \overline{X})^2$. This sum is then divided by the number of scores $\Sigma\ (X\ -\ \overline{X})^2/N$, and the square root of the result

$$\sqrt{\frac{\Sigma\ (X\ -\ \overline{X})^2}{N}}$$

is the standard deviation. Table 6.4 makes this formula clearer.

Remember that the mean in Table 6.3 was 70. Using the same scores and mean for Table 6.4, you must line up each score with the mean and then subtract the mean from each score. Next, you must square each of the "differences" from the mean and add up the squared values. When you insert all this information into the formula, you find that the result for this example is 14.41. Let's now return to the definition.

I claimed that the standard deviation is a sort of average (ignoring the squaring and the square root, notice that you are adding something up and then dividing by $N$ – similar to what you did to calculate the mean) of the differences of all scores from the mean (so it turns out that what you are averaging is the difference of each student's score from the mean). Thus, the standard deviation is a sort of average of the differences of all scores from the mean. These differences are also called their *deviations* from the mean – hence the name standard deviation. What this sort of average tells you will be explained more fully in the next chapter. Just keep in mind that it is a good indicator of dispersion. It is often better than the range because it is an averaging process. By averaging, the effects of any extreme scores that are not attributable to

TABLE 6.4. THE STANDARD DEVIATION

| Students (Group J) | Score (X) | Mean ($\overline{X}$) | Difference ($X - \overline{X}$) | Difference squared ($X - \overline{X}$)$^2$ |
|---|---|---|---|---|
| Jan | 40 | − 70 | = − 30 | 900 |
| Jakob | 67 | − 70 | = − 3 | 9 |
| Jaime | 67 | − 70 | = − 3 | 9 |
| Jimmy | 70 | − 70 | = 0 | 0 |
| Juanita | 76 | − 70 | = + 6 | 36 |
| Jean | 80 | − 70 | = + 10 | 100 |
| Jacques | 90 | − 70 | = + 20 | 400 |

$$\Sigma\ (X - \overline{X})^2 \quad = \quad 1454$$

$$SD = \sqrt{\frac{\Sigma\ (X - \overline{X})^2}{N}} = \sqrt{\frac{1454}{7}}$$

$$= 207.71 = 14.41$$

performance on the test (e.g., Jan's personal problem) are generally minimized.

## Putting the picture together

To review briefly, then, two aspects of group behavior normally are described: the central tendency and dispersion. Central tendency indicates what the middle, or typical, behavior is on a given measure in the form of the mean (arithmetic average), mode (the most-often-received score), and the median (the score that splits the group 50/50). Which of these indicators is presented in a particular study will depend on the type of data and analyses in that study. But, in most cases, you will find at least one of them.

Likewise, you should look for an indication of the dispersion of scores, or the way individuals varied from the typical behavior of the group. This variation may be presented as the range (the difference between the highest and lowest scores, including both) or the standard deviation (a sort of average of how far individuals varied from the mean). Again, this information, in one form or another, is usually presented, and you should look for it so you can picture how the group or groups performed.

Such information is particularly useful in comparing the behavior of several groups on a particular measure. In Table 6.5, for instance, two groups – J and K – are clearly involved, and fairly complete information is presented on the typical behavior within each group and on how the individuals varied from that typical behavior. You should now be able

TABLE 6.5. GROUPS J AND K ON MY EXAM

| Group | Central tendency | | | Dispersion | | | |
|-------|-----|------|--------|-----|------|-------|-----|
| | $\overline{X}$ | Mode | Median | Low | High | Range | SD |
| J | 70 | 67 | 70 | 40 | 90 | 51 | 14 |
| K | 60 | 55 | 62 | 55 | 68 | 14 | 2 |

to answer the following questions about the behavior of these two groups.

1. Which group did generally better on the exam?
2. Which group had the single lowest score?
3. Which group had the widest spread of scores?
4. Which group was the most homogeneous on the test?
5. Which group was the most intelligent?

To answer Question 1, you should have looked at all three indicators of the central tendency. Clearly, Group J is higher on all three indicators and, therefore, performed better as a group on the examination. In Question 2, you should have looked at the low–high figures (remembering that they are probably single scores in this case) and found the lowest score (40). For Question 3, you should have noted that the range for Group J was considerably higher than that for Group K. This would tell you that Group J had the widest spread of scores. The answer to Question 4 will be found by looking at the standard deviations. The one for Group K is considerably lower, which indicates that the scores of the group were more tightly grouped around the mean than those of Group J. Thus Group K is considerably more homogeneous. But why look at the standard deviations rather than the ranges? Remember that extreme scores can occur for reasons other than the performance of the group on the measure. Since the standard deviation is a sort of averaging process, such aberrations affect it less. Therefore, it is the better indicator of the relative homogeneity of a group.

You should have seen through Question 5 immediately. You have no idea what the test in this example is like. How, then, can you decide whether it is measuring intelligence at all, much less whether Group J is more intelligent than Group K? This is an example of how the numbers should *not* be misinterpreted by you or by the authors you read. The numbers are just numbers, and it is your responsibility to look at them and determine what they mean. This is a task you should now be able to do. But it should become even easier and clearer in the next chapter because you will see more precisely how central tendency and dispersion relate, how they can go awry, and how they can help you – the teacher, tester, and reader of language studies.

## Terms and symbols

| | |
|---|---|
| abscissa | mean ($\overline{X}$) |
| bar graph | median |
| bimodal distribution, trimodal | mode |
| distribution, and so forth | $N$ |
| central tendency | ordinate |
| descriptive statistics | range |
| deviations | standard deviation ($SD$) |
| dispersion | $X$ |
| frequency | $x$-axis |
| frequency distribution | $y$-axis |
| frequency polygon | $\Sigma$ |
| histogram | |

## Review questions

1. What is central tendency? What are three indexes of central tendency? Which index is the best indicator?
2. What is dispersion? What two indexes are usually used to estimate dispersion? Which index is the best indicator?
3. Why should group behavior on a measure usually be described in terms of both the central tendency and dispersion?
4. What is a frequency distribution? And what is the advantage of a frequency distribution?
5. Can you label the abscissa and ordinate on the axes below?

6. Which of the three graphic representations at the top of page 73 is a histogram? A bar graph? A frequency polygon?

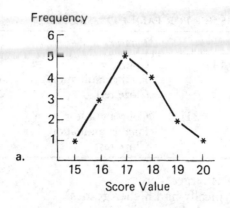

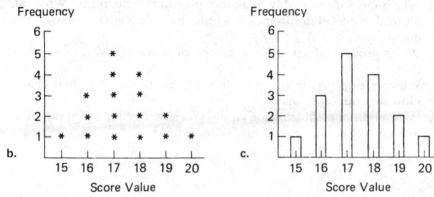

## Application

The table on page 74 is adapted from Figure 5.7 in Chapter 5. Look it over, then answer the questions that follow.

DESCRIPTIVE STATISTICS FOR FALL 1977 SAMPLE

| Group | Measure | $\overline{X}$ | SD |
|---|---|---|---|
| Placed Students ($n = 133$) | Course grade | 2.99 | .62 |
| | Final examination | 67.83 | 9.89 |
| | Cloze test | 22.97 | 4.56 |
| Continuing Students ($n = 31$) | Course grade | 2.04 | 1.04 |
| | Final examination | 55.31 | 9.66 |
| | Cloze test | 15.87 | 4.57 |

1. Which group was larger?
2. Which group typically had higher grades?
3. Which measure probably had more possible points on it? What additional piece of information would have helped to answer this question?
4. Which group performed better on the cloze test? How do you know that?
5. Which group performed more heterogeneously on the final exam? How do you know that?
6. What additional information would you have liked to see in this table to help you interpret the groups' behaviors?

# 7 Patterns in human behavior

Whether you believe that events are planned by a supreme being or are essentially random, you will probably accept the notion that there are certain patterns that occur in your life and in the lives of your students. Descriptive statistics, in addition to helping you visualize group behavior in terms of central tendency and dispersion, can help you understand these patterns and how individuals relate to them. To help you get a grip on how these patterns work, I will first explore the following concepts and how they interrelate: probability, distribution, normal distribution, and standardized scores.

## Probability

Short of taking you on a group trip to Monte Carlo or Las Vegas, perhaps the best way to demonstrate probability is to ask you to take out a coin and start flipping it. What did you get? Heads or tails? You no doubt recognize that there was a 50 percent chance of getting tails. How did you know that? You probably observed, or were taught, that there is a fairly predictable pattern to events like flipping a coin.

In more formal terms, the *probability* of getting heads on any given flip is 1 in 2, or 50 percent. This probability is determined by dividing the number of *expected outcomes* by the number of *possible outcomes* (heads or tails). Thus, one expected outcome (of heads) is divided by the two possibilities (of heads or tails) to yield .50, which indicates a 50 percent probability of getting heads.

What, then, is the probability of getting a five on a single roll of a six-sided die? Again, you need only divide the number of expected outcomes (one) by the total number of possible outcomes (the total of six sides). One divided by six is .166, or about .17. Hence there is about a 17 percent probability of getting a five on a single roll.

Why go through all this arithmetic to explain probability? There are three good reasons. First, it is important to realize that the probability of a given event is the ratio of the expected outcomes to the number of possible outcomes. This ratio, which ranges from 0 to 1.0, is commonly stated in percentages. Second, and perhaps more important, this explanation will help if you are ever asked to bet one month's salary on a flip of a coin or a roll of a die. Which would you choose – the .50 (or 50 percent) probability of a flip of a coin or the .17 (17 percent) probability of rolling a particular number on a die? Third, and more seriously, the purpose of discussing probability is to look at how it is related to descriptions of patterns in events, that is, how it is related to distributions.

## Probability and distribution

Another way to look at the probabilities and patterns is to plot them out as they occur, often in the form of a histogram like the one in Figure 6.2a, with the proportion of actual outcomes labeled on the ordinate and the possible outcomes demarked on the abscissa. Figure 7.1 shows how a scatterplot might look for flips of a coin if they were to occur as follows: heads, tails, tails, tails, heads, heads, tails, heads, tails, tails.

Notice that in Figure 7.1a an asterisk has been marked for each actual outcome. The result is a visual representation of the *distribution* of those outcomes. Perhaps you also thought that something was wrong with this distribution. If the probability of getting heads on any flip is .50, or 50 percent, would you not expect the heads and tails columns to be the same height? This apparent anomaly points to three important characteristics of probability (or frequency) distributions. First, the 50 percent probability of heads applies to (or starts over for) each flip. So heads may occur repeatedly or not at all for a number of flips. Second, in a small number of actual outcomes, the distribution may appear lopsided, as it does in Figure 7.1a. However, as the number of outcomes increases, to say 100 or 1,000, one would expect any such differences to decrease to meaningless proportions. Third, and perhaps most important, a visual examination of the scatterplot gives us important information about the distribution of the events involved. It is through such a visual examination that the patterns in human language-related events will be explored in the remainder of this chapter.

In purely mathematical terms, distributions of outcomes could theoretically occur with a greater number of possible events. Consider, for instance, the possibilities for outcomes of heads only for two coins (Figure 7.1b) and three coins (Figure 7.1c). Notice that the distributions have become a bit more complex. These two examples show limited versions of what is known as the *binomial distribution*. If the number of coins were increased, the distribution of events would obviously grow. If I were to plot a histogram of the number of occurrences of heads for 10 coins and connect the tops of each

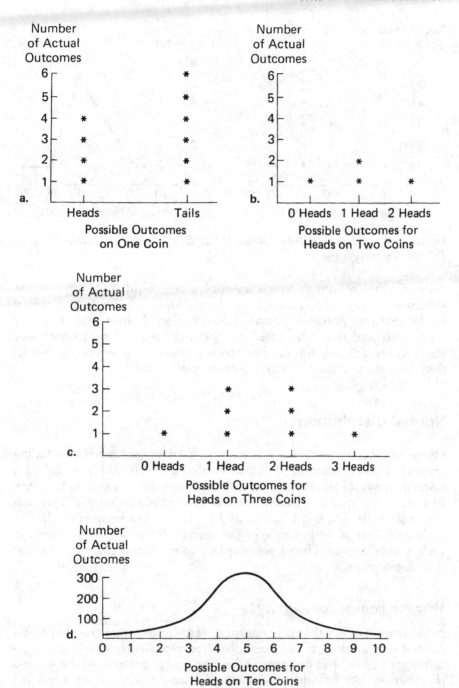

Figure 7.1   *Scatterplot of 10 coin flips*

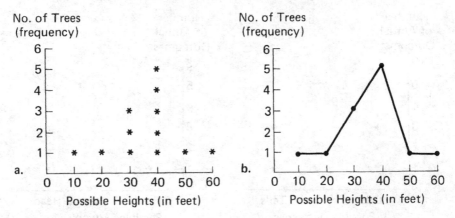

*Figure 7.2  Height of trees around J.D.B.'s house. a: Scatterplot. b: Frequency polygon.*

column, the resulting frequency polygon would take the shape shown in Figure 7.1d. Figure 7.1d should look familiar to you if you know anything about the normal distribution. Notice that it occurs with coins and that it is based on the mathematical probabilities of those coins coming up in the various possible numbers of heads; thus, you do not need to flip a coin to plot it out.

## Normal distribution

I have found considerable resistance among language teachers (including myself) to the notion of normal distribution. Whether it is called a normal curve, a bell curve, or normal distribution, this notion has been forced on us by well-meaning testers and administrators ("You *will* assign so many A's, B's, C's, D's, and F's for the grades in your class"). Let's look first at why people in the social sciences seem to believe in such a distribution. Then I will explain some of the characteristics of that distribution.

### Why the normal distribution?

Aside from the fact that the binomial distribution takes the shape of a normal distribution, it has been observed repeatedly that living organisms grow, live, and perform in the predictable patterns of the *normal distribution*. For example, there are 15 trees growing in my yard. If I measure each of them, I find that their heights can be plotted roughly as shown in Figure 7.2a. Each tree is represented by an asterisk on the

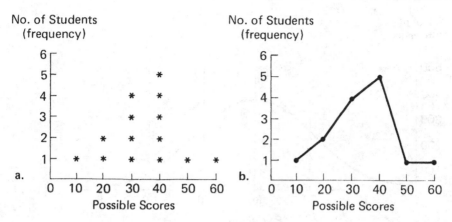

*Figure 7.3   Students' scores on a hypothetical language test. a: Scatterplot. b: Frequency polygon.*

10-foot height closest to the actual height of the tree. Notice that the result is a histogram of the distribution of heights among my trees. Such a visual representation could be accomplished equally well by using a frequency polygon (as shown in Figure 7.2b). Notice that the shape of the curve in the polygon looks suspiciously, but not exactly, like the normal curve.

The point is that the numbers along the abscissa could just as well represent the scores of your students on a 60-point language test, as shown in Figure 7.3. In other words, it would not be unusual to find something close to a normal distribution among your students. In fact, the probability would be high on certain types of tests. This would likely be true of their ages, heights, and IQ scores as well.

However, what is often forgotten by planners and decision makers are the three points I just raised about the distribution of flips of a coin: (1) the probability of finding this distribution starts over for each measurement of each group of trees, people, or whatever, (2) in a small number of outcomes, the distribution may be lopsided, as in Figures 7.2 and 7.3, but it becomes increasingly clear, or "normal," as the number of outcomes increases, and (3) a visual examination of each distribution yields information about the events involved (e.g., just how lopsided or normal the distribution is). At the intuitive level, you may have felt that forcing the grades or scores on your students to fit the normal curve was unfair. And you were right, according to the three points I previously mentioned. Typically, a class is too small a group to expect a perfectly normal distribution. But it would not hurt to sit down and plot the students' test scores or grades, as I have done here. After all, you have seen how such a scatterplot or frequency polygon can help depict group

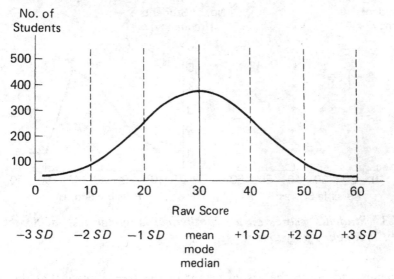

Raw Score: $\overline{X} = 30$; $SD = 10$.

*Figure 7.4   Mean and standard deviation in a normal distribution*

behavior, and looking at it does not mean that we teachers must forget the individuals.

However, the expected form of the normal distribution often actually occurs when the number of students is sufficient. It would, therefore, be irresponsible to dismiss the notion out of hand. With a group of 6,000 students taking a hypothetical language test, you could reasonably expect a normal distribution that would look something like the frequency polygon shown in Figure 7.4. This frequency polygon is, indeed, the typical theoretical form of the normal distribution, a pattern that occurs and recurs in nature, as well as in human behavior. It is also a pattern that helps statisticians sort out the confusion in the world around us. Now let's see how certain characteristics of this pattern interrelate and how they provide the researcher with useful tools to explore language learning and teaching.

## Characteristics of the normal distribution

Two of the most important characteristics of the normal distribution – central tendency and dispersion – are already familiar to you from the previous chapter. A third characteristic is based on the commonsense notion of percentage. These ideas will be explained in terms of an ideal distribution, but exceptions to this ideal will also be discussed later in the chapter.

## CENTRAL TENDENCY

As you may recall, central tendency indicates the typical behavior of a group, and there are three ways to estimate it: the mean, the mode, and the median. You would expect to find all three somewhere near the center, or middle, in a normal distribution. In fact in a theoretical normal distribution, we would find that all three would converge on exactly the same score value, as shown in Figure 7.4 – right in the middle of the distribution (mean = mode = median = 30).

### DISPERSION

Like central tendency, dispersion is predictable in a normal distribution. Remember that dispersion shows how the individual scores disperse, or are spread out around the central tendency. Dispersion is commonly estimated by the range and standard deviation. In a theoretical normal distribution, as in Figure 7.4, you would expect the lowest score on the test (0) and the highest score (60) to be exactly the same distance from the center, or mean. This distribution apparently occurs in the example; both scores are 30 points above or below the mean. Thus, the *range* is symmetrical.

The other indicator of dispersion is, of course, the standard deviation. Conveniently, the standard deviation in the example is a round number, 10. It also turns out that the standard deviation falls in the pattern shown in Figure 7.4. One standard deviation above the mean ($+ 1\ SD$) will fall on the score that is equal to $\overline{X} + 1SD$, or, in this case, $30 + 10 = 40$. Similarly, two standard deviations below the mean will fall on the score that is equal to $\overline{X} - 2SD$, or $30 - 10 = 20$. In short, the *standard deviation* is a regular distance that is expressed in score points that can be thought of as marking off certain portions of the distribution, each of which is equal in length along the abscissa.

Let's take another example just to make sure these important concepts are clear. You have administered an intelligence (IQ) test to a group of 100 students. The mean, mode, and median all turned out to be 100, and the standard deviation was 15 with a range of 91 points (the low score was 55 and the high score was 145). Can you picture what such a distribution of scores would look like under these extraordinarily ideal conditions? Try to draw the distribution, at least approximately. Be sure to include a vertical line for the mean (assuming that mean = mode = median), as well as for each of three standard deviations above the mean and below it. Now compare your distribution to the one shown in the

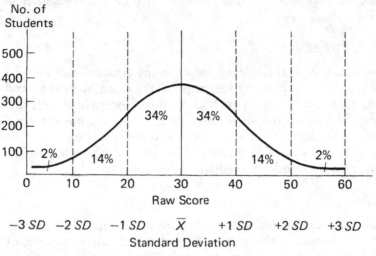

Raw Score: $\overline{X}$ = 30; $SD$ = 10

*Figure 7.5  The approximate percentages falling throughout the normal distribution. Note: More precise percentages would be 2.14, 13.59, and 34.13.*

first problem in the Application section of this chapter. They should look about the same.

PERCENTAGES

Once central tendency and dispersion in a normal distribution are understood, we can go on to percentages. First, you should remember that mean, mode, and median should be the same in the distribution and that the median is the score below and above which 50 percent of the cases should fall. So, in a normal distribution, you can predict with fair assurance that 50 percent of your students' scores will fall above the median (or mean, or mode). In like manner, approximately 34 percent of the scores will fall within one standard deviation above the mean, as shown in Figure 7.5. That means that about 34 percent of the students will score between 30 and 40 points on that test. Since this bell-shaped curve is symmetrical, you can reasonably expect another 34 percent of the students to score between 20 and 30 points on the test, or within one standard deviation below the mean.

You can now account for the 68 percent of the students (34% + 34% = 68%) who fall within one standard deviation of the mean, plus or minus. But that leaves 32 percent of the students (100% − 68% = 32%) yet to be accounted for in the distribution. Notice in Figure 7.5

that approximately 14 percent of the students will have scores that fall between the first and second standard deviations ($+1$ *SD* to $+2$ *SD*) above the mean, or between 40 and 50 raw score points. Likewise, 14 percent will score between one standard deviation below the mean ($-1$ *SD*) and two standard deviations below the mean ($-2$ *SD*), or between 10 and 20 raw score points.

You can now account for about 96 percent of the students in the distribution ($34\% + 34\% + 14\% + 14\% = 96\%$). The remaining 4 percent of students' scores are evenly divided above and below the mean: a little less than 2 percent in the area between the second and third standard deviations above the mean ($+2$ *SD* to $+3$ *SD*) and about 2 percent in the area between the second and third standard deviations below the mean ($-2$ *SD* to $-3$ *SD*). If the sample is large enough, this pattern of percentages for students' scores within the various areas of the normal distribution will be fairly regular and predictable. A great deal can be learned from such patterns, as you will see next.

## What can be learned from distributions?

I have stressed that these ideas are based on a "theoretical normal distribution" only as a caution to be kept in mind, not as an indicator of skepticism about the existence of such distributions or about their characteristics. I know that they exist in mathematical probability distributions (e.g., the binomial distribution) and have seen them occur far too often in my own data to be a doubter. And I am not alone. They have been observed by countless researchers in many disciplines. They really occur, just as 50 percent of coin flips will be heads and 50 percent tails if the numbers involved are large enough (see Chapter 9).

If you can accept this pattern, you will find that there is much that can be learned from it. You can discover what percentages of students will score within certain score ranges on a measure. You can learn what percentiles mean in terms of exactly where an individual student falls within a normal distribution. Most important, you can learn what happens when something goes wrong (when the distribution is *not* normal) and what language testers and researchers do when things depart from the normal distribution.

### Using percentages

There is nothing tricky about the concept of percentage. For example, you probably can easily figure out what percentage of your paycheck goes to taxes every month. You would simply divide the amount of money paid to the government by the total amount earned. Likewise, you should now be able to answer the following questions, which are based on Figure 7.5:

1. What percentage of students have scores below the mean?
2. About what percentage have scores falling between 30 and 40 points (or between the mean and one standard deviation above the mean)?
3. Approximately what percentage fall within one standard deviation of the mean, plus and minus (between 20 and 40 points)?
4. And roughly what percentage have scores below 40 (or below the first standard deviation above the mean)?

To answer Question 1, you need only recall that 50 percent of the students should fall below the mean and 50 percent should fall above it. Or a more cumbersome approach would be to add up all the percentages shown in Figure 7.5 that fall below, or to the left, of the mean (2% + 14% + 34% = 50%). Question 2 is even simpler because you need only look at the percentage shown in the space between 30 and 40 points in the example to know it is 34 percent. Question 3 requires that you add the two percentages shown in the spaces between 20 and 40 points (34% + 34% = 68%). Question 4 is a bit more complex because you must combine the types of reasoning that you used in all three of the previous questions. To find out what percentage of the students have scores of 40 points or less, you might simply recall that 50 percent will be below the mean and then add the 34 percent shown between the mean and 40 points (50% + 34% = 84%). Or you might add up all the percentages shown to the left of a score of 40 points (2% + 14% + 34% + 34% = 84%). Either way, you will be correct. In short, you can infer many things about students' performances from the observed patterns in the normal distribution. One of these is a student's percentile within the distribution.

## Percentiles

Percentiles are not any more tricky than are percentages. In fact, you have already dealt with percentiles when you answered Question 4 about what percentage of students scored below 40. The answer was 84 percent. Another way to phrase this question would be, What percentile is a score of 40? The answer would be the 84th percentile. So *percentile* can be defined as the total percentage of students who scored equal to or below a given score.

Given this definition, what percentile would a score of 20, 30, or 50 represent in Figure 7.5? (About 16th, 50th, and 98th percentile, respectively.) To bring this concept even closer to home, can you recall the percentile of your score on any standardized tests, such as the TOEFL, ACT, SAT, or GRE? What percentage of the other students involved scored below you? I recall once scoring in the 84th percentile on the GRE (Graduate Record Exam) quantitative subtest. This meant to me (even then) that my score was equal to or higher than 84 percent of the other people taking the test but lower than 16 percent of the people.

When you encounter the concept of percentile in a language study, it should now be clear to you. But be careful not to confuse it with the notion of percentage, which has a different meaning.

## Standard scores

Some interesting things are done by language testers and researchers with all the concepts that I have discussed so far. Among them are the conversion of raw scores or weighted scores on a test into standard scores. *Raw scores* are the actual number of questions answered correctly on a test. It is these scores that we in the field most often deal with. *Weighted scores* are scores that are based on different weightings being given to the questions in a test – perhaps two or three points for some questions but only one point for others. This type of procedure should also be familiar to you. Standard scores are yet a third way to report results. Standard scores seem to be cloaked in mystery for many language teachers. Since research studies often investigate and report standard scores, let's make sure this concept is clear.

Stepping back briefly, recall that percentiles, or *percentile scores*, tell you how a given student's test score relates to the scores of all the other students. A student with a percentile score of 98 had a score equal to or higher than 98 percent of the other students in the distribution and a score equal to or lower than 2 percent. Other types of *standard scores* express, in terms of standard deviations, a student's score in relation to how far it differs from the mean of a test. Recalling that standard deviations define units in the normal distribution, let's look at the three most commonly reported types of standard scores before trying to clarify that definition. They are $z$ scores, $T$ scores, and CEEB scores.

### Z SCORES

This type of standardized score tells you how far a given raw score is from the mean in standard deviation units. To calculate the $z$ score for any particular student, you apply the following formula:

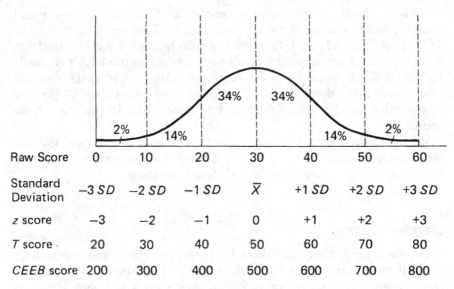

*Figure 7.6  Comparison of standard score distributions*

$$z = \frac{X - \overline{X}}{SD}$$

In other words, to find a student's z score, you subtract the mean from the student's score and divide the result by the standard deviation for the test. If a student scored 60 on a test where $\overline{X} = 50$ and $SD = 10$, the z score for that student would be as follows:

$$z = \frac{60 - 50}{10} = \frac{10}{10} = 1 = +1.0$$

So this student's z score was +1.0. In other words, the student's raw score was one standard deviation unit above the mean. But let's look at another student who scored 30 raw score points on the same test. This student's z score would be

$$z = \frac{30 - 50}{10} = \frac{-20}{10} = -2 = -2.0$$

This student with a z score of $-2.0$ is two standard deviations below the mean.

Now look at Figure 7.6. Notice that z scores are labeled three rows below the bottom of the distribution and that they are the same as the positions marked off for the standard deviations. Notice, too, that the mean for z scores is zero and, logically, the standard deviation would be 1.0. Looking at Figure 7.6, you should now be able to answer the following questions (notice that the raw scores have an $\overline{X} = 30$ and $SD = 10$);

1. How many standard deviations above the mean would a raw score of 40 be? Plus one, right? (So a raw score of 40 would represent a z score of $+1.0$.)
2. How many standard deviations below the mean would a raw score of 10 be? (Minus 2, right? $z = -2.0$)
3. Now for the tricky one: How many standard deviations above or below the mean would a raw score of 30 be? (Remember that in this example the mean is 30, so a raw score of 30 is neither above nor below the mean; it is the mean, $z = 0$.)

To sum up, the z score is simply the number of standard deviations that a particular score is from the mean – plus if above the mean and minus if below the mean.

T SCORES

When reporting z scores to students and their parents, you may find that several problems may arise. One is that such scores can turn out to be positive or negative. The other is that they are small in magnitude and may turn out to include decimals. How would you like to tell your students that they scored $-1$, 0, or, worse yet, $+3.67$ on a test? These scores would be hard for them to understand. One way around this problem is to convert the z scores into *T scores*. The researcher does this by arbitrarily multiplying the z score by 10 and adding 50. The formula for these operations is as follows:

$$T = 10z + 50$$

The resulting *T* scores for the $-1$, 0, and 3.67 z scores just mentioned would work out this way:

$$
\begin{aligned}
T &= 10(-1) + 50 \\
&= \quad -10 + 50 \\
&= 40 \\
T &= 10(0) + 50 \\
&= \quad 0 + 50 \\
&= 50 \\
T &= 10(3.67) + 50 \\
&= \quad 36.7 + 50 \\
&= 86.7
\end{aligned}
$$

Such scores look more like "real" scores and would probably be easier to explain to your language students. Notice in Row 4 of Figure 7.6

that the mean for $T$ scores is 50 and the standard deviation is 10 for the distribution of $T$ scores. This will always be true.

### CEEB SCORES

The College Entrance Examination Board (CEEB) scores that are often used in the United States are similar to $T$ scores. To convert $z$ scores to CEEB scores, the tester simply multiplies a given score by 100 and adds 500, or

$$\text{CEEB} = 100z + 500$$

The result for, say, a $z$ score of $-1$ would be this:

$$\begin{aligned} \text{CEEB} &= 100(-1) + 500 \\ &= -100 + 500 \\ &= 400 \end{aligned}$$

To convert from a $T$ score to a CEEB score, the tester need only add a 0 (if $z = -1$ and $T$ equals 40, then CEEB = 400). The mean for a distribution of CEEB scores is 500 with a standard deviation of 100. Row 5 of Figure 7.6 illustrates this.

Standardized scores are useful to know about for three reasons. First, most standardized tests report standard scores, often $T$ or CEEB scores, and/or percentiles (for example, scores on the subtests of the Test of English as a Foreign Language are $T$ scores, but the total TOEFL score is a CEEB score). Second, a researcher who wishes to compare the mean performances of different groups on two or more tests will find it difficult to compare the performances if the tests are of different lengths. But if the scores are first standardized and then compared, the problem of different lengths would be avoided, as shown in Figure 7.7. Notice that in Figure 7.7, the performances of graduate foreign students are compared with those of undergraduates on six different ESL tests, all of which were of different lengths, by converting raw scores to standard scores ($T$ scores in this case). But the other types of standard scores could have been used as well. Third, standard scores can be used to compare the relative position of a particular student on different tests or on different administrations of the same test. All in all, then, standard scores are common and very useful. Therefore, it is important for readers to understand the concepts underlying them.

### Skewed distributions

We have explored the primary characteristics of normal distributions and some of the inferences that can be drawn from such distributions. But what happens when things do not turn out normally? There are a

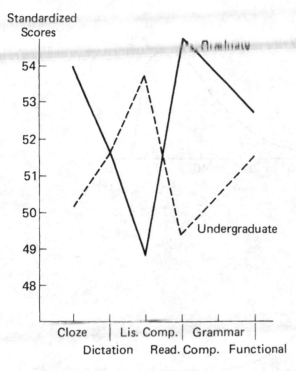

Figure 7.7   *Difference owing to university status in the performance of students on the study measures. (From: "Measure of language proficiency from the learner's perspective," by H. Farhady, 1982, TESOL Quarterly, vol. 16(1), p. 49. Copyright 1982 by Teachers of English to Speakers of Other Languages.)*

number of possibilities, but the most common is that the distribution is skewed.

## SKEWEDNESS

A *skewed* distribution is most evident to the researcher and reader alike when it is plotted. It does not have that nice symmetrical "bell" shape to it. In nontechnical terms, a distribution is skewed when the scores are, for some reason, "scrunched up" (Popham 1981), either toward the higher scores (Figure 7.8a) or toward the lower scores (Figure 7.8b). Such distributions characteristically have a tail that points in one of the two possible directions. When the tail is pointing in the direction of the lower scores (−), it is considered *negatively skewed*. When the tail points toward the higher scores (+), it is termed *positively skewed*.

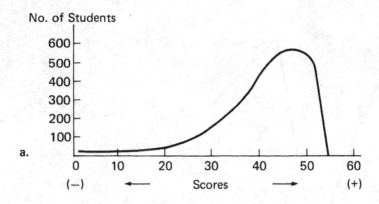

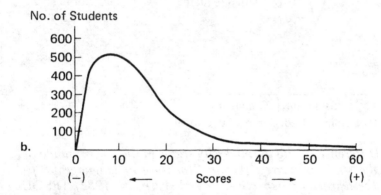

*Figure 7.8  Skewed distributions. a: Negatively skewed distribution. b: Positively skewed distribution.*

Let's consider what skewedness means. First, many of the statistics used in research assume a normal distribution, largely because they depend on comparisons of the variation in scores (related to dispersion). But when the distribution is skewed, let's say negatively, the researcher finds that most of the students scored well. In certain situations, like your end-of-term final exam, this might be desirable. But when applying many of the common statistical techniques, the researcher will have much more difficulty interpreting results based on skewed distributions. You as a reader should, therefore, be wary when you encounter such distributions.

When you look at the descriptive statistics for a study, you should now be able to picture the distributions clearly. Let's say you encounter a test which the researcher reported had a range of 70 raw score points

(31–100), a mean of 70, and a standard deviation of 10 (600 students took the test). What would the distribution look like? Can you picture it? Try sketching it out. (It should look normal.)

What if the range for the same test was still 70 points (31–100), but the mean was 90 and the standard deviation was 8.5? You should spot the skewedness of this distribution simply by realizing that there is room for only a little over one standard deviation of 8.5 above the mean ($\overline{X}$ = 90) because the top score is 100. Which way (positive or negative) would this distribution be skewed?

PEAKED DISTRIBUTIONS

Even if the researcher determines that a distribution is not skewed, it should be checked to make sure that its overall shape is not unusual. *Kurtosis* is the degree to which the curve in the middle of a distribution is steep, or peaked. If the height of the peak, relative to the width, departs too much from what would be expected in a normal distribution (it is either too peaked or too flat), problems may ensue in any statistical analyses that are based on that distribution. Therefore, for some statistics, researchers will report having checked this condition. They are simply looking at the degree to which the distribution in question departs from the normal shape.

Because abnormally skewed or peaked distributions may be signs of trouble in a statistical study, you should verify that the researcher has at least checked for such possibilities. Phrases like "the distribution of scores was examined for skewedness and kurtosis and was found to be normal" are comforting in this regard.

# Patterns among students

The concepts explored in this chapter are central to all statistical research, and are sometimes forgotten by researchers. It would seem, therefore, that you should be particularly careful that you understood the main points made here. This information will not only be useful to you as you read through this book and through research studies, but it should help you in your teaching situation because these patterns occur among your students. Thus, concepts like probability, normal distribution, raw scores, percentile scores, standard scores, and skewedness may help you on the job, but only if you look at the data generated by the students in your teaching situation. So why not plot those scores and try to analyze what is going on among your students?

## Terms and symbols

binomial distribution
central tendency
College Entrance Examination Board
  (CEEB) scores
dispersion
distribution
expected outcomes
kurtosis
negatively skewed
normal distribution
percentage (within ideal normal
  distribution)
percentile
percentile scores
positively skewed

possible outcomes
probability
range
raw scores
scatterplot
skewed
standard deviation (*SD*)
standard scores
*T* scores
weighted scores
$\overline{X}$
*z* scores

## Review questions

1. What is the probability of drawing an ace of spades from a deck of 52 cards? How many expected outcomes are involved? How many possible outcomes? What is the probability?
2. Can you draw an ideal normal distribution? Be sure to represent the mean, mode, and median with a vertical line. Also include six vertical lines (perhaps dotted) for each of three standard deviations above the mean and below the mean. And don't forget to label those standard deviation lines ($-3\ SD$, $-2\ SD$, $-1\ SD$, $0$, $+1\ SD$, $+2\ SD$, $+3\ SD$).
3. Can you determine the approximate percentages of students that you would expect to score within each of the standard deviation units?
4. Can you label the main *z* scores that would correspond to the standard deviation lines?
5. Can you label the equivalent *T* scores and CEEB scores for each of these *z* scores?
6. About what percentage of students would you expect to score within one standard deviation of the mean, plus *and* minus?
7. About what percentage of students would you expect to score below a *z* score of $-1$? Below a *T* score of 60? Below a CEEB score of 500?

8. What would be the percentile score for a z score of +2? A T score of 40? A CEEB score of 300?
9. What would a positively skewed distribution look like? And one that was negatively skewed?
10. Do you now believe that normal distribution occurs? If not, why not collect some data, plot them, and decide whether they are in a normal distribution. Remember to collect a large number of scores, or ages, or heights, or whatever.

## Application

A. Look at the frequency polygon and answer the questions that follow:

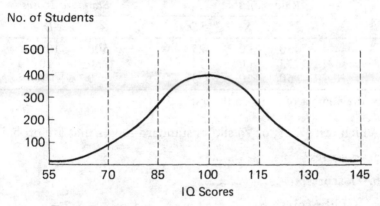

No. of Students

$\bar{X}$ = 100; *SD* = 15.

1. What percentile score would an IQ score of 85 represent?
2. About what percentage of students scored between 85 and 115?
3. If Iliana scored 175 on this test, how many standard deviations would she be above the mean?
4. What would Iliana's z score be? T score? CEEB score?

*Application continues on next page*

B. In the following table, the raw score mean is 10 ($\overline{X}$ = 10) and the raw score standard deviation is 4 ($SD$ = 4). You should now be able to fill in all the blank spaces on the basis of what you know.

| Student | Raw score | z score | T score | CEEB score |
|---------|-----------|---------|---------|------------|
| A | 10 | | 50 | |
| B | 6 | | | |
| C | | +1 | | |
| D | 18 | | | 700 |

C. Study the following table and answer the questions.

| Test | Raw scores $k^a$ | $\overline{X}$ | $SD$ | Standard scores $\overline{X}$ | $SD$ |
|------|------|------|------|------|------|
| X | 130 | 60 | 25 | 500 | 100 |
| Y | 75 | 60 | 12 | 50 | 10 |
| Z | 50 | 10 | 3 | 0 | 1 |

$^a k$ = the number of items on the test.

1. Which test (X, Y, or Z) shows standard scores that are probably

   a. z scores? ........

   b. T scores? ........

   c. CEEB scores? ........

2. In raw scores, which test has

   a. the largest standard deviation? ........

   b. the lowest mean? ........

   c. the largest number of items? ........

   d. a negatively skewed distribution? ........

3. In test Z,

   a. a raw score of 10 would equal what z score? ........

   b. a raw score of 7 would equal what T score? ........

   c. a raw score of 16 would equal what CEEB score? ........

# 8 Statistics for testing

The majority of statistical studies must be based on tests or question-naires. The descriptive statistics and patterns found in the distribution of the data are important concepts for understanding these measures, so the researcher should present such information. However, a test can have excellent descriptive statistics, create a classic normal distribution, and still be problematic. As with measuring a person's height, the mea-surement on a test should be the same every time it is done, it should assess exactly what it is supposed to, and the procedures for measuring should be practical. For height, this would mean that (1) if the person being measured is 5'5" today, he or she will not turn out to be 5'10" the next day, (2) if you are measuring distance in feet and inches, it will not turn out that you are measuring weight in pounds and ounces, and (3) the tools for making the measurement are not cumbersome (e.g., you will not use a ruler that is only a half inch long or a yardstick that has feet marked off but no inches). In terms of testing, these considerations are called (1) test consistency, (2) test validity, and (3) test practicality, respectively. The first two will be the primary focus of this chapter. Before going into them, I will discuss two preliminary topics that must be considered so test reliability and validity will be easier to understand.

## Preliminary considerations

The first consideration is that two basic types of tests are used for different purposes in language programs. The second consideration is the concept of correlation. Both are central to understanding the rest of this chapter.

### Two types of tests

Although there are numerous ways to classify and categorize language tests, all such tests basically fall into one of two major types: *norm-referenced tests* (N-RTs) or *criterion-referenced tests* (C-RTs). This dis-tinction is based on differences in the way the tests are built and in the way the results are interpreted. On the one hand, an N-RT, as the name implies, is used primarily to spread students out into a normal distribution so their performances may be compared in relation to *each other*. If, for instance, a researcher's purpose is to separate students into three levels of language proficiency, an N-RT would be appropriate. On the other hand, a C-RT is used principally to find out how much of a clearly defined domain of language skills or material the students have learned. Thus, the focus is on how the students achieve in relation to *the material*, rather than to each other. A common example of a C-RT is a final examination for a language course with clearly defined objectives that are tested in that exam.

The tests in statistical language studies have, by and large, been N-RTs because N-RTs spread students out and tend to show the normal distribution, while C-RTs may not. On C-RTs, all the students may score 100 percent if they have learned all the material. Hence, you can expect a dispersion of scores on N-RTs but not necessarily on C-RTs. The blunt fact is that the most powerful statistical techniques do not work well without dispersion of scores; that is why N-RTs are the most common types of measures for studies in our field. Therefore, in the rest of this chapter, I will concentrate on N-RTs. This does not mean that C-RTs should not be investigated but, rather, that they usually are not studied in our field.

## Correlation coefficient

Dispersion is important to statistical concepts in general because we often compare how two tests order students. One way to do so is to look at the *correlation* of the two sets of scores (how they go together). Figure 8.1a presents two sets of scores side by side. Notice that the two sets are in exactly the same order; that is, the student who scored highest on Test A also scored highest on Test B, and the same is true for the second highest, third highest, and so on.

The degree to which two such sets of scores *covary*, or vary together, can be estimated by calculating a *correlation coefficient* (symbolized by $r$). Such a coefficient can have a positive value as high as $+1.0$ if the relationship is perfectly direct, as shown in the scatterplot in Figure 8.1a, in which the students obtained nearly the same scores on Tests A and B. Notice that each asterisk in the scatterplot represents the points at which the two scores for each student intersect (e.g., the student who scored 50 on Test A scored 51 on Test B, so the asterisk representing her is at the point where the two scores meet).

A correlation coefficient can have a negative value as high as $-1.0$ only if the relationship between the two sets of scores is in exactly the opposite order, as shown in Figure 8.1b. The negative sign before the correlation coefficient indicates that the relationship is in this opposite order. Nevertheless, the relationship between the two sets of scores is

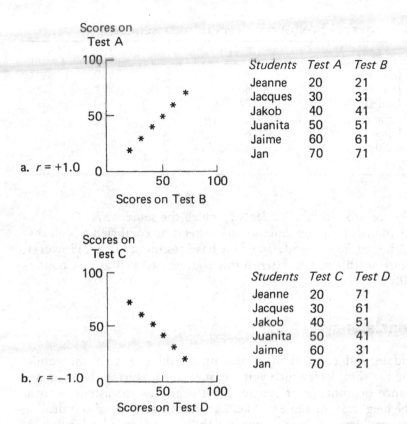

| Students | Test A | Test B |
|----------|--------|--------|
| Jeanne   | 20     | 21     |
| Jacques  | 30     | 31     |
| Jakob    | 40     | 41     |
| Juanita  | 50     | 51     |
| Jaime    | 60     | 61     |
| Jan      | 70     | 71     |

| Students | Test C | Test D |
|----------|--------|--------|
| Jeanne   | 20     | 71     |
| Jacques  | 30     | 61     |
| Jakob    | 40     | 51     |
| Juanita  | 50     | 41     |
| Jaime    | 60     | 31     |
| Jan      | 70     | 21     |

*Figure 8.1  Scatterplots of two correlation coefficients*

strong (correlation) because students who have high scores on Test C have low scores on Test D, and vice versa.

If there were no relationship between two sets of scores, the coefficient would be 0. And, of course, weak relationships, either positive or negative, would produce coefficients up to perhaps $+.40$ or $-.40$, respectively. Likewise, strong correlations might range from $+.80$ to $+1.0$, or $-.80$ to $-1.00$, depending on whether they are positive or negative. For the moment, it will suffice to remember that as coefficients get further away from 0 toward $+1.0$ or $-1.0$, the relationship they represent between the two sets of scores is getting stronger.

Table 8.1 presents a slightly more realistic situation because the scores do not line up perfectly. The coefficient used here is called the Pearson product-moment correlation coefficient. It is appropriate for comparing two sets of interval data. In this case, it is .97. Thus, it can be said that there is a strong positive correlation between these two sets of scores,

TABLE 8.1. CORRELATION OF TWO SETS OF TEST SCORES

| Students | Test E | Test F |
|---|---|---|
| Jacques | 90 | 100 |
| Jean | 80 | 91 |
| Juanita | 76 | 80 |
| Jimmy | 70 | 75 |
| Jaime | 67 | 71 |
| Jakob | 67 | 70 |
| Jan | 40 | 51 |

since they are ordering the students in much the same way.

For the moment, this explanation of correlation coefficients is all that you need. It is enough to understand the basic testing statistics. However, I will return to this notion later in this chapter, as well as in Chapters 9 and 10.

## Test consistency

One fundamental concern in measuring anything is that the results should be the same every time you measure it. Measuring the language performance or aptitude of people is not nearly as consistent as measuring the height of the same people. Language testers go about dealing with this problem in two ways: reliability and standard error of measurement.

### Reliability

The reliability of a test is defined as the extent to which the results can be considered consistent or stable. Let's say that you have just given a placement test to your students. Of course, you would like it to be reliable because an unreliable test might produce wildly different scores if it was taken again, and you could not be sure that you had placed the students in the right levels.

The degree to which a test is reliable can be estimated with a *reliability coefficient* ($r_{xx}$). This is how researchers commonly report the reliability of the measures they have used in a study. A reliability coefficient works much like a correlation coefficient in that it can go as high as $+1.0$ for a perfectly reliable test. But it is also different because it can only go as low as 0 (after all, how could a test have less than no reliability?).

Theoretically, we would like to know what score a student is likely to obtain if he or she were to take the test over an infinite number of times. This score would be called the student's *true score*, and it could be estimated by computing the average of an infinite number of scores for each student. Since a true score obviously is impossible to achieve, we must settle for estimating how close the students' scores on our test came to the ideal true scores. The reliability coefficient, then, is the way researchers estimate the percentage of variation in the *observed scores* (the scores that are actually obtained on a test) that can be attributed to true score variation.

For example, a reliability coefficient of .85 indicates that 85 percent of the variation in observed scores was due to variation in the true scores and the remaining 15 percent cannot be accounted for and is called *error*, or unsystematic variation, from chance alone. So, if a test has a reliability coefficient of $r_{xx} = .91$, what percentage is due to the variation among true scores? What if $r_{xx} = .40$, or $r_{xx} = .99$? And what percentage would be considered error for each of these?

## WAYS OF ESTIMATING RELIABILITY

In language testing, reliability has most often been estimated in three ways: test-retest, equivalent forms, and internal consistency reliabilities. *Test-retest reliability* is usually estimated by administering the same test twice to one group of subjects and then calculating a correlation coefficient between the pairs of scores from the two administrations. *Equivalent forms reliability* is estimated by administering two equivalent tests (say Forms A and B of a test) to one group of subjects and calculating the correlation coefficient between the scores on the form. Internal-consistency reliability can be estimated in a number of ways, but the easiest method to understand conceptually is the *split-half method*, in which (1) the even-numbered and odd-numbered items on a test are scored separately, (2) the correlation between these two subtests is calculated, and (3) the resulting coefficient is adjusted for full-test reliability using a formula called the Spearman-Brown prophecy formula. The many other variations of this type of reliability include the commonly reported Kuder-Richardson formula 20 (K-R20) and Cronbach alpha ($\alpha$). Internal-consistency estimates are the ones most often reported in language studies because they have the distinct advantage of being estimable from a single form of a test administered only once – in contrast to test-retest and equivalent forms reliabilities, which require either two administrations or two forms.

You may encounter two other types of reliability in language studies: interrater and intrarater reliabilities. These types of reliability commonly arise in language-testing situations, such as with compositions or oral interviews, in which raters are required to make judgments on the language produced by students. *Interrater reliability* is essentially a variation of the equivalent forms type of reliability in that the scores are usually produced by two raters and a correlation coefficient is calculated between them. *Intrarater reliability* is closely related to the test-retest type in that two sets of scores are produced by the same rater on two separate occasions for the same group of students and a correlation coefficient is calculated.

It should be clear at this point that it is important that researchers report the degree to which any measures used in a study were reliable. It is also crucial that the researcher explain the type of reliability estimate that he or she employed and that you consider not only the degree to which the measures were reliable but the appropriateness of the method or methods that were utilized to estimate the reliability.

However, regardless of the type of reliability involved, your interpretation of the coefficients will be about the same. You should be concerned with how consistent the test is in terms of the percentage of the reliable variation in scores, as opposed to error. If $r_{xx} = .30$, then 30 percent of the variation is reliable (related to variation in true scores), and the remaining 70 percent is error (owing to chance). In short, a coefficient of $r_{xx} = .30$ indicates that the test is not reliable and that another one should have been used.

## Standard error of measurement

Reliability coefficients, then, are one way of looking at the consistency of a test. They can be used to estimate how consistent the test is in percentage terms. Another, perhaps more concrete, approach is called the *standard error of measurement* (SEM). This concept can be used to determine a band around a student's true score within which that student's observed scores would probably fall if a test were administered repeatedly. On the basis of the percentages in a normal distribution, as discussed in Chapter 7, it can also estimate the percentage of the time that those scores can be expected to fall within the band.

Let's say that the standard error of measurement for a 100-item test is 3 (SEM = 3). From this SEM, you can conclude that Hans, who got a score of 70, would score within a band of one SEM plus (70 + 3 = 73) or minus (70 − 3 = 67) 68 percent of the time if he were to take the test an infinite number of times (this percentage is based on the percentages in the normal distribution). This conclusion is derived from the notion that the SEM is the standard deviation of the hypothetical distribution of these infinite test scores. Thus, you can be fairly sure that Hans would consistently score between 67 and 73 points, 68 percent of the time. If you wanted to be even more certain of this band, you could extend it out further to two SEMs (3 + 3 = 6) plus (70 + 6 = 76) or minus (70 − 6 = 64) the raw score actually observed. You could then be relatively sure that his score would consistently be between 64 and 76, with 95 percent confidence (also based on the percentages in the normal distribution).

A corollary is that the narrower the band, the more accurately the raw scores represent the theoretical true scores. Hence, a test with a smaller SEM can be considered more consistent. In a sense, the SEM is easier to interpret than a reliability coefficient because it is expressed in terms of raw score bands rather than the more abstract percentage terms represented in reliability estimates.

For decision-making purposes, the SEM has some interesting applications. It is especially useful in deciding the "fate" of borderline cases – students who are right on or near the cutoff point for some decision that will affect their lives. For example, perhaps the test that Hans took was for the purpose of placing students in one of four levels of college Spanish. This decision would be important for Hans. After all, if the test inaccurately placed him at a level below his real proficiency, it could unjustly cost him not only one semester of his time but extra tuition fees. Therefore, his placement should be as accurate and fair as possible.

Unfortunately, Hans scored 70 and the cutoff point between second- and third-semester Spanish was 72. In which level should he be placed? Hans is clearly within one SEM of the cutoff point, so he might score above it if he were to take the test again. A responsible decision in such a case would probably involve getting more information about Hans's proficiency in Spanish through an additional composition or an oral interview before making the decision about this borderline case. That is why the SEM is often important and should be reported along with reliability coefficients.

## Test validity

Consistency is a desirable and necessary quality for a good test, but it is not the only quality that is important. For instance, the *Test of English as a Foreign Language* (Educational Testing Service 1987) is considered a reliable test of proficiency in English as a foreign language because the reliability coefficients tend to be high and the SEM tends to be low. If the test were administered to a group of foreign students as a test of mathematical ability, however, it would probably remain reliable but would obviously not be valid in any logical sense for the purpose of testing mathematical ability. Hence, reliability and validity, although related, are different characteristics of tests.

*Test validity* is defined as the degree to which a test measures what it claims to be measuring. If a test claims to measure the ability to read French, then it should test that ability. Researchers must likewise use tests that actually tap the variables of interest in the study exactly as they were operationalized.

## Types of validity

There are basically three ways to look at the validity of a test: content validity, construct validity, and criterion-related validity. Any or all these approaches may be used to defend the validity of a given test. Logically, however, the validity of a test should be examined only after the reliability of the test is determined to be acceptable.

### CONTENT VALIDITY

To demonstrate the content validity of a test, the test developer must answer the question, Is the test a representative sample of the content of whatever the test is claiming to test? To answer this question, someone almost inevitably ends up making a judgment. For instance, let's consider how a test developer might go about establishing the content validity of a test of proficiency in reading Spanish. The first step would be to decide what the test should really claim to measure. In other words, decisions must be made about what components make up proficiency in reading Spanish. In defining these components, the test developer is not only explaining what the elements, or subtests, on the test will be but also how proficiency in reading Spanish is being defined as the content of the test. The developer might consider such proficiency to be made up of reading for facts, reading for inference, reading for vocabulary, or any number of other possible elements.

To establish the content validity of such a test, items would be written for all the elements in approximately the proportions that they are considered to be important to proficiency in reading Spanish. A panel of experts would then be convened to judge the degree to which the items on the test actually represented the elements in question. If those experts disagreed that the items represent proficiency in reading Spanish and its underlying elements, the test developer would have to return to the drawing board. If they agreed, the test would be considered content valid for the purposes of testing proficiency in reading Spanish as the test developer defined it. Unfortunately, this procedure is accurate only to the extent that the biases of the "experts" do not interfere with their judgments. Furthermore, this type of validity does not consider students' performance on the test, that is, how the test is related to the talents of the particular group of students in question. So you should carefully read about content validity, with a view to making sure that the experts were truly experts in the appropriate field and that their judgments were not biased for any reason.

## CONSTRUCT VALIDITY

To understand construct validity, you must understand another related concept – *psychological construct*. A psychological construct is a theoretical label that is given to some human attribute or ability that cannot be seen or touched because it goes on in the brain. Consider, for example, love. Love is a name that is given to a complex emotion that goes on in the brain (not in the heart as commonly reported). Other more pertinent constructs might include the ability to speak Russian, the aptitude for languages, and intelligence.

Notice that each of these constructs goes on in the brain, so it must be observed indirectly, if at all. It is through tests that such constructs are measured indirectly. But researchers cannot take the constructs out and show that the tests are measuring them. Therefore, they do the next best thing: They try to demonstrate experimentally that a given test is measuring a certain construct. Such a demonstration is how researchers go about establishing the construct validity of a test. The experiment may take numerous forms but, most commonly, it is in the form of a differential-group or intervention experiment. A *differential-group experiment* might compare the performance of two groups on a test: one group that obviously has the particular construct and another group that clearly does not. Let's consider the construct second-year reading ability in Russian. To demonstrate the construct validity of a test developed to measure this construct, a researcher might seek out a group of second-year Russian students and a group of first-year Russian students from a variety of U.S. universities and colleges and administer the test to all these students. If the second-year students scored high on the test and the first-year students scored low, this would be one argument for the construct validity of the test, that is, those who have the construct (second-year students of Russian) score higher on the test than those who do not have the construct (first-year students of Russian).

Another approach would be to perform an *intervention experiment*, which is a similar strategy but is performed with only one group of students. Let's say that the researcher administered the test of reading ability in second-year Russian to a group of students at the end of their first year of Russian study and then readministered the test to this same group at the end of their second year of study. If the students performed much better on the second administration than they did on the first, the researcher would have a basis for arguing the construct validity of the test, that is, those who have the construct (second-year students of Russian) score much higher than do those who do not (first-year students).

There are numerous ways to go about establishing the construct validity of a test, but the basic strategy is always the same. The test developer sets up an experiment to demonstrate that a given test is indeed testing the construct that it claims to be testing. Such construct validation is a process – an accumulation of concurring evidence from a variety of experiments and other sources. Such demonstrations can be convincing or unconvincing. So, in the end, you will have to make your own judgments as to the worth of arguments for the construct validity of a given test.

## CRITERION-RELATED VALIDITY

This concept (not to be confused with the criterion-referenced tests described earlier) is basically just a subset, or variation, of the notions discussed under construct validity. The demonstration of criterion-related validity usually involves setting up an experiment in which the subjects take two tests: the test being developed and a well-established test of the construct involved. For instance, to demonstrate the criterion-related validity of a new test called the Test of Overall ESL Proficiency (TOESLP), we might administer it to a group of foreign students who wish to study English in the United States. As a *criterion measure*, we might also administer the *Test of English as a Foreign Language*, also known as the TOEFL. We would choose this particular test because it is a well-established test of the construct under investigation. We could then calculate the correlation coefficient between the two sets of scores and determine the degree to which they go together, or overlap. For instance, a *validity coefficient* ($r_{xy}$) of .91 would indicate a strong relationship between the two sets of scores; in other words, the scores on the two tests would be spreading the subject out in almost exactly the same way. It could then be argued that TOEFL is a well-established measure of overall ESL proficiency, the TOESLP measures virtually the same things as the TOEFL, and, therefore, the TOESLP is a valid test of overall ESL proficiency. In short, the criterion-related validity of the TOESLP would be demonstrated. If you believe that the criterion measure, in this case the TOEFL, is valid, then you really must believe that the TOESLP is, too.

To understand this kind of validity, it helps to know that the squared value of a validity coefficient can be directly interpreted as the percentage of overlap between the two measures. For instance, if it were shown that scores on the TOESLP were correlated at $r_{xy} = .90$ with those on TOEFL, one could only say that this is a strong relationship because .90 is a lot closer to a perfect correlation of 1.00 than to a correlation of zero. If the .90 value was squared ($r_{xy}^2 = .90^2 = .81$), one could say that the TOESLP overlaps about 81 percent with TOEFL. This squared value is called the *coefficient of determination*.

Sometimes the criterion-related validity will be called concurrent or predictive validity in studies. These are just variations on the same theme. *Concurrent validity* is criterion-related validity, but it indicates that both measures were administered at about the same time, as in the foregoing example. *Predictive validity* is also a subtype of criterion-related validity, but the two two sets of scores are collected at different times. For predictive validity, the purpose of the test should logically be "predictive." Can you imagine an aptitude test for French being interpreted in terms of students' course grades in French after one semester? If so, a correlation coefficient between scores on the test and course grades would be an indication of how well the test predicts grades (predictive validity).

## Importance of testing statistics

Whether you are for or against tests in general, you must recognize that they are here to stay. Certainly in the studies you read in our field, tests are often important because the quantities representing variables in the data of a study are often based on them. Hence the operationalization of the variables – indeed, the entire meaning of the results of a study – may depend on tests. And a study can be no better than the measures on which it is based.

Given what you have learned about consistency and validity in this chapter, you are now in a position to make sure that the authors of the studies you read have demonstrated that the tests reliably measured what the researcher claimed they measured. It is the author's responsibility to provide such information. You will most likely find it in the Materials section of the study, or in the Results section if testing issues were included in the original research questions.

## Terms and symbols

coefficient of determination

concurrent validity

construct validity

correlation coefficient

covary

criterion measure

criterion-referenced tests (C-RTs)

criterion-related validity

Cronbach alpha

differential-group experiment

equivalent forms reliability

error

internal-consistency reliability

interrater reliability

intervention experiment
intrarater reliability
Kuder-Richardson formula 20
  (K-R20)
norm-referenced tests (N-RTs)
observed scores
predicative validity
psychological construct
$r$
$r_{xx}$
$r_{xy}$
$r_{xy}^2$
reliability coefficient

Spearman-Brown prophecy
  formula
split-half method
standard error of measurement
  (SEM)
test consistency
test reliability
test-retest reliability
test validity
true score
validity coefficient
$\alpha$

## Review questions

1. Would a C-RT or an N-RT be best suited to spreading students out on a continuum of general proficiency in Spanish? Which type of test would best determine the degree to which the students in a class had learned the material in Chapter 13 of their Portuguese textbook?
2. What is a correlation coefficient?
3. Does a strong relationship between two sets of scores necessarily have to be a positive correlation (e.g., $+.98$), or can it also be negative (e.g., $-.98$)?
4. What is test reliability? What are the three basic types of reliability?
5. What are interrater and intrarater reliability? For what types of tests would they be most appropriate? Which of the three basic types of reliability is the interrater approach most like? And the intrarater approach?
6. What is the SEM? For decision-making purposes, is it better to have a large or small SEM?
7. What is validity? And what are the three basic types of validity? Which one is usually based on expert opinion? Which is an experimental demonstration of an underlying psychological construct? And which is based on a correlation of scores on a new test with scores on a well-established test of the same thing?
8. What are the necessary characteristics of a good test?
9. Why are good studies dependent on good tests?

## Application

Examine the following table on the Modern Language Association's Proficiency Test and answer the questions that follow.

TEST STATISTICS: MLA FOREIGN LANGUAGE PROFICIENCY TEST FOR FOREIGN AND ADVANCED STUDENTS — FRENCH[a]

| Test statistics | Listening | Speaking | Reading | Writing |
|---|---|---|---|---|
| Number of items | 36 | — | 50 | 60 |
| Posttest data | | | | |
|   Mean – Form A | 42.0 | 83.6 | 47.4 | 46.9 |
|   SD – Form A | 8.4 | 17.1 | 10.5 | 12.5 |
| Reliability | | | | |
| coefficient | .91 | — | .93 | .94 |
| SEM | 2.5 | — | 3.0 | 3.1 |
| Intercorrelations | | | | |
|   Listening | — | .784 | .800 | .781 |
|   Speaking | | — | .739 | .804 |
|   Reading | | | — | .858 |
|   Writing | | | | — |

[a]Based on approximately 1,500 French teachers who attended the 1961 National Defense Education Act Language Institutes.
*Source:* Adapted from Educational Testing Service (1964: 32).

1. How is it possible that the mean on the listening test is 42 when the number of items is 36?
2. Can you tell from the information given here what type of standardized scoring was used?
3. Which test appears to spread the French teachers out the most and why?
4. Which test appears to be the most reliable?
5. Is the type of reliability clear in the adaptation? Would you be more comfortable if it had been?
6. Why is no reliability coefficient reported for the speaking test?
7. Would it have been possible to calculate interrater and intrarater reliabilities if the speaking test was an interview procedure?
8. Which test has the "best" SEM? Is it best because it provides the widest or narrowest band around the subjects' scores?
9. What evidence is provided for the validity of the test or tests?
10. Are you satisfied with the information provided here, or would you want more information? What else would you like to know?
11. Would you accept the results of the study on the basis of this description of the test?

# 9 Statistical logic

So far in this book, I have discussed the fundamental considerations underlying the design and organization of research reports, as well as the basic descriptive and testing statistics that are necessary to understand what is going on in a study. The remainder of the book will be devoted to showing you how to interpret and critique the statistical logic underlying such reports. This chapter discusses that logic in general terms and provides definitions and explanations of the central ideas. Each of Chapters 10 through 12 will then use a sample study to illustrate how that logic is applied in the three most commonly reported families of statistical studies: (1) those that explore the strength of relationships between variables, (2) those that compare group means, and (3) those that compare frequencies.

It should be noted that the organizational pattern of research reports (shown in Chapter 5) corresponds to the five stages of statistical logic that are described in this chapter. Therefore, a research report should guide you straight through the logic, step by step. So it is a good idea to keep this overall logic in mind as you read this chapter and the remaining chapters, and especially when you read actual research reports. Now let's peek inside the researcher's head and explore the logic that should be going on in most statistical research.

## Stage 1: focusing the study

Language teaching is riddled with problems, not to mention some frustration. Statistical research is one way of attacking these problems. The first stage involved in the statistical logic of such research includes (1) noticing a problem, (2) identifying and operationally defining the constructs to be examined, and (3) formulating research questions and hypotheses. Let's look at how most researchers do this.

### Identifying a problem

The inspiration for a study may come from many sources, but it is often derived from classroom teaching experiences or from reading the literature in the field. Regardless of the source, the researcher must first

108

notice a problem that is worthy of a solution – one for which the answer will be indirectly useful to teachers in theory building or more directly for actual language teaching.

## Operationalizing constructs as variables

However, noticing a problem is just the beginning. The researcher must next attempt to identify all the constructs that are pertinent to solving the problem at hand. This procedure often requires a great deal of hard thought because studies of language learning and teaching are highly complex and have many variables. It can be frustrating because many constructs that are important to language learning (e.g., students' motivation and students' drive or ambition) may be difficult to measure or otherwise operationalize as variables. Yet, the failure to identify or operationalize such key constructs in the form of variables in the beginning (see Chapters 2–4) could threaten the entire framework and logic of a study.

## Research hypotheses

Knowing that there is a problem and what variables are associated with it is still not focused enough for the application of statistical logic. As I noted in Chapter 5, a research report should contain at least one of the following: a clear statement of the purpose of the study, precise research questions, and precise research hypotheses. My bias is that all three should be included. However, if only one is present, it really should be the hypotheses.

*Hypotheses* are statements about the possible outcomes of a study. Hence, they show the different ways that the researcher envisions the study will turn out. For instance, a scholar who investigates the degree of relationship between two variables – one independent and one dependent – would probably do correlational analysis, as discussed in Chapter 8. To focus the study, the researcher would have to consider all the possible outcomes, that is, the different ways that the study might turn out – a task that is most easily accomplished by formulating hypotheses. Two strategies can be followed to achieve clearly stated hypotheses: one results in directional hypotheses and the other, in nondirectional hypotheses. Let's consider how these strategies would be applied to a study of the degree of correlation between two sets of interval data collected on two variables (a criterion measure as the dependent variable and a new language test as the independent one).

A *directional hypothesis* can be formulated when there is a sound theoretical reason, usually based on previous research, to hypothesize that the relationship, if there is any, will be in one direction or the other.

This hypothesis has come to be known as a *one-tailed hypothesis* because it predicts a relationship only in one direction or the other. For a correlational study in which the correlation, if any, is believed (for sound theoretical reasons) to be positive, the hypothesis under investigation would take the following form:

> $H_1$: There is a positive relationship between the two variables ($r$ is greater than 0).

Conversely, if the correlation in a study is believed, on the basis of previous research, to be negative, the hypothesis would take this form:

> $H_1$: There is a negative relationship between the two variables ($r$ is less than 0).

If there is no reason to hypothesize that an existing relationship will be in one direction or the other, positive or negative, the researcher may take the more conservative path of formulating a *nondirectional hypothesis*, which leaves open the possibility of the relationship being in either direction. Such a hypothesis is also called a *two-tailed hypothesis* because it predicts possible relationships in two directions. It would be formulated like this:

> $H_1$: There is a systematic relationship between the dependent and independent variables ($r$ does not equal 0).

This nondirectional hypothesis essentially says the same thing as the following two directional hypotheses, but much more efficiently:

> $H_1$: There is a positive relationship between the two variables ($r$ is greater than 0).
> $H_2$: There is a negative relationship between the two variables ($r$ is less than 0).

All these hypotheses are statements about the possible outcomes of a study if the results indicate the existence of a relationship between whatever variables are involved. There is always the possibility that the results will show no relationship between the variables. This possibility leads to the need for a special type of hypothesis called a *null hypothesis*, which is essentially a hypothesis of no relationship in a correlational study:

> $H_0$: There is no systematic relationship between the dependent and independent variables ($r$ equals 0).

A null hypothesis is always implicit for each statistical decision in a study even if it is not explicitly stated. This will be discussed in much greater detail later.

In all these types of hypotheses, which should be stated clearly and unequivocally, the posited relationships are considered the only possible outcomes for the study. The difference between the directional and non-directional sets of hypotheses might, at the moment, seem trivial, but, as you will discover in the next chapter, when the time comes to make statistical decisions, the difference can become important.

In addition to the *null hypothesis* ($H_0$), which posits no relationship, there are hypotheses, termed *alternative hypotheses* ($H_1$, $H_2$, $H_3$, and so on), that state other potential outcomes. Both types are considered in the logic of a study, as you will see. In any study, there should be at least one null hypothesis and one alternative hypothesis for each pair or set of variables being studied. This is true for correlations between variables (discussed further in Chapter 10), as well as between pairs of group means (Chapter 11) and between different frequencies of responses in survey data (Chapter 12). Of course, more than one set of hypotheses may be under investigation in a given study. Whether they are stated explicitly or are left for the reader to guess, the hypotheses are central to the underlying logic of all statistical studies. Therefore, they deserve some thought on the part of the reader. Particularly at the end of the literature review, where you would expect some statement of the purpose of the study as well as an enumeration of the research questions, it is important to stop and think about the formal null and alternative hypotheses, even if they are not openly presented.

## Stage 2: sampling

To investigate which of the hypotheses to accept, the researcher turns to a primary source of information and gathers data. In our field, this source is usually students who are studying a language. Unfortunately, few researchers are in a position to study, for instance, the entire population of Anglophone students in Canadian high schools who are studying French. Thus, most researchers prefer *sampling*, that is, working with more limited data from a sample or subgroup of the students in a given population. Only then can data be efficiently and practically collected and organized. Samples are commonly drawn from populations for language studies by random sampling and stratified random sampling, both of which have the same goal: to create an accurate *sample*, or group, that is representative of the population.

The point of a *random sample* is to ensure that each member of the population has an equal chance of being selected for the sample. One set of procedures for making such a selection might be to (1) identify the population to which the results will be generalized, (2) assign a number to each, and (3) use a table of random numbers to choose as many subjects as are needed. A *table of random numbers*, which can be found in appendixes of most introductory statistics books, is simply a list of numbers generated to contain no systematic biases. The use of such a list eliminates biases in the researcher's choice of subjects. The subjects can then be assumed to represent the population from which they are selected if a large enough sample is selected. Some researchers utilize more practical, but equally acceptable, procedures, such as pulling numbers out of a hat or using dice or a deck of cards to pick subjects for a study or place them in groups within the study. The point is that each subject must have an equal chance of being selected so that any biases of the researcher are obviated.

A slightly different strategy, called a *stratified random sample*, is occasionally employed in language studies. In this case, the population must not only be identified, but subgroups, or strata within the population, must also be precisely defined. This form of identification is usually done with clear-cut specifications of the characteristics of that subgroup, for instance, sex (male/female), type of school attended (public/private), location (urban/rural), economic status (family income), and their proportions in the population. Given this information about the population, the researcher can randomly select from each of the different groups, or strata, in proportion to their occurrence in the population. The resulting sample should thus have about the same proportional characteristics as the whole population. This procedure also requires random selection but adds a certain amount of precision to the representativeness of the sample and allows for the use of the identified characteristics as variables.

Which strategy a particular researcher chooses to use in a given study will depend on a number of factors, but, generally, the following issues are the most important considerations. The stratified random sampling procedures are most useful when the population to be sampled or separated into groups is heterogeneous. In such situations, purely random sampling might not representatively sample each level or subgroup within the population, particularly when the samples to be used are small or the groups to be formed are of unequal sizes. If properly done, random sampling has the advantage of letting the characteristics of the population, not the researcher, determine the strata to be sampled. If the samples are to be relatively large and the population fairly homogeneous, purely random sampling is much easier to do because there is no need to define strata. The researcher must, however, be willing to assume that the sample represents the population from which it was taken. This assumption is widely held to be a reasonable one, but it is counterintuitive for some people.

Questions often arise about how large a sample must be to be "big enough." There is no quick and easy answer to this question, but there is little doubt that the larger the sample, the better. I think it is reasonable that a sample that includes all but one member of a population is more representative than one that contains 50 percent, 10 percent, or 2 percent of it. But how many is enough? That depends on the situation and on the statistic or statistics that are involved. So rules of thumb that are proposed (e.g., N should equal at least 28 or 30 per group or per variable) are imprecise. Your best strategy is to check that the researcher mentions the rationale/reasoning behind the sample size involved, that the population is clearly delineated, and that the sampling procedures make sense. Thus, the sample should seem large enough to be representative. All of which is to say that this issue is necessarily subjective but nevertheless important.

The notions involved in sampling are crucial to the underlying logic of statistical studies because you want to know how well the results generalize beyond the study itself. Recall that the *generalizability* of a study is the degree to which the results can be said to be meaningful beyond the study. The central question to ask yourself in checking generalizability is, What is the largest population that the sample can be said to represent, given the sampling procedures? The results of a study based on a single class of second-year French students can be generalized only to that class (except in the unlikely event that these students were randomly selected into this particular class). Because the students of this class belong to an intact group, there is a real danger that their characteristics might be different from those of other classes. Similarly, combining all classes from a given school will probably produce results that are generalizable only to that school. The school is the entire population because other schools might be different. But you may want to think about how much that school is like your situation and consider the generalizability of the study accordingly. Again, there are no hard and fast rules.

## Stage 3: setting up statistical decisions

Once the study is defined through the formulation of hypotheses and data have been correctly sampled, the real fun begins. On the basis of the research hypotheses, the researcher must (1) select the correct statistical procedures, (2) formulate statistical hypotheses, and (3) select an alpha decision level.

### Choosing the correct statistics

Perhaps the single most difficult part of a researcher's job is the selection of the appropriate statistical procedures. It is difficult because the investigator must be aware of many possible statistical approaches and if

he or she chooses the wrong one, the results, although impressive looking, may be nonsense.

The options that are available to the researcher are constrained within
a given study by a number of factors, particularly the sizes of the samples
that are used and the types of scales that are involved. Of course, the
first consideration is that the correct family of statistical analyses is used.
And the family that is chosen will depend on the type of research questions that are posited. Is the investigator interested in the degree of
relationship between two variables, as in Chapter 10; in comparing
means, as in Chapter 11; or in comparing frequencies, as in Chapter
12? These families are perhaps an oversimplification, but they are the
most common types of questions that are investigated statistically in the
language teaching field. Thinking in terms of these families should help
you understand what a particular study is doing. Remember that a given
research report may include statistics from one, two, or even all three
of the families mentioned here.

Once you are sure about the appropriate family, the charts provided in
each of these chapters will help you check that the correct statistic was
used. This judgment will be based on clear thinking about (1) how many
variables there are, (2) which variables are dependent, independent, moderator, or control variables, and (3) which scales (nominal, ordinal, and/or
interval) are used for each. You will then have to decide the appropriateness of the statistics that the researcher used. Perhaps the value of the information in Chapters 2–4 is now more obvious to you.

## Statistical hypotheses

Researchers use a shorthand for expressing hypotheses. Sometimes they
do so simply for their own benefit and other times they include it in the
research report. From the set of possible hypotheses shown previously,
we can formulate the following shorthand versions:

$H_0$: $r = 0$ (*r* equals zero)
$H_1$: $r > 0$ (*r* is greater than zero)
$H_2$: $r < 0$ (*r* is less than zero)
$H_3$: $r \neq 0$ (*r* does not equal zero)

If you ponder these statements, you will notice that they represent the
same ideas as the more lengthy written hypotheses.

Recall that the researcher has selected a sample to study a population
more efficiently. Let's briefly review this notion to gain a better understanding of statistical hypotheses and how they are studied. A *population*
is the entire group that is of interest in a study. A *sample* is a subgroup
taken from that population to represent it. When calculations are made
to describe a sample, they are called *statistics* (as shown in Chapters 6–

8). If the same calculations were actually done for the entire population, they would be called *parameters*. Parameters would clearly give the best picture of what is going on in a given population. It has also been argued, however, that sample data may provide better information than census data (e.g., a survey of all homes in the United States) in that a sample can be more easily and accurately identified and controlled than can an entire population. For reasons of economy, practicality, and accuracy, then, parameters are seldom used.

Researchers prefer to work with samples. If a sample is drawn correctly, rational estimates can be made of the parameters for the population. Thus, statistics are used to describe samples as well as to make inferences about populations. But such estimates may be in error. Thus, in addition to allowing researchers to make inferences about populations from samples, statistical theory makes it possible to estimate the probability that such inferences are incorrect. This key concept will be explored in greater depth later.

To accommodate the conceptual differences between statistics and parameters, researchers often use two sets of symbols: one to represent various statistical measurements and the other to represent parameters. The statistical symbols are usually Roman letters (e.g., $\overline{X}$ and $SD$ for the sample mean and the standard deviation), while the parameters are most often symbolized by Greek letters (e.g., $\mu$ and $\sigma$, for the population mean and the standard deviation). Remember that the statistics are what the researcher actually computes from the data. Inferences drawn from those statistics to represent the parameters are only estimates and will have a certain probability of being in error.

## Alpha decision level

Since the researcher is typically using statistics to investigate parameters, there is always some chance that the results based on the sample do not represent the population, that is, that they are in error; this is one way that probability fits into the picture. There are also situations in which the researcher wants to determine whether two events or sets of data are related or different. There is always a chance that observed relationships occurred by chance alone or that differences in means or frequencies between sets of data are chance occurrences. This, then, is another way that probability enters the picture.

In many cases, the researcher is concerned with the *probability* ($p$) that the alternative hypotheses are correct, for example, that the correlation is different from zero. Unfortunately, the alternative hypotheses cannot be tested directly. The existing mathematical and statistical models make it necessary that a much more indirect form of logic be used. The researcher begins by investigating the probability that rejecting

115

the null hypothesis will be an error, or not represent the actual state of affairs in the population. Current statistical theory can help with this problem. In fact, when you see $p < .01$ in a study for a given result, it is indicating the answer to just this type of question. It is saying that the probability $(p)$ is less than $(<)$ 1 percent $(.01)$ that rejecting the null hypothesis will be an error; that is, the probability is less than 1 percent that the results are due to chance alone. (There will be much more about this later.)

Consider the correlation example discussed earlier and recall that the null hypothesis was $H_0$: $r = 0$. The problem is that the two sets of data could be related, at least to some degree, by pure chance. For instance, if two people were to draw 30 cards each (while keeping track and replacing them) from a well-shuffled deck, a small correlation might be observed. The question is, How high a correlation is it necessary to observe before you can be reasonably sure that it did not occur by chance alone? The mathematics of probability theory can be applied to answer this question. Thus, you can compute the theoretical magnitude of a correlation that you might expect to find at some probability level, say 1 in 100 (1/100), for a given sample size. If the correlation that you actually calculate is greater than the one you would expect to find by chance alone, you could conclude that the one you calculated is probably (99/100) due to factors other than chance.

In testing the null hypothesis, then, you are asking how different the correlation coefficient must be from 00.0 (in either the positive or negative directions) with a given sample size to reject the null hypothesis that it really is equal to 00.0 or at least differs from 00.0 only by chance.

In simple terms, the purpose is to determine the probability that the correlation (alternative hypothesis) found in the data is "real" (alternative hypothesis) or is due to chance alone (null hypothesis). The researcher bases the decision of whether to reject the null hypothesis on such probabilities. But how does the investigator decide what probability is acceptable?

In language studies, the *significance level* is typically set at $p < .01$ (1/100) or at $p < .05$ (5/100), depending on whether the researcher is willing to accept only 1 percent error or tolerate up to 5 percent error, respectively. These two levels are used by convention in most of the social sciences. Statistical decisions in some fields, in which lives or millions of dollars may hang in the balance, may set considerably more conservative alpha levels, say $p < .00001$ (the probability of error in rejecting the null hypothesis is less than 1 in 10,000 — a pretty safe decision). Note that when the decision level is initially determined, it is traditionally symbolized by $\alpha$, rather than $p$ (e.g., $\alpha < .01$; the alpha level is set at .01 or less). It is when the results are reported that $p$ is used, as in $p < .01$. Both $\alpha$ and $p$ represent essentially the same thing but at different points in the researcher's thinking and reporting.

## Stage 4: necessary considerations

All the preliminaries are now completed, and the researcher is finally ready to perform the actual statistical calculations. Four types of information must now be found: (1) the observed statistics, that is, those that were actually calculated, (2) whether the assumptions underlying those statistics were met, (3) the degrees of freedom involved for each statistic, and (4) the critical values for each statistic.

### Observed statistics

Whether the results are a straightforward Pearson $r$ or a complicated-looking analysis of variance table based on $F$ ratios (see Chapter 11), the researcher does a lot of adding, subtracting, dividing, and multiplying to get there. Often, he or she does so with a mainframe computer, using statistical software like the *Statistical Package for the Social Sciences* (1975) or the *Biomedical Computer Program: P-Series* (1977). Other researchers prefer to do the calculations by hand or with a calculator or on a personal computer. In all cases, however, errors can be made. Therefore, you should always check to make sure that the reported statistics make sense, especially in relation to the descriptive statistics that are presented (e.g., $\overline{X}$ or $SD$).

The result of the calculations will be *observed statistics*. These are the actual figures found for the sample (e.g., $r_{observed} = .91$, or $F_{observed} = 4.67$) – that were actually observed and calculated in a study. And it is on these numbers that all decisions and inferences are based.

### Assumptions

Before calculating observed statistics, however, the investigator should have checked to see that the assumptions for each statistic were met. An *assumption* is a precondition that must be met for the particular statistical analysis to be accurately applied. For instance, one of the assumptions that underlies the proper application of the Pearson product-moment correlation coefficient ($r$) is that each set of scores is on an interval scale. This means just what it says. The scales involved must *not* be nominal or ordinal. If they are other than interval scales, other statistics may be applied, but the Pearson product-moment correlation coefficient assumes an interval scale. This and the other three assump-

117

tions that are crucial to the application of *r* will be explained more thoroughly in the next chapter. For the moment, the most important thing to keep in mind is that the proper application of most statistics depends on first meeting certain assumptions. It is the researcher's job to check the assumptions. And it is up to you to make sure that the assumptions were not only checked, but met in a manner that is satisfactory and clear to you. Details of the assumptions underlying the most common types of analyses will be discussed in the chapters that follow.

## Degrees of freedom

For logical reasons developed over many years, statistical decisions will vary because of differences in the size of the sample, the number of groups, and so forth. To adjust for these differences, the researcher uses *degrees of freedom* (*df*). This concept is related to the assumption of independence discussed earlier. The existence of the concept of degrees of freedom is due in large part to the fact that statistics are calculated on the basis of sample means and standard deviations. Let's consider the sample standard deviation for a moment. Recall that the formula was as follows:

$$S = \sqrt{\frac{\Sigma(X - \overline{X})^2}{N}}$$

There are several interesting things about this formula. Recall that the sum of the deviations from the mean on a measure, or $\Sigma (X - \overline{X})$, will always turn out to be zero. That is why *z* scores always have a mean of zero. It is also why we have to square the deviations before summing them up to calculate the standard deviation.

Let's now take a simple example (in which $N = 4$). If I were to ask you to guess the deviations on a test, you might first guess a deviation from the mean of 6. Thus, for the first guess, $X_1 - \overline{X} = 6$. You could also guess $X_2 - \overline{X} = 2$ for the second deviation and, maybe, $X - \overline{X} = -4$ for the third deviation. So far, these have all been guesses. But for the fourth and last deviation, no guesswork is necessary. Notice that if the first three deviations are 6, 2, and $-4$, the last one must also be $-4$ because all the deviations must add up to zero. Since $6 + 2 + (-4) +$ "fourth guess" $= 0$ is the expected relationship, the last number to be guessed, "fourth guess," in this case, will always be fully predictable. In other words, for that fourth value, you are not free to guess any number you want to because that last value is not independent of the other three. It must be $-4$ so that the deviations add up to zero [$6 + 2 + (-4) + (-4) = 0$]. This leads to the realization that you had three (or $N - 1 = 4 - 1 = 3$) free guesses, or degrees of freedom, and one that was not free to vary. You will see $N - 1$ appearing in many statistical formulas; it is usually there to adjust for degrees of freedom. In fact, you will often see the following formula for the standard deviation;

$$S = \sqrt{\frac{\Sigma(X - \overline{X})^2}{N - 1}}$$

Here the $- 1$ in $N - 1$ is present to adjust for just the issue discussed in the previous paragraph. It is especially important in the standard deviation formula when the sample on which it is based is small, say 28 or less. Because this issue is involved in virtually all statistics, degrees of freedom will be an essential part of calculating observed statistics and will affect the determination of critical values as well.

### Critical values

One last bit of information is necessary before the researcher can make the long-awaited statistical decision – the critical value for whatever statistic is involved. The *critical value* is the value that the researcher might expect to observe in the sample simply because of chance. In most cases, an observed statistic must exceed the critical value to reject the null hypothesis and thereby accept one of the alternative hypotheses. This critical value will vary from study to study even for the same statistic because the degrees of freedom will usually vary, largely owing to differences in the size of samples. To account for all this, the researcher turns to readily available tables (as will be shown in later chapters) and determines the critical value for a given statistic on the basis of the degrees of freedom that are allowable and the alpha decision level of the particular study. Now let's turn to how a discussion of all this fits together into a statistical decision.

## Stage 5: Statistical decisions

A statistical decision involves everything that has been discussed so far in this chapter. It is based on (1) hypothesis testing (not to be confused with the common meaning of "testing"), (2) the careful interpretation of the results, and (3) an awareness of the potential pitfalls for a particular statistical test.

### Hypothesis testing

The researcher has now collected all the information that is necessary for testing the hypotheses in question. Such information is listed in Table

TABLE 9.1. INFORMATION NECESSARY FOR HYPOTHESIS TESTING

| Type of information needed | Example |
| --- | --- |
| The problem | Degree of relationship between two language tests |
| Statistical hypotheses | $H_0 : r = 0$ (null) |
| | $H_1 : r > 0$ (alternative) |
| | $H_2 : r < 0$ (alternative) |
| Alpha decision level | $\alpha < .01$ |
| Number of individuals (pairs of scores) | $N = 100$ |
| Observed statistic ($r$) | $r_{obs} = .91$ |
| Assumptions met? | Yes |
| Degrees of freedom ($df$) | $N - 2 = 98$ |
| Critical value of the statistic | $r_{crit} = .27$ |
| | (at $p < .01$; $df = 98$) |

9.1. The information in the right column of the table is based on the relatively simple problem of determining the degree of relationship between two language tests.

The steps followed by the researcher in testing a hypothesis are shown in Table 9.2. Keeping the statistical hypotheses and the alpha decision level in mind, the researcher compares the observed value of the statistic to the critical value. If the observed statistic is smaller than the critical statistic, the null hypothesis is accepted. There is probably no relationship between the variables and the hypothesis testing is finished. If the observed statistic is greater than the critical value for that statistic, then the null hypothesis is rejected. Having rejected the null hypothesis, one of the two alternatives is automatically accepted. The researcher must decide which of them is most reasonable on the basis of simple logic. If $H_1$ is accepted, then it can be said on the basis of the alpha level that there is a $p$ level of probability that the observed statistic occurred by chance alone. Let's try all these steps one more time using the information from the example cited earlier in the chapter:

1. The researcher ponders the hypothesis $H_0$, that the correlation is zero (or, even if higher, is due entirely to chance); $H_1$, that the correlation really is greater than zero (or positive and probably is not due to chance alone); $H_2$, that the correlation is really less than zero (or negative and probably is not due to chance alone).
2. The researcher must also remember that the $\alpha < .01$ decision level means that only 1 percent error will be acceptable. Thus, the results must be 99 percent sure.

TABLE 9.2. HYPOTHESIS TESTING

| Steps | Example |
|---|---|
| 1. Look at the hypothesis. | $H_0$: $r = 0$ <br> $H_1$: $r > 0$ <br> $H_2$: $r < 0$ |
| 2. Look at the alpha level. | $\alpha < .01$ |
| 3. Compare the observed statistic and the critical value. | $r_{obs} = .91$ <br> $r_{crit} = .27$ |
| 4. a. If the observed statistic is less than the critical value, it could be due to chance. Therefore, we accept the null hypothesis and stop. | Not so here. |
| b. If the observed statistic is greater than the critical value, the probability is .01 or less (alpha level) that it is due to chance. We can, therefore, reject the null hypothesis and continue. | $r_{obs} > r_{crit}$ $(.91 > .27)$, so reject $H_0$. |
| 5. Decide which alternative hypothesis is more logical. | $r_{obs} = .91$, a positive value, so $H_1$: $r > 0$ is more logical. |
| 6. Interpret the results in terms of the $p$ level. | $H_0$ is rejected at $p < .01$ and $H_1$ is accepted. So there is only a 1% probability that $r_{obs} = .91$ occurred by chance alone, or a 99% probability that $r_{obs}$ is due to other than chance factors. |

3. The researcher can now compare the $r_{observed}$ ($r_{obs}$) with the $r_{critical}$ ($r_{crit}$), obtained from the appropriate table.

4. (a) If the $r_{obs}$ is less than the $r_{crit}$, $r_{obs}$ could be due to chance, and the null hypothesis must be accepted. (b) If the $r_{obs}$ is greater than the $r_{crit}$, the probability is .01 or less that $r_{obs}$ is due to chance, so the null hypothesis can be rejected. In this case, $r_{crit} = .91$ and $r_{obs} = .27$. Since .91 is greater than .27, the null hypothesis is rejected.

5. Because this is the outcome, one of the alternative hypotheses must be accepted. The $r_{obs}$ in this case is positive, so it is logical to accept the first alternative hypothesis (that $r_{obs}$ is greater than zero).

6. Having rejected the null hypothesis at $p < .01$ and accepted the first alternative hypothesis, the researcher correctly explains these results as follows: There is only a 1 percent probability that $r_{obs}$ at .91 occurred by chance alone, or there is a 99 percent probability that $r_{obs}$ is due to other than chance factors.

## Interpretation of the results

The hypotheses have now been tested, but the investigator is not finished. Results can be *significant* ($H_0$ rejected at $p < .01$ or $p < .05$) without being particularly interesting or meaningful. Notice that with an $r_{crit}$ of .27 (at $\alpha < .01$), an $r_{obs}$ of .30 would be found to be significantly different from zero. This finding would mean only that the researcher is 99 percent sure that the relationship between variables did not occur as a fluke — that it was due to other than chance factors. It is what is referred to as *significance*, that is, that the observed relationship between variables was probably (95 percent or 99 percent, depending on whether the alpha was set at .05 or .01) not an accidental, or chance, occurrence.

The notion of significance does not necessarily imply meaningfulness. The *meaningfulness* of a particular result will depend on a number of factors. For instance, recall that the previous chapter showed that the squared value of $r^2$ (or $r_{obs}^2$) indicates the percentage of overlap between two sets of scores. In the example under consideration here, there is a statistically significant correlation coefficient, $r_{obs} = .30$. But $r_{obs}^2 = .30^2 = .09$. So the significant coefficient, although it probably (99 percent sure) did not occur by chance alone, is indicating a relationship that amounts to only 9 percent of the covariance, or variation, shared by either of the sets of scores with the other. Since the remaining 91 percent of the variation is not shared by the two sets of scores, it would be difficult, indeed, to argue that this "significant" correlation coefficient is meaningful. There are, however, situations in which such a relationship would be meaningful and interesting, so there are no absolute rules.

The important thing to remember is that significance and meaningfulness are separate issues. Logic would dictate that a statistic must be statistically significant before it can be meaningful because chance occurrences do not reveal meaningful patterns and relationships. But the reverse is not necessarily true; just because a result is statistically significant does not mean it is necessarily meaningful. It is up to you to make sure the researcher did not overinterpret the results in terms of meaningfulness.

## Potential pitfalls

Every statistical procedure has certain pitfalls. Good researchers are aware of them and avoid such traps. Some of the most common pitfalls will be enumerated in the chapters that follow so that you can discern them as well. But, for the moment, the overinterpretation just mentioned will serve as an example that cannot be overemphasized.

Overinterpretation is a trap into which language researchers often fall. You will encounter studies that use "significant" to mean "meaningful."

You will see studies that do not appear to recognize that a significant correlation coefficient of .30 is indicating only a very weak (although nonchance) relationship between variables. But, worst of all, you will find studies that argue that one finding is "more significant" at $p < .0001$ than another at $p < .05$.

Traditionally, the alpha level was always decided in advance and viewed as a decision point for accepting or rejecting the null hypothesis at a predesignated probability level. Alpha (or the resulting $p$) was considered rigid – neither a sliding scale nor a yo-yo. When you see it used as either, you might want to consider the possibility that the researcher does not understand the logic of statistical reasoning.

However, the traditional view of statistical decision levels seems to have changed in recent years because computers calculate the actual probability levels involved. When researchers report the actual probability levels (e.g., $p < .025$), it is the reader's responsibility to judge whether the level is acceptable. In a sense, it is now up to the reader to decide the alpha level that is acceptable for a given study, expecially if the researcher has not indicated any such level.

## Related analyses

The last section of Chapters 10–12 list and discuss other analyses that are related to the family of analyses covered in the respective chapters. The focus of these discussions will be on how the particular analysis is related to or differs from what you already know from reading the chapter. The analyses are listed alphabetically for easy reference, and other names for the same statistical tests are cross-referenced. This strategy was chosen so you will be able to find at least a brief description of the most common statistical analyses that you are likely to encounter in your reading.

## Terms and symbols

| | |
|---|---|
| alpha decision level | meaningful results |
| alternative hypotheses ($H_1$, $H_2$, etc.) | nondirectional hypothesis |
| assumption | null hypothesis ($H_0$) |
| critical value | observed statistic |
| degrees of freedom ($df$) | one-tailed hypothesis |
| directional hypothesis | parameters |
| generalizability | population |
| hypothesis | probability ($p$) |
| hypothesis testing | random sample |

sample
sampling
significance level
significant
statistical hypothesis
statistical logic
statistics

stratified random sample
table of random numbers
two-tailed hypothesis
$\alpha$
$\mu$
$\sigma$

## Review questions

1. What are the five basic stages involved in the logic of a statistical study?
2. If you had to choose, which strategy for clarifying the intent of a study would you consider most important: the statement of purpose, the research questions, or the research hypotheses?
3. What is the difference between a null hypothesis and alternative hypotheses? Which type must be rejected before the other is accepted?
4. What is the difference between random sampling and stratified random sampling? What are the advantages and disadvantages of each? What is an adequate sample size?
5. What is generalizability? How does it relate to sampling? And why is it important to think about it in terms of you and your students?
6. What is the difference between a population and a sample?
7. What are the three families of statistical studies?
8. What are the considerations that you must keep in mind when deciding whether the correct statistic has been used in a study?
9. What does $\alpha < .01$ mean in terms of statistical decision making? How does $\alpha < .01$ relate to $p < .01$ and to the null hypothesis?
10. What pieces of information must the researcher have before the hypotheses can be tested? What are the steps involved in testing a hypothesis?

## Application

A. Reread the study presented in Examples 5.1–5.11 in Chapter 5.
1. Did the researcher cover each of the steps involved in statistical logic?
2. If any steps are missing, how does this fact affect the logic of the study and the value of the study?

3. Studies in second language learning (especially ESL) often involve samples made up of various nationalities. Do you think the sampling procedures are adequate in the study? To what population, if any, can the study be generalized?

B. Find a statistical study of particular interest to *you* and apply everything you have learned so far to reading it critically. Focus particularly on the issues raised in the checklist given in Chapter 5 and those raised in Table 9.2. In the end, you should decide what you think of the study in terms of its value to you and your field.

# 10 Correlation

We are all familiar with correlation in one form or another, whether it is the degree to which smoking cigarettes is said to be correlated with the incidence of cancer or the degree of relationship between variables like the percentage of unemployed people and the number of felony crimes that are committed. Because they can reveal interesting and useful patterns in data, statistical studies of correlation have led to medical breakthroughs, social change, and even new strategies for language teaching. One problem, however, is that some researchers and readers misinterpret statistical results. Statistics are neither absolutes nor truths. Whether they are statistics of correlation or the other statistics covered in this book, they are, as you saw in the last chapter, the backbone of a straightforward form of logic − a logic that limits itself to drawing conclusions about the world around us in probabilistic terms. Let's now look at this family of analyses in more detail so you can continue to temper your understanding of the concepts without rejecting them out of hand.

## Stage 1: focusing the study

### Identifying a problem

In general, correlational studies are designed to investigate the nature and strength of functional relationships among the variables of interest to the researcher. Thus, they are the statistics of *covariance*, or the degree to which sets of data vary together, that is, in the same way. In our field, these statistics are usually applied to support hypotheses regarding logical theoretical relationships among psychological constructs that are related to language learning. One example of this kind of study was illustrated in the previous chapter. Some of the common uses for correlational statistics include the demonstration of the criterion-related validity of language tests, the exploration of the relationship between two variables, and the establishment of the existence of a relationship before making predictions.

This last application of correlation − *prediction* − is one of the many statistical tools within the larger family of statistics that have practical uses. It is often used to estimate the performance on one variable from the performance on another (e.g., predicting achievement in language classes from a language aptitude test) or to equate scores on one test with those on another (e.g., a score on Test A of 92 is about equal to a score of 555 on TOEFL, 80 = 503, 75 = 492, and so on). You will find many other tools in this family of statistics at the end of the chapter listed alphabetically and explained briefly under Related Analyses.

The following abstract of a hypothetical study uses both correlation (Sentences 1 and 5) and prediction (Sentences 1 and 6) to explore two typical problems probabilistically. (I will refer to this study throughout the chapter in my discussion of various points):

EXAMPLE IO.I. HYPOTHETICAL STUDY OF RELATIONSHIPS BETWEEN CLASS HOURS AND PROFICIENCY IN FRENCH

(1) This study investigates the questions of whether there is a systematic relationship between the number of class hours of French study and proficiency in French, as well as how accurately proficiency can be predicted from class hours. (2) "Class hours" is defined as the total number of hours spent studying French at the secondary level and "French proficiency" is defined as the scores on the French proficiency test. (3) The Pearson product-moment correlation coefficient is used to test the null hypothesis of no significant relationship ($H_0$: $r_{xy} = 0$) at $\alpha < .01$ directional (because any correlation found was expected to be positive). (4) The study is based on a random sample of students ($N = 102$) drawn from the entire population ($N = 5,432$) of French students in the Megalopolis Unified School District. (5) All assumptions for the statistical test were found to be met and the correlation coefficient that was obtained ($r = .65$) was significant ($p < .01$). (6) Predictions of the scores on the French proficiency test are also made from the number of class hours. (7) The results are discussed in terms of how meaningful the relationship and resulting predictions are and what they may mean to planners of a high school curriculum in French.

## Operationalizing variables

This family of analyses can deal with all types of scales – interval, ordinal, or nominal. As you will see later, the very choice of statistics depends primarily on the number and type of scales that are involved. And, of course, the results will be no better than the tests, questionnaires, or definitions of categories that operationalize the constructs as variables.

The way the variables are viewed also has a great deal to do with the accurate interpretation of results. The dependent variable should be viewed as the *criterion variable*, or that which is predicted, and will normally be labeled Y. The independent variable should be considered a *predictor variable*, or the basis for prediction, and will normally be labeled X.

127

Notice how the constructs have been operationalized in Example 10.1. What are the two variables of interest? How are they operationalized? Should any other variables have been included? What type of scale is involved for each? Which is the dependent variable and which is the independent variable? Which is the criterion variable (Y) and which is the predictor variable (X)? (Only two variables are involved here and both are interval scales: (1) proficiency in French, as measured on the test, is the criterion variable, Y, and (2) the number of class hours is the independent (predictor) variable, X.)

### Research hypotheses

The hypotheses of such a study will normally take about the same form as those shown in the previous chapter. For Example 10.1, the null and alternative hypotheses that are implicit in the first sentence are these:

$H_0$: There is no significant systematic relationship between the number of class hours of French and the scores on the French proficiency test.

$H_1$: There is a significant positive relationship between the number of class hours of French and the scores on the French proficiency test.

Notice that these hypotheses express a directional decision, that is, the researcher must have a sound theoretical reason for expecting that if any relationship exists, it will be positive.

## Stage 2: sampling

As with all statistics, the manner in which the data are gathered – the Procedures – is important. Of course, sampling procedures will affect the generalizability of the results. But in this family of analyses, it is particularly important that all information that is gathered for each individual is independent of the information for all the other subjects in the study. Practically speaking, this usually means that the researcher must limit the possibility of "cheating" or "cooperating" on tests or questionnaires. This possibility must be considered well in advance during the design and data gathering stages.

Notice how the sampling and data gathering are described in Sentence 4 of Example 10.1. Are you satisfied with this description? Perhaps Sentence 5 is an indication that the issues of cheating and cooperating were adequately handled.

128

## Stage 3: setting up statistical decisions

*Choosing the correct statistic*

The choice of the statistic to be used in a study depends largely on the number of variables, the types of scales, and how each variable is viewed conceptually (as dependent, independent, or whatever). Table 10.1 shows in boldface type the options that are most commonly used by language researchers to explore questions involving correlation and prediction. Notice that the dependent variables are shown vertically in rows while the independent variables are presented horizontally in columns. Within each type of variable, then, the three types of scales are shown: interval, ordinal, and nominal. The number of such variables within each type of scale is also given as "0, 1, or more than 1."

To see how Table 10.1 works, let's once again consider Example 10.1. The hypothetical study it describes had only two variables. The dependent variable, scores on the French proficiency test, is an interval scale, as is the independent variable, the number of class hours of French study. If you look across from one interval scale dependent variable and down from one interval scale variable in Table 10.1, you will find that simple regression and the Pearson *r* correlation are the correct forms of analysis. But what if both dependent variables had been ordinal scales or nominal scales? What if there had been four variables – one dependent and three independent – and all had been interval scales?

In your critical reading, you are not actually making such a decision. Therefore, it might be more useful to look for the statistic that is used in a study and work backwards to the number of variables, type of scale, and dependent/independent labels. In Example 10.1, this would mean that you would first find the types of analyses (Sentence 3), which are simple regression and the Pearson product-moment correlation coefficient. Next, you would locate the box containing those categories of analysis (simple regression and Pearson *r*) and check to see that the design conditions are correct: one interval scale dependent variable and one interval scale independent variable. Is this the case in Example 10.1? What design conditions would be necessary for the phi coefficient or the Spearman rho to be correctly applied (see Table 10.1)? Once again, if the analyses involved are other than simple regression and Pearson *r*, you will find more information at the end of this chapter in the Related Analyses section.

### Statistical hypotheses

It should be no mystery to you by now that the statistical hypotheses for the study abstracted in Example 10.1 should be about the same as those shown in the previous chapter:

TABLE 10.1. COMMON ANALYSES FOR CORRELATION

Type and Number of Independent Variables

| | | Interval | | Ordinal | | Nominal | | |
|---|---|---|---|---|---|---|---|---|
| | | 1 variable | More than 1 | 1 variable | More than 1 | 1 variable — 2 levels | 1 variable — more | More than 1 |
| **Interval** | 0 | | | Transform the ordinal variable into a nominal variable and use *C-1*, or transform the interval variable into an ordinal variable and use *B-2*, or transform both variables into nominal variables and use *C-3*. | | | | |
| | 1 | **Simple regression and Pearson r** | **Multiple regression and Multiple R** | | | z stat. (large sample), t test (any sample) | One-way ANOVA | Two-way ANOVA, three-way ANOVA, etc. *(Row 1)* |
| | More than 1 | **Multiple regression and Multiple R** | | Multivariate analyses | | Multivariate analyses | | Multivariate analyses |
| **Ordinal** | 0 | Transform the ordinal variable into a nominal variable and use *C-1*, or transform the interval variable into an ordinal variable and use *B-2*, or transform the interval variable into a nominal variable and use *C-2*. | | | **Kendall's W** | Median test, U test | Kruskal-Wallis test | Friedman's two-way ANOVA *(Row 2)* |
| | 1 | | | **Spearman rho** **Kendall's tau** | | | | |
| | More than 1 | | | | | | | |

| Nominal | | Column A | Column B | Column C | Row 3 |
|---|---|---|---|---|---|
| | 0 | | | | Chi-square |
| | 1 | Biserial, Point-biserial correlation | (see C-2) | Phi coefficient, tetrachoric corr., Fisher exact test Chi-square | |
| | More than 1 | (see C-1) | (see C-2) | | |

*Note:* Boldface indicates the common analyses for correlation. C-1 stands for Column C, Row 1.
*Source:* Adapted from Tuckman (1978: 255).

$$H_0: r = 0$$
$$H_1: r > 0$$

If these hypotheses do not make sense to you, go back and review what was said about them in the previous chapter.

### Alpha decision level

Likewise, making the decision about what alpha level is acceptable will follow the traditional pattern. The language researcher should set a conservative level ($\alpha < .01$) if only 1 percent chance of error is acceptable and a more liberal level ($\alpha < .05$) if 5 percent chance of error can be tolerated. In Example 10.1, the decision level was clearly set at $\alpha < .01$ (see Sentences 3 and 5).

As was pointed out, this decision level was *directional* (Sentence 3) in Example 10.1. When only a positive correlation is expected as a possible alternative outcome, the researcher may choose to use only $H_0$ and $H_1$. However, such an expectation should be based on logic or the results of previous research that support the directionality. When either a positive or negative outcome is possible, all three hypotheses ($H_0$, $H_1$, and $H_2$) should be used. This is called a *nondirectional* decision. Recall also that directional decisions are sometimes called *one-tailed*, while nondirectional decisions are called *two-tailed*.

## Stage 4: necessary calculations

From this point on, I will stay with the type of analysis (Pearson $r$) chosen for the study in Example 10.1. But remember that the other possible types of analyses in this family have basically the same logic.

### Observed statistics

The Pearson $r$ correlation coefficient was defined in Chapter 8 as an estimate of the degree to which two sets of interval scale scores go together (covary or vary in a similar manner). It can range from a perfect positive relationship of $+1.0$ to no systematic relationship at 0.0 to a perfect negative relationship of $-1.0$.

It was also pointed out that when such a coefficient is further away from 0.0. toward $+1.0$ or $-1.0$, the relationship represented between the two sets of scores is stronger. One of the uses of such coefficients is to examine the degree of relationship between two variables. On the basis of this examination, predictions can then be made.

For the sake of clarity, let's extend the hypothetical study in the

TABLE 10.2. SIX-STUDENT STUDY

| Students | French Class Hours (X) | Scores on the French Proficiency Test (Y) |
|---|---|---|
| Jimmy | 850 | 95 |
| Jaime | 800 | 90 |
| Juan | 750 | 85 |
| Joanne | 700 | 80 |
| Jake | 600 | 70 |
| Jerry | 550 | 65 |

b. Descriptive Statistics

| | | |
|---|---|---|
| $\overline{X}$ | 708.3 | 80.83 |
| SD | 115.8 | 11.58 |
| Low–high | 550–850 | 65–95 |
| Range | 300 | 30 |

c. Regression Statistics
Intercept $(a)$ = 10.0
Slope $(b)$ = .10
$r$ = 1.0

abstract into a perfect make-believe world in which proficiency scores in French are due entirely to the number of class hours – a world unlike the real world in which explanations of human behavior are often complex. Let's say that data have been gathered on six students, so I will, therefore, call this the "Six-Student Study." The students' scores and the number of hours are shown in Table 10.2a. The first thing you should do in such a case is to look at the descriptive statistics (see Table 10.2b) to get a feel for how the two distributions look (skewed or normal). Then you will have to examine the regression statistics (Table 10.2c): slope, intercept, and correlation coefficient.

To understand all this, let's look at a scatterplot of Jerry's scores on the proficiency test with the number of class hours (Figure 10.1). Jerry attended 550 hours of French classes, so a line was drawn up from 550 hours on the abscissa. He also scored 65 on the proficiency test, so a horizontal line was drawn across from that score on the ordinate. Where the two lines meet, an asterisk can be placed to represent Jerry. If the same is done for all six students, the result turns out as in Figure 10.2. Notice that in this figure, there is a set of asterisks that form a straight line. If a line, called the *regression line*, is drawn to connect these points, some interesting inferences can be made.

Let's take another student, who attended 650 hours of French classes but did not take the test. Can you use the line in Figure 10.2 to predict that student's score on the French proficiency test? Just draw a straight

133

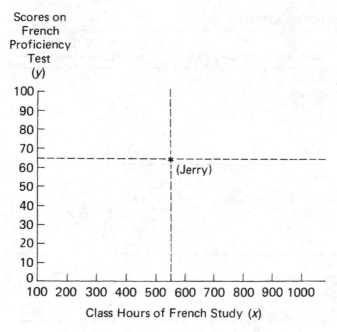

*Figure 10.1   Jerry*

line up from where 650 is marked on the abscissa; where it meets the regression line for the plotted scores, draw another horizontal line over to the ordinate. The lines should cross at about 75. Hence, a reasonable prediction of the student's score on the proficiency test, based on 650 hours of classes, would be 75.

Unfortunately, the real world does not work in such a perfect manner. First, the sample size in this example is entirely too small to make a sound prediction. Second, an exactly straight-line relationship of the asterisks is seldom, if ever, obtained.

More often, you find situations like the one in Example 10.1. A scatterplot of the results of that study is presented in Figure 10.3. The 102 students constitute a considerably better sample size, and the cluster of asterisks is more typical than is a straight line. The best that the researcher can do to make predictions is to estimate where the straight line would pass through the middle of the scores. To do this properly, the researcher calculates the slope, the intercept, and the correlation, each of which gives important information about the estimated line. The *slope* indicates the angle of the line in terms of how many y points the line goes up for each x point change on the other axis. In Table 10.3, notice that the slope is .10, which means that there is a one-tenth of a point rise in scores on the proficiency examination for every hour of

134

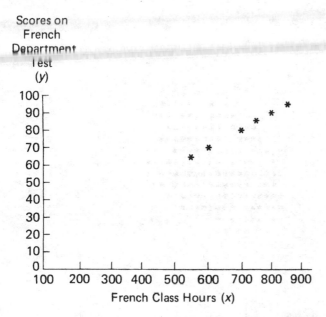

*Figure 10.2   Scatterplot of the six student study*

French class (or one point for every 10 hours). The *intercept* of 10 in this case is estimating where the line will cross the ordinate, or y-axis. Notice that the regression line crosses the y-axis at 10 in Figure 10.3.

The *correlation coefficient* provides additional information about the degree to which the data actually fall on a straight line. In Figure 10.2, on the one hand, the correlation was 1.0 because there was a straight-line relationship between the two sets of scores and all asterisks fell exactly on the line. In Figure 10.3, on the other hand, the correlation is only .65. This correlation indicates that the straight-line relationship is less than perfect and that some asterisks fall fairly far from that line.

The *regression equation* can be used to make the actual predictions of Y scores from X scores without the scatterplot. This equation takes the form:

$$\hat{Y} = a + bX$$

where $\hat{Y}$ = estimated Y score, $a$ = intercept, $b$ = slope, and X = X variable score.

Applying this formula to Figure 10.3 and Table 10.3, let's try to predict what a new student with 650 hours of French classes would score on the proficiency test. We know that the slope ($b$) is .10, the intercept ($a$) is 10, and the number of hours ($X$) is 650. Plugging these into the regression equation, we get the following result:

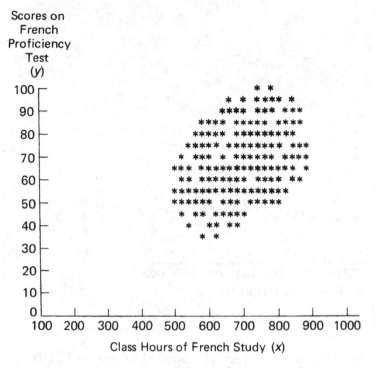

Figure 10.3  *Scatterplot of the study in example 10.1*

$$\hat{Y} = a + bX$$
$$= 10 + .10(650)$$
$$= 10 + 65$$
$$= 75$$

In other words, the estimated score on the proficiency test ($\hat{Y}$) for a student with 650 hours of class is 75.

All this yields a correlation coefficient ($r_{observed} = .65$) and a regression, or prediction, equation ($\hat{Y} = 10 + .10X$) for the hypothetical study presented in Example 10.1. But before the researcher can interpret these observed statistics, the assumptions must be considered.

## Assumptions

The assumptions underlying the Pearson product-moment correlation coefficient are that

1. each pair of scores is independent from all other pairs;
2. each of the two variables involved is normally distributed;

TABLE 10.3. HYPOTHETICAL DESCRIPTIVE STATISTICS FOR THE STUDY
IN EXAMPLE 10.1

| Statistic | Class hours of French study (X) | French Proficiency Test (Y) |
|---|---|---|
| N | 102 | 102 |
| X̄ | 683.30 | 78.33 |
| SD | 134.50 | 14.10 |
| Low–high | 500–900 | 35–100 |
| Range | 400 | 65 |
| Regression[a] | | |
| Slope (b) | | .10 |
| Intercept (a) | | 10.00 |
| r | | .65 |
| $r^2$ | | .42 |
| SEE | | 8.34 |

[a]Regression equation: $\hat{Y} = a + bX$
$\hat{Y} = 10 + .10(X)$

3. each of the two variables involved is measured on an interval scale;
4. the relationship between the two sets of scores is linear.

Let's look at these separately.

## INDEPENDENCE

The assumption of independence for each pair of scores from all others requires that the scores can be lined up in two columns, that no student took the tests twice (and thus created two pairs of scores related to each other), and that no student copied from another student (which would also create related pairs). This assumption precludes the analysis of scores for a single student who takes a pair of tests repeatedly over the course of, say, three years. In short, there must be no connection between pairs of scores for a correlation analysis to be properly applied. You can usually check for this assumption by carefully reading the author's explanation in the Procedures section of a study.

## NORMAL DISTRIBUTION

The second assumption is that each of the variables must be *normally distributed*. Another way to state this assumption is that neither of the two distributions should be skewed. This assumption can usually be checked by judging the scales and descriptive statistics for each variable. The importance of checking for skewedness is further amplified later in this chapter in the section on Potential Pitfalls.

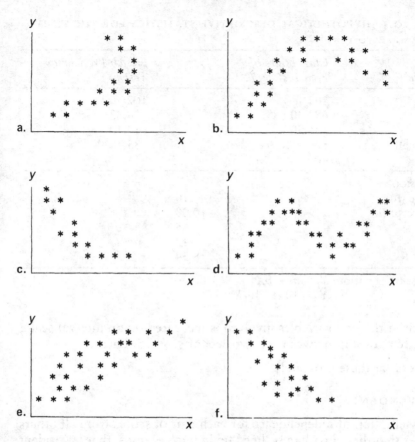

*Figure 10.4   Curvilinear (a–d) and linear (e and f) relationships*

### INTERVAL SCALES

As was mentioned in the previous chapter, this assumption simply requires that both of the scales involved be interval scales rather than ordinal or nominal ones. This is not to say that correlational analysis cannot be applied to nominal and ordinal scales. It can, but other statistics (explained at the end of this chapter) must be used to do so.

### LINEAR RELATIONSHIP

The most important of the three assumptions is that the relationship must be linear, that is, a straight regression line through the points on the scatterplot must make sense. Figure 10.4 depicts different situations that may arise in sets of data. The sections a–d of Figure 10.4 are examples of *curvilinear* relationships. As they stand, they could not be

138

properly analyzed with a Pearson *r*. The curvilinear relationship is most frequently a problem when one of the variables is a function of time. Consider, for instance, a study in which the number of simple addition problems computed per minute was plotted on the *y*-axis and the number of minutes plotted on the *x*-axis. I think it is reasonable that a postive relationship would be shown for the first few minutes while the subjects became increasingly proficient at the addition problems. However, the number of problems per minute would begin to decrease after a certain amount of time as the subjects became tired and bored with the tasks. This last phenomenon would produce a negative plot. The positive and negative relationships combined into the same scatterplot would produce a curvilinear relationship like that shown in Figure 10.4b, largely because one of the variables was a *function of time*.

The relationships represented in Sections e and f of Figure 10.4, however, are the form that a scatterplot would take for the linear relationship of a strong positive or negative correlation. The best way to check this assumption is by a visual examination of the scatterplots. You should, therefore, look for some indication from the author that they were examined and that the relationship was found to be linear. With regard to Example 10.1, you may assume that the researcher is correct in saying that all assumptions were found to be met (Sentence 5).

## Degrees of freedom

The degrees of freedom that the researcher in Example 10.1 would be concerned with at this point would be those that are necessary for determining the critical value for the Pearson *r* coefficient. They are the number of pairs of data minus two (as you can see in the heading for Column 1 of Table 10.4). A pair is the number of class hours and the proficiency score for each student. There are 102 students, so $df = N - 2 = 102 - 2 = 100$. The *df* for the conditions present in Example 10.1 are, therefore, 100.

## Critical values

Given that the researcher in Example 10.1 has set the alpha level at $\alpha < .01$ directional and knows that $df = 100$, the next step is to turn to a table of critical values for Pearson *r*, as shown in Table 10.4. To find the critical value for this particular study, first look for the appropriate row of alpha levels at the top for directional (one-tailed) decisions. In that row, look for the heading of Column 4 − .01. Now go down the column until you reach the row for 100 degrees of freedom. You should find the number to be .2301. That is the critical value for this statistic

**TABLE 10.4. CRITICAL VALUES OF THE PEARSON PRODUCT-MOMENT CORRELATION COEFFICIENT**

| | *Level of significance for a directional (one-tailed) test* | | | | |
|---|---|---|---|---|---|
| | *.05* | *.025* | *.01* | *.005* | *.0005* |
| | *Level of significance for a nondirectional (two-tailed) test* | | | | |
| *df = N − 2* | *.10* | *.05* | *.02* | *.01* | *.001* |
| 1 | .9877 | .9969 | .9995 | .9999 | 1.0000 |
| 2 | .9000 | .9500 | .9800 | .9900 | .9990 |
| 3 | .8054 | .8783 | .9343 | .9587 | .9912 |
| 4 | .7293 | .8114 | .8822 | .9172 | .9741 |
| 5 | .6694 | .7545 | .8329 | .8745 | .9507 |
| 6 | .6215 | .7067 | .7887 | .8343 | .9249 |
| 7 | .5822 | .6664 | .7498 | .7977 | .8982 |
| 8 | .5494 | .6319 | .7155 | .7646 | .8721 |
| 9 | .5214 | .6021 | .6851 | .7348 | .8471 |
| 10 | .4973 | .5760 | .6581 | .7079 | .8233 |
| 11 | .4762 | .5529 | .6339 | .6835 | .8010 |
| 12 | .4575 | .5324 | .6120 | .6614 | .7800 |
| 13 | .4409 | .5139 | .5923 | .6411 | .7603 |
| 14 | .4259 | .4973 | .5742 | .6226 | .7420 |
| 15 | .4124 | .4821 | .5577 | .6055 | .7246 |
| 16 | .4000 | .4683 | .5425 | .5897 | .7084 |
| 17 | .3887 | .4555 | .5285 | .5751 | .6932 |
| 18 | .3783 | .4438 | .5155 | .5614 | .6787 |
| 19 | .3687 | .4329 | .5034 | .5487 | .6652 |
| 20 | .3598 | .4227 | .4921 | .5368 | .6524 |
| 25 | .3233 | .3809 | .4451 | .4869 | .5974 |
| 30 | .2960 | .3494 | .4093 | .4487 | .5541 |
| 35 | .2746 | .3246 | .3810 | .4182 | .5189 |
| 40 | .2573 | .3044 | .3578 | .3932 | .4896 |
| 45 | .2428 | .2875 | .3384 | .3721 | .4648 |
| 50 | .2306 | .2732 | .3218 | .3541 | .4433 |
| 60 | .2108 | .2500 | .2948 | .3248 | .4078 |
| 70 | .1954 | .2319 | .2737 | .3017 | .3799 |
| 80 | .1829 | .2172 | .2565 | .2830 | .3568 |
| 90 | .1726 | .2050 | .2422 | .2673 | .3375 |
| 100 | .1638 | .1946 | .2301 | .2540 | .3211 |

*Source:* From Fisher and Yates (1963).

under the conditions of this study. This value will, of course, vary from study to study, but you can still use Table 10.4 to check those critical values. Please note that the increasing use of computers has freed many researchers from having to refer to such tables. The concepts, however, have not changed.

## Stage 5: statistical decisions

### Hypothesis testing

The customary steps for hypothesis testing with Pearson $r$ are much like those shown in the previous chapter. For the sake of economy, they are summarized in Table 10.5. Notice that the primary differences are as follows:

1. Because the decision is directional (or one-tailed), only one alternative hypothesis is present ($H_1: r > 0$). This is logical in situations in which previous research or logic would support the idea that any existing correlation would be positive.
2. The $r_{observed} = .65$.
3. The $r_{critical} = .23$ because any $r$ lower that this could have occurred by chance alone with this sample size (with $N = 102$, $df = N - 2 = 100$.

Make sure this example makes sense to you before pushing on. If not, you should review the previous chapter.

### Interpretation of results

The interpretation of results in a study such as Example 10.1 involves two parts. The separate issues of significance and meaningfulness must both be considered. Only then can the actual predictions of test scores from hours of study be correctly interpreted.

Table 10.5 shows that the null hypothesis was rejected and the alternative hypotheses accepted. Thus, the results can be said to be significant, since there is only a 1 percent probability that the observed correlation of .65 occurred by chance alone. Notice in Table 10.3, however, that the squared value of $r = .65$ is $r^2 = .42$. Thus the variation in class hours accounts for about 42 percent of the variation among proficiency scores in the hypothetical study. It is now up to you to decide if that is meaningful. Of course, the researcher should address the issue as well. What do you think? The overlapping variation of 42 percent is less than half, so the relationship is relatively weak. Yet, it is still interesting and, to some degree, meaningful in the sense that one simple variable (class

TABLE 10.5. HYPOTHESIS TESTING (PEARSON $r$)

| Steps | Hypothetical study in the abstract |
|---|---|
| 1. Look at the hypotheses. | $H_0$: $r = 0$<br>$H_1$: $r > 0$<br>Directional decision (only one alternative hypothesis) |
| 2. Look at the $\alpha$ level. | $\alpha < .01$. Directional (one-tailed) decision |
| 3. Compare the observed and critical statistics. | $r_{obs} = .65$<br>$r_{crit} = .23$<br>when: $\alpha < .01$.<br>Directional (one-tailed)<br>$df = 100$ |
| 4. a. If the observed statistic is less than the critical statistic, accept the null hypotheses and stop. | Not so here. |
|    b. If the observed statistic is greater than the critical statistic, reject the null hypothesis and continue. | $r_{obs} > r_{crit}$<br>$(.65 > .23)$, so reject $H_0$ |
| 5. Decide which alternative hypothesis is more logical. | Because only a positive correlation was expected, there was only one alternative hypothesis: $H_1$: $r > 0$ |
| 6. Interpret the results in terms of the $p$ level. | $H_0$ is rejected at $p < .01$ and $H_1$ is accepted. So there is only a 1% probability that $r_{obs} = .65$ occurred by chance alone, or a 99% probability that the observed correlation is due to other than chance factors. |

hours) seems to explain at least some of the other highly complex variable (French proficiency). Again, what do you think? Even very low correlations of say .09 may be interesting under certain conditions. So this issue is far from clearcut.

One application of the obtained correlation coefficients is shown in Table 10.6, which shows the class hours (at 50-hour intervals) in the left column and the resulting predicted proficiency scores in French in the second column. These predictions were based on the regression equation, $\hat{Y} = a + bX$, where the intercept $a = 10$ and the slope $b = .10$. To predict an estimated proficiency score from say 800 class hours, you simply plug these figures into the equation as follows:

TABLE IO.6. ESTIMATED FRENCH PROFICIENCY SCORES PREDICTED
FROM THE NUMBER OF CLASS HOURS

| Class hours (X) | Estimated proficiency scores ($\hat{Y}$) | Range for ± 1 SEE (68% confidence)[a] | Range for ± 2 SEEs (95% confidence) |
|---|---|---|---|
| 500 | 60 | 51.66 − 68.34 | 43.32 − 76.68 |
| 550 | 65 | 56.66 − 73.34 | 48.32 − 81.68 |
| 600 | 70 | 61.66 − 78.34 | 53.32 − 86.68 |
| 650 | 75 | 66.66 − 83.34 | 58.32 − 91.68 |
| 700 | 80 | 71.66 − 88.34 | 63.32 − 96.68 |
| 750 | 85 | 76.66 − 93.34 | 68.32 − 101.68 |
| 800 | 90 | 81.66 − 98.34 | 73.32 − 106.68 |
| 850 | 95 | 86.66 − 103.34 | 78.32 − 111.68 |
| 900 | 100 | 91.66 − 108.34 | 83.32 − 116.68 |

[a]SEE = 8.34.

$$\hat{Y} = a + bX$$
$$= 10 + .10(800)$$
$$= 10 + 80 = 90$$

To predict each of the estimated proficiency scores shown in Table 10.6, it is only necessary to repeat this process for 500 hours, 550, 600, and so on.

However, calculating the predicted scores is not enough. Notice that the researcher called them *estimated proficiency scores*. That is because the scores do not form a perfectly linear relationship (some of the asterisks in the scatterplot of these scores did not fall exactly on the regression line). This is indicated, among other things, by the correlation coefficient ($r = .65$) and, of course, by its squared value ($r^2 = .42$). The latter coefficient indicates that the variation in the two sets of scores overlaps about 42 percent. But what about the other 58 percent ($100\% − 42\% = 58\%$)?

To account for this 58 percent, called error or random variation, the researcher must incorporate a concept called the *standard error of estimate* (SEE) to make responsible predictions. The SEE is an estimate of the margin of error in real score points – usually $Y$ score points, or French proficiency points in Example 10.1. Similar to the standard error of measurement discussed in Chapter 8, the SEE can be used to determine a band of $Y$ score points on either side of the regression line within which the asterisks will diverge from the line. Also, like the SEM, there is about 68 percent probability that actual scores will fall within one SEE (plus or minus) of the regression line. There is about 95 percent probability if the bands are extended out two SEEs (plus or minus) and about 98 percent if the bands are moved out three SEEs (plus or minus). This is, of course, all based on the percentages under the normal distribution discussed at length in previous chapters.

Notice in Table 10.6 that the SEE for the estimates of the proficiency scores predicted from class hours is 8.34 proficiency score points. To be 68 percent confident for a prediction of a score of say 75, the researcher must concede that the predicted proficiency score may fall within one SEE plus or minus of 75 (75 − 8.34 = 66.66 and 75 + 8.34 = 83.34), or between 66.66 and 83.34. To be 95 percent confident, would require two SEEs plus or minus of 75 (75 − 16.68 = 58.32 and 75 + 16.68 = 91.68), or between 58.32 and 91.68.

These bands of one and two SEEs are shown for each predicted score in Columns 3 and 4 of Table 10.6. Some thought about how much the bands of adjacent proficiency score estimates overlap each other should illustrate just how imprecise each seemingly precise prediction is if you are to have even 68 percent confidence in them. This is due, in large part, to the relatively weak degree of relationship between the variables here ($r = .65$). In general, the higher the correlation coefficient, the more precise the prediction in terms of confidence or probability bands, as represented by the SEE. So, again, you should ask yourself just how meaningful are the predictions in Table 10.6, rather than let the impressive rows of numbers simply convince you.

## Potential pitfalls

Aside from the error of not checking the underlying assumptions for correlation analysis, there are three other potential pitfalls of which a researcher must be wary in a correlational study: *restriction of range*, *skewedness*, and *causality*.

### RESTRICTION OF RANGE

If an investigator chooses to base a correlational study on a sample with fairly homogeneous language proficiency, say students from one level out of the five in a one-year French program, the sample itself can have dramatic effects on the analysis. Unwittingly, the range of talent has been restricted, and this will tend to make any resultant correlation coefficients lower. The degree to which this restriction can affect results is shown in Table 10.7. In this table are real testing statistics for a single cloze test that was administered to different samples. These results are systematically arranged here to have narrower and narrower ranges of talent as you move down the table.

Notice that the ranges of talent are generally reflected in both the standard deviations and the ranges. Both statistics get much smaller as

TABLE 10.7. RANGE OF TALENT IN RELATIONSHIP TO RELIABILITY AND
VALIDITY OF A CLOZE TEST

| Sample | S | range | $r_{xx}$ | $r_{xy}$ |
|--------|------|-------|------|------|
| 1978a | 12.45 | 46 | .95 | .90 |
| 1978b | 8.56 | 33 | .90 | .88 |
| 1981a | 6.71 | 29 | .83 | .79 |
| 1981b | 5.59 | 22 | .73 | .74 |
| 1982a | 4.84 | 22 | .68 | .59 |
| 1982b | 4.48 | 20 | .66 | .51 |
| 1982c | 4.07 | 21 | .53 | .40 |
| 1982d | 3.38 | 14 | .31 | .43 |

*Source:* Adapted from Brown (1983b).

you move down the columns. Notice also the dramatic relationship
between this restriction and the reliability and validity coefficients. In
this example, the effect is so great that the particular cloze test in question
may appear to be either the most highly reliable and valid cloze test ever
created or a hands-down loser as the worst, depending mostly on differences in the ranges of talent among the samples. The message is that
descriptive statistics should always be presented when such analyses are
reported. And you should look particularly at the dispersion in relation
to any correlation coefficients that are reported. You may often notice
things that the researcher did not – things that can change how you
interpret the researcher's results and the study as a whole.

SKEWEDNESS

A skewed distribution in one or both of the variables will likewise depress
the values of correlation coefficients. This is why the assumption of
normality in each variable is so important. Again, you can spot skewedness by looking at the descriptive statistics for both variables. It is particularly useful to compare the means and standard deviations. Say, for
instance, that you encounter a 100-point test with a mean of 20 and a
standard deviation of 19. Do you see how such a distribution must be
positively skewed? There simply is not room for scores to be distributed
two standard deviations below the mean – much less three. What about
a test with a mean of 80 out of 100 and a standard deviation of 15?
That would be a negatively skewed distribution, right? A normally distributed set of scores typically will have a mean of about 55 out of 100
with a standard deviation of 12 or 15.

Another good indicator of skewedness is that the mean and median
in a normal distribution will be similar, if not the same. Hence, a distribution that has a mean that is radically different from its median is

probably skewed. And remember that skewedness tends to depress correlation coefficients. Perhaps you should reexamine the descriptive statistics in Table 10.3 to see if skewedness might have affected the results of the study described in the abstract.

CAUSALITY

It is also a mistake to view a high correlation between a criterion and predictor variable as indicating a causal relationship. One variable, although highly related to another, may not be "causing" it. This is easily illustrated by considering that there is probably a strong relationship, or correlation, between scenes of crimes and the number of police officers who are present at them. Yet it would not be fair to say either that the police officers cause the crime scenes or that the crime scenes cause police officers. So researchers should carefully interpret any causal relationships that they try to show, and you should view such stated relationships with a critical eye.

# Related analyses

Other forms of analysis that are in the same family as those discussed in this chapter are listed alphabetically and briefly described in this section. They are related in form and logic to what you have just read. However, they are meant only to be used as a reference when you encounter strange-looking statistical analyses in your reading, so you should probably move on to the next family of analyses until you need the specific information provided here.

## Biserial correlation

The biserial correlation coefficient $(r_{bi})$ is considered a good estimate of Pearson $r$. It is appropriately applied when two interval scales are involved, but, for some logical reason, one of the two is more sensibly interpreted as a dichotomy (nominal scale). For instance, a researcher might be interested in determining the degree of relationship between passing a first-semester course in Spanish and scores on a language aptitude test. To do so, the researcher might separate the grades at the end of the course (A, B, C, D, and F) into two groups: pass (A, B, C, D) and fail (F). The degree of relationship between this new dichotomy and the interval scores on the language aptitude test could then be determined by using the $r_{bi}$ coefficient. Aside from the scales involved, the assumptions and interpretation of the resulting coefficient are virtually the same as those for the Pearson $r$.

146

## Kendall tau

Kendall tau is interpretable for our purposes much like the Spearman rho. It is used on the same types of ordinal, or rank-ordered, data. Apparently, tau provides a more generalizable test of the null hypothesis $H_0$: tau = 0 than does Spearman rho when $N$ is greater than or equal to 8. Spearman rho is much more commonly used in language studies.

## Kendall W

The Kendall $W$, or coefficient of concordance, is appropriately used to determine the tendency of agreement among three or more sets of ordinal data. If, for instance, a study were to be made of the way four teachers agree in ranking students' ability to speak Russian, Kendall $W$ could be used. Note that $W$ ranges from 0 to 1.0. By definition, it cannot be negative. The null hypothesis $H_0$: $W = 0$ can be tested. And the coefficient can be interpreted as an estimate of the average of correlations between all pairs of ranks. Such an interpretation should be carefully applied as an estimate of the *tendency* of agreement, or concordance, among the ranks.

## Multiple regression

A full explanation of multiple regression is clearly beyond the scope of this book. Nevertheless, this type of analysis occurs in language studies and so must be discussed here at least briefly. Multiple regression is similar to simple regression. Remember that simple regression is used to predict values on a dependent variable ($Y$) from those on an independent variable ($X$). Often, things are not that simple, particularly in language studies. Predictions of the dependent variable ($Y$) can often be more accurate if they are made from two or more independent variables ($X_1$, $X_2$, and so on). For example, the prediction of ESL achievement scores at the end of two years of study might be much more accurately predicted from three independent variables than from one. In other words, ESL achievement might be more fully predicted from (1) overall proficiency scores in English, (2) language aptitude scores, and (3) some measure of individual motivation to learn language than it would be from any one of these three.

Like simple regression, there is a formula for multiple regression that should help you to understand the concept:

$$\hat{Y} = a + b_1 X_1 + b_2 X_2 + b_3 X_3 + e$$

Notice that this is just a more complex version of the simple regression formula and that it takes more independent variables into consideration ($X_1$, $X_2$, $X_3$, and so forth).

TABLE 10.8. RELATIONSHIP BETWEEN $\beta$ AND $R$

| Variable | $\beta$ | $r$ (with Y) | $\beta r$ | $R^2$ (with Y) |
|----------|---------|--------------|-----------|----------------|
| $X_1$ | .40 | .60 | .24 | .24 ($X_1$ with $\hat{Y}$) |
| $X_2$ | .37 | .55 | .20 | .44*($X_1$ and $X_2$ with $\hat{Y}$) |
| $X_3$ | .21 | .40 | .08 | .52*($X_1$, $X_2$, and $X_3$ with $\hat{Y}$) |

*$p < .01$.

Similar to simple regression, the researcher is interested in the degree of relationship among all variables and with each other, as reflected in simple Pearson $r$ coefficients. Therefore, you should expect to see a table reporting these coefficients, as well as the coefficients of determination ($r^2$). But the investigator is also concerned with the *multiple correlation* ($R$) between the dependent variable and various combinations of independent variables. Here, too, there are *coefficients of multiple determination* that help you to understand the multiple results. Both $R$ and $R^2$ are interpreted much like the corresponding $r$ and $r^2$, but with more independent variables.

Since more variables are involved, the interest is in the degree to which various combinations of independent variables correlate with the dependent variables. But these variables are themselves related in complex ways. To sort out this complexity, researchers use *beta coefficients*, or *beta weights* ($\beta$), sometimes called *standard partial regression coefficients*. They are standard because they would be applicable if all scores on all variables were changed to $z$ scores (see Chapter 7). They are *partial* because the effects of all other variables are held constant when examining beta for a given variable. They are important because they are used in calculating the $b_1$, $b_2$, $b_3$, and so forth in the regression equation, as well as the multiple $R^2$.

Table 10.8 illustrates how beta coefficients are used to calculate multiple $R^2$. Notice that for variables $X_1$, $X_2$, and $X_3$, the beta weights are .40, .37, and .21 in Column 2. Each of these is multiplied by the simple correlation coefficient ($r$) between each independent variable and the dependent variable in Column 3. The result ($\beta r$) is the proportion of $R^2$ that is accounted for by each independent variable, shown in Column 4. So $R^2$ for $X_1$ alone is .24. With $X_1$ and $X_2$ together, it is the sum of both $\beta r$ values, $.24 + .20 = .44$. With all three, $X_1$, $X_2$, and $X_3$, it is the sum of all three $\beta r$ values, $.24 + .20 + .08 = .52$. In short, one variable ($X_1$) only accounts for 24 percent of the variation in Y scores, while $X_1$ and $X_2$ considered together account for 44 percent, and $X_1$, $X_2$, and $X_3$ account for 52 percent.

Among other hypotheses that can be tested using multiple regression is $H_0$: $R = 0$ for all correlation coefficients. But the researcher can also test $H_0$: $R^2 = 0$. You may have also noticed the asterisks and $p < .01$ in Table 10.8. These indicate the results of testing the null hypothesis $H_0$: $R^2 = 0$ in terms of what is added to $R^2$ at each step, that is, with each additional variable. In the example, then, it appears that each variable adds to the $R^2$ because of other than chance factors. And the three of them taken together seem to explain more of the variation in the dependent variable scores than any one considered alone. The tables used to represent such results are often complex looking, but do not be intimidated. Just search out the beta coefficients, $r$ coefficients, and $R^2$ coefficients, and make sure the intepretation makes sense to you.

The pitfalls with this type of analysis are numerous. Although interval and nominal scales are appropriate as independent variables, the dependent variable should be an interval scale. If these conditions are met, the other assumptions underlying simple regression should be checked, along with two additional and important assumptions involving heteroscedasticity and multicollinearity. Data transformation is also central to understanding how the assumptions are often handled in this type of analysis.

### HETEROSCEDASTICITY

Essentially, the problem of heteroscedasticity occurs when the error variance is not constant over all observations. The researcher should indicate that scatterplots of the "residuals" against each independent variable were examined and that no systematic pattern was found. The assumption being checked is that of homoscedasticity, or constancy of error across observations.

### MULTICOLLINEARITY

The problem here is that independent variables may themselves be so highly correlated that the interpretation of which is predicting the most (or least) variation in dependent variable scores becomes virtually impossible to disentangle. This problem can be detected if a table of intercorrelations is presented in a study. Look for a pattern of Pearson $r$ coefficients that are $+.70$ or higher or $-.70$ or lower. Either is an indication that this problem exists in the analysis. If so, the author should explain in detail how it was dealt with. This is a serious problem in multiple regression.

### DATA TRANSFORMATION

If the data in a study violate one or more of the assumptions underlying multiple regression analysis, the researcher may have to transform the data to satisfy the statistical model. *Transformation* involves changing each score for one or more variables by some mathematical principle. For instance, the logarithm of each score might be used in place of the actual scores. Transformation can be used to satisfy the assumptions of linearity and homoscedasticity. It is the researcher's responsibility to explain why and how scores on a given variable were transformed and to interpret the results accordingly.

## Phi coefficient

The phi coefficient ($\Phi$) is logically applied when two variables are true dichotomies (nominal). For example, an investigator might be interested in the degree of relationship between being male or female (dichotomous) and whether students who study first-semester Spanish in college previously visited a Spanish-speaking country (dichotomous). The degree of relationship between the two dichotomies can be determined by using the phi coefficient. The interpretation of this coefficient is the same as for Pearson $r$, except that the magnitude of the coefficient can only reach $-1.0$ or $+1.0$ under certain ideal conditions. Therefore, the interpretation should be approached cautiously.

## Point-biserial correlation

The point-biserial correlation coefficient ($r_{pbi}$) is similar to the biserial correlation discussed above, but it is used to analyze the degree of relationship between an interval scale and a true dichotomy (nominal scale). For example, a researcher might want to investigate the degree of relationship between being male or female (dichotomous nominal scale) and achievement in French, as measured by the end-of-the-year departmental examination (interval scale). Aside from the scales involved, the assumptions and interpretation of the resulting coefficient are the same as for Pearson $r$. However, Pearson $r$ or the biserial correlation should be used, if possible (and logical), because they tend to give a better estimate of the relationship.

## Spearman rho

The Spearman rank-order (or rank-difference) correlation coefficient is usually represented by the symbol $\rho$, or rho. This coefficient is applied to ordinal data (rank ordered) only. Of course, interval data may be converted to ordinal data for the purposes of calculating rho, but some precision is lost in doing so. Typically, rho is applied to small samples (of less than 30) to test the same hypotheses as the Pearson $r$. The only assumption that must be met is that both sets of data be ordinal.

TABLE 10.9. HYPOTHETICAL RANKS AND SPEARMAN RHO

| Ranks A | | Ranks B | |
|---|---|---|---|
| 1 | | 4 | |
| 2 | | 3 | |
| 3 | | 2 | $\rho = -1.0$ |
| 4 | | 1 | |
| 5 | $\rho = .67^*$ | 5 | |
| 6 | | 9 | |
| 7 | | 8 | |
| 8 | | 7 | $\rho = -1.0$ |
| 9 | | 6 | |

*$p < .05$ (with $N = 9$).
*Source:* Adapted from Brown (1983a).

Interpretation of the resulting coefficients is roughly the same as that for Pearson $r$. The coefficients range from $-1.0$ through zero to $+1.0$, but do not necessarily represent a linear relationship between the two sets of ranks under analysis. As such, rho might be more safely interpreted as an estimate of the tendency of two ranks to be similar. For instance, Spearman rho has often been used in language studies to investigate the degree of similarity between morpheme acquisition rank orders (see, for example, Krashen 1977).

One pitfall that illustrates just how carefully rho must be interpreted is represented in the hypothetical situation shown in Table 10.9. Notice that the overall rho for all nine rankings is .67 ($p < .05$ with $N = 9$). But, clearly, the rho coefficients calculated for parts of the ranks (shown to the right) are also significant at $p < .01$. This hypothetical example points to the necessity for careful and logical interpretation. It should also be noted that squaring the rho coefficients to determine overlapping variation is not appropriate and that confidence intervals and SEEs cannot be calculated for Spearman rho estimates. All in all, this is a weak but sometimes useful procedure if it is properly handled and interpreted.

## Tetrachoric correlation

The interpretation of tetrachoric correlation is similar to that for the phi coefficient. However, the tetrachoric correlation is appropriate in lieu of phi when the dichotomies (nominal) involved have been created by artificially reducing interval data for each variable to two categories. In other words, if a researcher were interested in the degree of relationship between passing Spanish 101 and having been absent 10 or more times from class, the tetrachoric correlation coefficient would be appropriate. Each of the variables (grades A–F and the number of absences) was originally an interval scale. However, they have been converted to artificial dichotomies: passing versus not passing and 1–9 absences versus 10 or more absences. The resulting coefficient, like so many of those already discussed, is an approximate estimate of Pearson *r*.

## Terms and symbols

| | |
|---|---|
| *a* | one-tailed decisions |
| *b* | Pearson *r* |
| causality | prediction |
| correlation coefficient | predictor variable |
| covariance | regression equation |
| criterion variable | regression line |
| curvilinear | restriction of range |
| directional decisions | skewedness |
| estimate | slope |
| independence | standard error of estimate (SEE) |
| intercept | two-tailed decisions |
| interval scale | $X$ |
| linear | $X$ (variable) |
| linear relationship | $Y$ (variable) |
| nondirectional decisions | $\hat{Y}$ |
| normal distribution | |

## Review questions

1. What types of problems are addressed or explored using regression and correlational analyses?
2. What type of analysis should be used to investigate the degree of relationship between two or more independent variables when one dependent variable is considered (see Table 10.1)?
3. What types of scales and what number of dependent and independent variables would you expect if a researcher stated that Kendall's tau was used in a study (see Table 10.1)?
4. Can you list the null and two alternative hypotheses for Kendall's tau according to the patterns you have seen so far?
   $H_0$:
   $H_1$:
   $H_2$:
5. What would the estimated $Y$ be for the following regression equation? (You should not even need a pencil.)

$$\hat{Y} = a + bX$$
$$\hat{Y} = 100 + 10(2)$$
$$\hat{Y} = ?$$

6. Which is the slope in the regression equation? The intercept? The value of the $X$ variable? The estimated $\hat{Y}$ value?
7. What are the four primary assumptions underlying regression and correlational analyses?
8. Can you list the six steps that are necessary to test the hypotheses in a correlational analysis?
9. What is the standard error of estimate? How is it applied? And how does it relate to probability?
10. What are the three most common pitfalls that you may encounter with this family of analyses? And why are they pitfalls?

## Application

Find a study of interest to you — one that contains correlational or regression analyses. Then systematically look at the study on the basis of what you have learned up to this point. Especially keep in mind the issues raised in Chapter 5, as well as those in Chapter 9 and this one. The ultimate question you should answer is, What value does the study have for you and your field?

# 11 Comparing means

If studying the degree of relationship between variables is popular, comparing the means is clearly a close runner-up in language research. Recall from Chapters 6 and 7 that the central tendency of groups is often described in terms of means or medians. Comparing the performance of groups will often involve looking at one or both of these two basic characteristics. This chapter introduces the family of statistics used for this purpose.

## Stage 1: focusing the study

### Identifying a problem

The simplest type of comparisons of means involves the performance of two groups on a test or some other measure. A study often is designed so that the groups themselves are different on the basis of some variable – one which is likely to produce variations in their performances. Statistical logic is then put into motion to determine the probability that observed differences in group means are due to chance alone. The problems that can be studied and the ways that investigations are designed or set up are numerous. More than ever, you should examine each study to decide whether the ways the groups were selected and labeled make sense. Three common uses are the pretest-posttest design, the experimental/control group design, and the naturally occurring groups design.

In the *pretest-posttest design*, the researcher gives a pretest (e.g., French vocabulary) to a group of students, provides some sort of treatment to the group (e.g., classroom instruction in French vocabulary), then gives them a posttest. The pretest and posttest means are then compared to determine whether learning took place. Although such a study can provide useful information, there is often no way of determining whether any observed gain in means was due to the treatment itself, to normal classroom teaching, or perhaps even to the effect of having taken the test twice. But with a careful design, such problems can be controlled.

*Experimental/control group designs* are one way to disentangle such ambiguities. A sample of students might be randomly drawn from all the French students at a certain high school. The students in this sample could then be randomly assigned to two groups: one experimental and one control. The experimental group might then be provided with some treatment (e.g., two hours per week of instruction in French vocabulary by a computer program), while the control group would receive the traditional in-class explanation of vocabulary and a word list to memorize each week. Mean scores for the two groups on an end-of-term vocabulary test would then be compared to determine whether the treatment (computer-instruction in French vocabulary) caused the experimental group to score higher than the control group. [Example 11.1 is similar to this design.]

EXAMPLE 11.1   HYPOTHETICAL STUDY OF THE
EFFECTIVENESS OF EXTRA LANGUAGE LABORATORY
TRAINING IN FRENCH

(1) This study investigates the effectiveness of supplementary laboratory training in French language study at the university level. (2) Of the 350 students taking French at all levels at Mount Rainier University in Longmire, Washington, 200 were randomly selected for this study. (3) These 200 students were further randomly divided into experimental and control groups of 100 subjects each. (4) The experimental group received two hours of supplementary language laboratory training per week, while the control group did not. (5) Both groups were tested on the French proficiency test at the end of the semester of study. (6) A one-tailed mean comparison was made, using the *t*-test, of the null hypothesis that the means of the experimental and control groups would be equal at $\alpha < .01$. (7) All assumptions for the *t*-test were found to be met. (8) The $t_{observed}$ was 3.25, which was significant ($p < .01$). (9) These results are discussed in terms of how meaningful the actual mean difference was and what the ramifications are for policy decisions on the use of the language laboratory.

*Naturally occurring group designs*, sometimes called *quasi-experimental designs*, are similar to the experimental/control group approach except that they make comparisons between the mean performances of groups that occur normally. These are groups into which subjects would not usually be randomly assigned because individuals naturally belong to one group or the other. This would clearly be the case, for instance, in comparing the performances of students in naturally occurring classrooms.

There are innumerable designs other than these three to which this family of analyses – comparing group means – can be applied. But, in general, the types of issues involved are similar to those just discussed. The more complex the design, the more difficult it will be to understand – for you and for the researcher. Possibly for this reason, it is this family of analyses that is most often misused or abused by researchers. It is also a common type of study, so it is particularly important to understand the statistical logic underlying such studies and to examine them carefully.

There is one important difference between the pretest-posttest designs, on the one hand, and the experimental and quasi-experimental designs, on the other hand. The pretest-posttest designs generally yield scores that are *dependent* because the same students have taken both tests. Thus, the two sets of scores are dependent, or related (not *independent* of each other). Experimental and naturally occurring group designs, however, usually yield sets of scores that are independent of each other because the students are different in each group. The importance of this distinction will become clearer in the discussion of the assumptions that underlie many of the statistics in this chapter.

## Operationalizing variables

Although all types of constructs may be analyzed, the one operationalized as the independent variable is normally a grouping factor, or nominal variable. The dependent variable, in contrast, will typically be on an interval or ordinal scale. The choice of the correct statistic will depend on (1) the number of groups involved, (2) the types of scales used, and (3) the sizes of the samples in each group. And, of course, the results of such studies will be no more reliable, valid, or meaningful than the tests, questionnaires, or definitions of categories that are provided to operationalize the constructs as variables. Hence, it is, once again, important to consider the variables involved in such a study.

For instance, the hypothetical study in Example 11.1 contains one dependent variable: overall proficiency in French, as reflected by scores on the French proficiency test, an interval scale. There is also one independent variable in the study: whether students were in the treatment group (extra laboratory training) or in the control group (no extra training). This variable would be a nominal scale.

Are you satisfied with the way these variables have been operationalized? Consider just the independent variable for a moment. How can you be sure that students in the control group did not sneak into the laboratory late at night or have their friends in the experimental group smuggle cassette tapes out? If either of these cases were true, the control group's scores might be higher than those of the experimental group but for reasons that are out of the hands of the researcher. Surely, a study of this size would be the talk of the French department. What effect might that have on the internal and external validity of such a study (see Chapters 3 and 4)? And why should you accept the French proficiency test at face value? The author says nothing about its reliability or validity as a test of French proficiency for this group. It is just such imprecision in the operationalization and design of research that you should be alert to in reading actual studies.

## Research hypotheses

The hypotheses formulated for this family of analyses take the same general form as those in the previous chapters. The researcher is still concerned with a null hypothesis and other possible outcomes for the study in the form of alternative hypotheses. For a study like the one in the abstract, the hypotheses might be stated as follows:

$H_0$: There is no significant difference between the means for the experimental and control groups.

$H_1$: The mean for the experimental group is significantly higher than that for the control group.

$H_2$: The mean for the experimental group is significantly lower than that for the control group.

As in the previous chapter, the hypotheses may state all the possible outcomes for studies comparing two means. But if this is the case, the decision is nondirectional, or two tailed. The two alternative hypotheses might also be expressed as one hypothesis, for instance, $H_1$: the mean for the experimental group is significantly different from that of the control group. Example 11.1 clearly states (Sentence 6) that the decision was one tailed, or directional. Although a rationale should have been given, it is still safe to assume that there was only one alternative hypothesis in this hypothetical study ($H_1$) and that the decision was directional. As usual, the focus of the statistical decisions in Example 11.1 was on the null hypothesis (Sentence 6).

## Stage 2: sampling

The procedures used to gather data, including sampling and the way variables are operationalized, greatly affect the generalizability and validity of any study that compares means. But it is particularly important for the statistic of focus in this chapter, the *t* test, that one variable be nominal with only two levels. The number of *levels* simply indicates how many groups are involved in the variable being studied. In this case, there are two levels because there are two groups, experimental and control. But the study could have been designed with three levels: two different experimental groups (one using the language laboratory and the other using computer-assisted supplemental training) and one control group.

Regardless of the number of levels, it is important that the members of each group were randomly sampled from the populations involved and that no person fell into both groups at the same time. You might also check to see that both samples were exactly the same size (as in Example 11.1). If they are not, the researcher should have mentioned that special statistical procedures were used to overcome the problem of groups of unequal sizes.

## Stage 3: setting up statistical decisions

### *Choosing the correct statistic*

As was mentioned before, the choice of the correct statistic will depend mostly on the number of groups, the types of scales, and the sizes of the samples. Table 11.1 is the same as the table shown in the previous chapter except that you will find only the statistics appropriate for comparing two means (or medians) in boldface type.

Applying what you know about the study in Example 11.1, let's review how the table works. Recall that the study had one dependent variable on an interval scale (the scores on the French proficiency test) and one independent variable that is a nominal scale. Looking across from one interval scale dependent variable and down from one nominal scale independent variable, you will find that you must choose between two levels and more than two levels. In the example, there were two *levels* of the independent variable. This simply means that this variable was divided into two groups, rather than into three or more. Just below "2 levels," you will find *z statistic* (large sample) and *t test* (any sample). If 100 students per group is considered a large sample, and it is here, was the researcher in Example 11.1 correct to choose the *t* test? Of course, it is applicable to a sample of any size.

But you probably will want to use the reverse strategy in your reading. Looking to the square containing the *t* test and working outward, you will find that (1) any sample size can be analyzed, (2) there should be one interval scale dependent variable, and (3) there should be one two-level nominal scale independent variable. Does all this make sense in the abstract? What conditions would you look for in a study that used the *z* statistic? The median test?

### *Statistical hypotheses*

The shorthand version for the hypotheses stated earlier is often given in terms of parameters rather than statistics. This correctly implies that, in most cases, the researcher is really interested in the population, rather than the sample. In other words, the sample statistics are being used to make generalizations about the population. So you may encounter hypotheses (directional in this case) that use $\mu$ for the mean. In others, $\overline{X}$ will be used as follows:

| Populations | Samples |
|---|---|
| $H_0$: $\mu_E = \mu_C$ or | $\overline{X}_E = \overline{X}_C$ |
| $H_1$: $\mu_E > \mu_C$ or | $\overline{X}_E > \overline{X}_C$ |

The subscript $_E$ is used here for the experimental group mean and the subscript $_C$ is used for the control group. These subscripts would also appear as $_1$ and $_2$ for Groups 1 and 2, or even $_A$ and $_B$. In all cases, they are just labels to help you keep straight which mean is for which group.

The statistical hypotheses are also sometimes stated as follows:

$$H_0: \mu_E - \mu_C = 0, \quad \text{or} \quad \overline{X}_E - \overline{X}_C = 0$$
$$H_1: \mu_E - \mu_C > 0, \quad \text{or} \quad \overline{X}_E - \overline{X}_C > 0$$

If you think about it for a moment, either way of formulating the hypotheses amounts to about the same thing.

### Alpha decision level

The language researcher should once again set the alpha decision level in advance. The level may be at $\alpha < .05$ or at the more conservative $\alpha < .01$, if the decisions must be more sure. Remember, the statistical test may be nondirectional (two tailed) if there is no logical or theoretical reason to expect one of the means to be higher than the other or directional (one tailed) if there is a sound logical or theoretical reason to expect one or the other of the means to be higher. This, too, should be decided in advance and stated early in a study.

## Stage 4: necessary calculations

At this point, the discussion will focus mostly on the $t$ test chosen for the study in Example 11.1. To understand how the $t$ test works, it will first be necessary to take a brief look at the $z$ statistic. Remember that other statistics used to compare means will follow the same basic logic, although the assumptions and calculations may differ for each (see the section on Related Analyses).

### Observed statistics

To begin with, it is important to realize that the mean for the behavior of even a single group may not always be the same on a given measure.

TABLE 11.1. COMMON STATISTICS FOR MEAN COMPARISONS

Type and Number of Independent Variables

| | | Interval | | Ordinal | | Nominal | | |
|---|---|---|---|---|---|---|---|---|
| | | 1 variable | More than 1 | 1 variable | More than 1 | 1 variable — 2 levels | 1 variable — more | More than 1 |
| **Interval** | 0 | | | Transform ordinal variable into nominal and use C-1, or transform the interval variable into ordinal and use B-2, or transform both variables into nominal and use C-3. | | | | |
| | 1 | Simple regression and Pearson r | Multiple regression and Multiple R | | | z stat. (large sample), t test (any sample) | One-way ANOVA | Two-way ANOVA, three-way ANOVA, etc. *(Row 1)* |
| | More than 1 | Multiple regression and Multiple R | | | | Multivariate analyses | Multivariate analyses | Multivariate analyses |
| **Ordinal** | 0 | Transform the ordinal variable into a nominal variable and use C-1, or transform the interval variable into an ordinal variable and use B-2, or transform the interval variable into a nominal variable and use C-2. | | | | | | |
| | 1 | | | Spearman rho Kendall's tau | | Median test, U test | Kruskal-Wallis test | Friedman's two-way ANOVA *(Row 2)* |
| | More than 1 | | | | Kendall's W | | | |

160

| Nominal | | Column A | Column B | Column C | |
|---|---|---|---|---|---|
| | 0 | | | | Chi-square |
| | 1 | Biserial, Point-biserial correlation | (see C-2) | *Phi* coefficient, tetrachoric corr., Fisher exact test Chi-square | |
| | More than 1 | (see C-1) | (see C-2) | | |

*Note:* Boldface indicates the common statistics for mean comparisons. *C-1* stands for Column C, Row 1.

*Source:* Adapted from Tuckman (1978: 255).

161

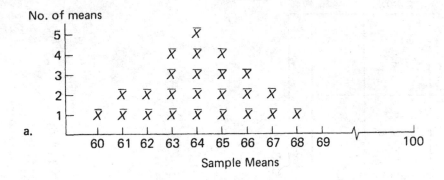

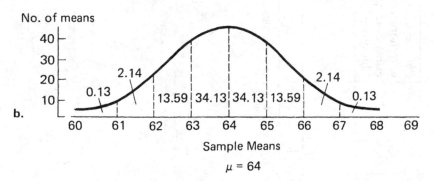

*Figure 11.1   Distribution of means. a: 25 means. b: 1,000 means.*

For example, a single sample of students taking the same test 10, 20, or even 25 times may produce a variety of mean scores (even if we could assume that no learning had taken place, there was no testing effect, and so forth). Individuals do not always perform the same. When grouped, a sample's behavior will vary from time to time as well.

Consider the hypothetical case of a 100-point test administered to the same group of 50 students 25 times. It would probably turn out that the 25 different means would not be the same. In fact, it is likely that the means themselves would be normally distributed – perhaps as shown in Figure 11.1a. By extension, 1,000 administrations of the same test would probably produce a distribution of sample means that would look like the now-familiar distribution shown in Figure 11.1b. Like individual scores on a single test, the distribution of sample means is reasonably predicted in terms of the normal distribution and the percentages that we now associate with that distribution.

In a similar manner, you can reasonably expect the mean scores of different samples drawn from the same population to vary on a given test. Each sample may, indeed, be randomly drawn from a particular

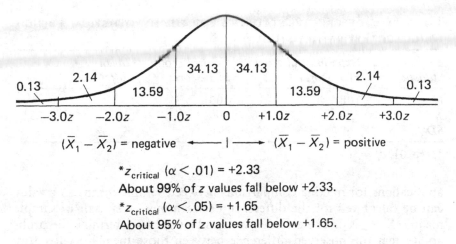

$$*z_{\text{critical}} \ (\alpha < .01) = +2.33$$
About 99% of $z$ values fall below +2.33.
$$*z_{\text{critical}} \ (\alpha < .05) = +1.65$$
About 95% of $z$ values fall below +1.65.

*Figure 11.2 Sampling distribution of differences between means as a z distribution*

population (and, therefore, be representative of it). Nevertheless, like individuals, the mean performances of samples can differ, as shown in Figure 11.1b. The mean of all possible samples (of equal size) drawn from a given population would be the population mean, or $\mu = 64$ in Figure 11.1b.

Let's say further that a pair of samples was drawn from this population. If the means for each of these samples were calculated, we would be able to find the difference $(\overline{X}_1 - \overline{X}_2)$ between the sample means of the two groups. Randomly selecting all possible pairs of means from the population and repeating the process of calculating the difference between each pair $(\overline{X}_1 - \overline{X}_2, \overline{X}_3 - \overline{X}_4,$ and so on) would lead to finding the differences between all such pairs. This is, of course, never actually done, but it is theoretically possible.

## THE Z DISTRIBUTION

The crucial concept here is that these differences between means, if plotted out, would themselves form a distribution. This distribution is called the *sampling distribution of differences between means.* Like so many others that we have considered, it will be normally distributed, have its own mean, and have something analogous to the standard deviation called the *standard error of the difference between means.* When the samples are large, this distribution is interpreted as a $z$ distribution with a mean of 0 and a standard deviation of 1.0 (see $z$ scores, Chapter 7), as shown in Figure 11.2.

The $z$ distribution of differences between means has some interesting

TABLE 11.2. DESCRIPTIVE STATISTICS FOR THE HYPOTHETICAL FRENCH
LANGUAGE LABORATORY STUDY

| Statistic | Experimental group FPT Scores | Control group FPT Scores | Mean difference | $z_{obs}$ |
|---|---|---|---|---|
| N | 100 | 100 | — | |
| $\overline{X}$ | 530 | 500 | 30 | 3.25* |
| SD | 60 | 70 | — | |

*$p < .01$, $df = 198$.

applications for making comparisons between sample means. A $z$ value can be calculated for the difference between any given pair of sample means $(\overline{X}_1 - \overline{X}_2)$. The $z$ value can then be used to determine the probability that the observed difference between those means occurred by chance alone. After all, we saw in Figure 11.1 that sample means can differ from each other just by chance under natural conditions. But the researcher in Example 11.1 wanted to know if the difference between the sample means was due to factors other than these chance differences.

To this end, a $z_{observed}$ $(z_{obs})$ score is calculated. On the basis of the descriptive statistics given in Table 11.2 for the example study, $z_{obs}$ would be 3.25. Notice that this value is positive. Then refer back to Figure 11.2. It should be clear to you that $z_{obs} = 3.25$ would fall far to the right of $z_{critical}$ $(z_{crit})$ $(\alpha < .01) = 2.33$. It is, therefore, safe to say that there is only a 1 percent chance that the observed differences between means belong to the sampling distribution of differences between means that would occur by chance alone. In other words, the $z_{obs}$ indicates that the probability is less than 1 percent $(p < .01)$ that the observed $\overline{X}_E - \overline{X}_C$ belongs within that distribution of chance differences. Hence, it would be safe to say that the null hypothesis $(H_0: X_E - X_C = 0)$ can be rejected. If $z_{obs}$ had turned out to be 1.3016, would the same be true?

It should be pointed out that everything discussed so far with regard to the $z$ distribution can be applied only to the task of comparing the means of two independent samples. Recall that independent samples are those in which the subjects selected into each group from the population are different people. Thus, the results of measuring the two groups are not related, or dependent on each other. This is usually the situation in an experimental design or a carefully designed quasi-experimental design. And it is the type of situation in which the comparison just described is used.

When the two samples are dependent (the same subjects are found in both groups), as in a pretest-posttest design, adjustments must be made by using a different formula that adjusts the standard error of the differences between the means to account for the fact that the two sets of scores are not independent and may be correlated. Without burdening you with the formula or the differences involved, I have brought this up so that you will check to see that the researcher has mentioned using the correct formulas, especially if you think the samples involved are dependent. Using the incorrect formula can make a big difference in the results. Consequently, you should place little faith in the results of a study of dependent means if the author does not mention having used a formula that adjusts for the correlation between the two sets of scores. This is equally true for the $t$ test, which will be discussed next.

The $t$ test has one distinct advantage over the $z$ statistic. Using the $z$ statistic requires large samples, while the $t$ test does not. The $t$ test applies regardless of the size of the two samples and is, therefore, much more commonly used in language studies. If the two samples are of equal size, the calculations for $t_{obs}$ are the same as those for $z_{obs}$. However, instead of looking at a single distribution of mean differences, as is done to find $z_{crit}$, the $t$ test has a family of distributions that differ according to the size of a sample. The particular distribution that is referred to by the researcher depends on the sample sizes. When the samples are large ($N = 62$ or more for each group), the values for $t_{crit}$ are the same as those for $z_{crit}$, whether the decision level is $\alpha < .01$ or $\alpha < .05$ for either directional or nondirectional situations. But the $t_{crit}$ necessary to reject the null hypothesis will increase as smaller and smaller samples are used (see the section on Critical Values later in this chapter).

Turning once again to the information given in Table 11.2, notice that the sample sizes ($N = 100$) are equal and each is large (larger than 62). Under these conditions, the results, form, and logic of the $t$ test are the same as those shown for $z$ ($t_{obs} = 3.2537$; $t_{crit} = 2.33$). However, when sample sizes are $N = 61$ or less or when the two samples are different in size, the $t$ test shows its flexibility. By using the $t$ test, the researcher can get around these problems that disallow the use of the $z$ distribution. Hence the $t$ test is much more often used in language studies.

As with the $z$ distribution, you must be aware that the basic $t$ test can be applied only if the two groups involved are independent. However, there are situations in which the researcher wants to compare the means in a pretest-posttest study that are not independent because the same students have taken both tests. One way for a researcher to handle this problem might be to divide the students' test papers randomly into two groups and then to use the pretest scores from one group and the posttest scores from the other group in the analysis. This procedure would mean that each student would be found in either the pretest or posttest groups but not in both.

Like the *z* distribution, special versions of the *t* test have been developed to adjust for the fact that the scores in two groups are related. If you find a situation in which both sets of scores come from the same group of subjects (the scores are not independent), you should look for some mention that a *t* test for correlated or paired means was used. Either version of the *t* test involves the application of a formula that compensates for the fact that the scores in each of the two sets are related. If you find comparisons being made between means that seem to be clearly correlated and you find that the author makes no mention of using the correct version of the *t* test, you should view the results skeptically. Remember, it is the researcher's job to convince you that the study was correctly conducted and analyzed.

## Assumptions

The assumptions underlying the *t* test are that

1. the scores in each group are normally distributed and
2. the variances for the scores of the two groups are equal.

Now, let's take a more detailed look at each assumption.

### NORMAL DISTRIBUTION OF SCORES

This assumption requires that the distribution of scores for each group be approximately normal. The researcher may indicate that the scores were plotted and examined, and that they appeared to be about normal. Or you can consider the means and standard deviations for each group. If they do not appear to be markedly skewed, the *t* test will most probably not be seriously affected by any existing violation of this assumption.

### EQUAL VARIANCES

This assumption is also referred to as the "homogeneity of variances." It means that the squared values of the standard deviations ($SD^2$) should be about the same (e.g., $SD^2_E = SD^2_C$). The violation of this assumption apparently has little effect on the results if the sample sizes are equal. If the sample sizes are seriously different (in a ratio of 3 or more to 1), the assumption should be tested empirically by the researcher before continuing with the analysis. The researcher should mention having done so with Hartley's $F_{max}$ test or the Cochran or Bartlett tests for homogeneity of variances (see Guilford and Fruchter 1973 for more on this topic). However, a glance at the descriptive statistics for a study should tell you if the group sizes are markedly different and, if so, the degree to which the standard deviations (and their squared values) are different for the groups involved.

## Degrees of freedom

The degrees of freedom (*df*) for the *t* test of independent means is the first sample size minus one plus the second sample size minus one. So for the study in Example 11.1, $df = (N_E - 1) + (N_C - 1) = (100 - 1) + (100 - 1) = 99 + 99 = 198$. This is important to know in finding the critical value for *t*, because the degrees of freedom are part of the adjustment made for the conditions existing in a particular study and will determine to which *t* distribution the researcher refers.

## Critical values

You know that the researcher in Example 11.1 set the alpha level at $\alpha < .01$ for a one-tailed, or directional, decision. You also know that the $df \doteq 198$. Armed with all this information, you can now turn to a table of critical values for *t* as shown in Table 11.3. To find the critical value of *t* for the example study, first find the row at the top of the table for one-tailed tests. Then find the column for $\alpha < .01$. Now move down the column until you reach the row that corresponds to a *df* of $\infty$ (this row is for any *df* over 120). The $t_{crit}$ you find should be 2.326, or about 2.33. That is the correct value under the conditions of that study. This value will, of course, vary from study to study. Notice the general trend in the table: as *df* gets smaller, $t_{crit}$ increases, and as $\alpha$ gets smaller, $t_{crit}$ increases as well. Hence, as the samples and $\alpha$ get smaller, larger and larger $t_{obs}$ values must be found to reject the null hypotheses. You should find this table useful in checking the $t_{crit}$ for any study you encounter as long as the study contains adequate information about the *df*, $\alpha$, and directionality.

## Stage 5: statistical decisions

### Hypothesis testing

The customary steps involved in testing hypotheses using the *t* test are the same as those shown in Table 11.4. These should now be clear to you. If not, turn back to the previous two chapters.

### Interpretation of results

As always, the interpretation of results for a study like that in Example 11.1 should have two parts: significance and meaningfulness. Here, the researcher has shown that the two means, $\overline{X}_E = 530$ and $\overline{X}_C = 500$, are significantly different. That is, the 30 points difference in means on

TABLE II.3. CRITICAL VALUES OF *t*

| df | Level of significance for one-tailed test | | | | | |
|---|---|---|---|---|---|---|
| | .10 | .05 | .025 | .01 | .005 | .0005 |
| | Level of significance for two-tailed test | | | | | |
| | .20 | .10 | .05 | .02 | .01 | .001 |
| 1 | 3.078 | 6.314 | 12.706 | 31.821 | 63.657 | 636.619 |
| 2 | 1.886 | 2.920 | 4.303 | 6.965 | 9.925 | 31.598 |
| 3 | 1.638 | 2.353 | 3.182 | 4.541 | 5.841 | 12.941 |
| 4 | 1.533 | 2.132 | 2.776 | 3.747 | 4.604 | 8.610 |
| 5 | 1.476 | 2.015 | 2.571 | 3.365 | 4.032 | 6.859 |
| 6 | 1.440 | 1.943 | 2.447 | 3.143 | 3.707 | 5.959 |
| 7 | 1.415 | 1.895 | 2.365 | 2.998 | 3.499 | 5.405 |
| 8 | 1.397 | 1.860 | 2.306 | 2.896 | 3.355 | 5.041 |
| 9 | 1.383 | 1.833 | 2.262 | 2.821 | 3.250 | 4.781 |
| 10 | 1.372 | 1.812 | 2.228 | 2.764 | 3.169 | 4.587 |
| 11 | 1,363 | 1.796 | 2.201 | 2.718 | 3.106 | 4.437 |
| 12 | 1.356 | 1.782 | 2.179 | 2.681 | 3.055 | 4.318 |
| 13 | 1.350 | 1.771 | 2.160 | 2.650 | 3.012 | 4.221 |
| 14 | 1.345 | 1.761 | 2.145 | 2.624 | 2.977 | 4.140 |
| 15 | 1.341 | 1.753 | 2.131 | 2.602 | 2.947 | 4.073 |
| 16 | 1.337 | 1.746 | 2.120 | 2.583 | 2.921 | 4.015 |
| 17 | 1.333 | 1.740 | 2.110 | 2.567 | 2.898 | 3.965 |
| 18 | 1.330 | 1.734 | 2.101 | 2.552 | 2.878 | 3.922 |
| 19 | 1.328 | 1.729 | 2.093 | 2.539 | 2.861 | 3.883 |
| 20 | 1.325 | 1.725 | 2.086 | 2.528 | 2.845 | 3.850 |
| 21 | 1.323 | 1.721 | 2.080 | 2.518 | 2.831 | 3.819 |
| 22 | 1.321 | 1.717 | 2.074 | 2.508 | 2.819 | 3.792 |
| 23 | 1.319 | 1.714 | 2.069 | 2.500 | 2.807 | 3.767 |
| 24 | 1.318 | 1.711 | 2.064 | 2.492 | 2.797 | 3.745 |
| 25 | 1.316 | 1.708 | 2.060 | 2.485 | 2.787 | 3.725 |
| 26 | 1.315 | 1.706 | 2.056 | 2.479 | 2.779 | 3.707 |
| 27 | 1.314 | 1.703 | 2.052 | 2.473 | 2.771 | 3.690 |
| 28 | 1.313 | 1.701 | 2.048 | 2.467 | 2.763 | 3.674 |
| 29 | 1.311 | 1.699 | 2.045 | 2.462 | 2.756 | 3.659 |
| 30 | 1.310 | 1.697 | 2.042 | 2.457 | 2.750 | 3.646 |
| 40 | 1.303 | 1.684 | 2.021 | 2.423 | 2.704 | 3.551 |
| 60 | 1.296 | 1.671 | 2.000 | 2.390 | 2.660 | 3.460 |
| 120 | 1.289 | 1.658 | 1.980 | 2.358 | 2.617 | 3.373 |
| ∞ | 1.282 | 1.645 | 1.960 | 2.326 | 2.576 | 3.291 |

*Source:* From Fisher and Yates (1963).

TABLE 11.4. HYPOTHESIS TESTING (*t* TEST)

| Steps | Example 11.1 |
| --- | --- |
| 1. Look at the hypothesis. | $H_0: \overline{X}_E = \overline{X}_C$<br>$H_1: \overline{X}_E > \overline{X}_C$ |
| 2. Look at the $\alpha$ level. | $\alpha < .01$, one-tailed (directional) decision |
| 3. Compare the observed and critical statistics | $t_{obs} = 3.25$<br>$t_{crit} = 2.33$ |
| 4. a. If the observed statistic is less than the critical statistic, accept the null hypothesis and stop. | Not so here. |
|    b. If the observed statistic is greater than the critical statistic, reject the null hypothesis and continue. | $t_{obs} > t_{crit}$ (3.25 > 2.33), so reject $H_0$. |
| 5. Decide which alternative hypothesis is more logical. | Because $\overline{X}_E$ was expected to be greater if there was any mean difference, there was only one alternative hypothesis: $H_1: \overline{X}_E > \overline{X}_C$. |
| 6. Interpret the results in terms of the $p$ level. | $H_0$ is rejected at $p < .01$ and $H_1$ is accepted. So there is only a 1% probability that the observed mean difference, $\overline{X}_E > \overline{X}_C$, occurred by chance alone, or a 99% probability that it was due to factors other than chance. |

the French proficiency test between the experimental group (who received the extra language laboratory training) and the control group (who did not) probably did not occur by chance alone (99 percent sure). But is a difference of 30 points meaningful? The researcher and the reader should consider this question carefully. Two hours of laboratory time for one semester (15 weeks) amounts to 30 hours. It appears that one point on average was gained by students for each hour in the laboratory. But whether that finding is meaningful depends on many factors that can be determined only within the context of the study. How many hours of class time in total were attended by both groups? How much does the language laboratory cost? Would the members of the experimental group have responded just as well if they had been required to spend (a much cheaper) two hours per week in a French study hall? I think I have made my point: You have not finished your critical reading just because you have found a study that was correctly and logically conducted from a statistical point of view.

### Potential pitfalls

I have already discussed two potential problems that you might encounter in this family of statistics. The first, as you will recall, was the potential error of not applying the correct formula for the *t* test (or *z* distribution) when the scores of the two groups were dependent, or correlated. As was pointed out, still other potential problems could arise if the researcher fails to check the assumptions underlying the *t* test. A third major pitfall, which I did not previously address, is that of multiple *t* tests, that is, the application of a number of *t* tests to analyze data collected from the same two groups. For instance, a researcher might want to compare the placement means, including four sets of subtest scores, of the males and females at a particular institution. In such a situation, it is tempting to make the comparisons between the means for males and females on each of the four subtests with four different *t* tests. Unfortunately, doing so makes the results difficult to interpret. Yet, I have seen studies in our literature that make 2, 3, 4, 5, and more comparisons of means on the same groups or test scores.

The problem is that as the number of *t* tests increases, so does the probability that one or more of the "significant" findings are due to chance alone. There is no way to know which or how many of these findings are spurious. Hence, it is impossible to determine which, if any, of the null hypotheses rejected by a researcher under these conditions was justifiably rejected, which creates tremendous problems in interpreting such results. They simply become increasingly meaningless as the number of comparisons grows. So you should probably keep an eye out for such multiple comparisons. They are *never* justifiable, especially since there are statistical means for properly addressing this problem (see the discussions of one-way analysis of variance and two-way analysis of variance in the next section, Related Analyses).

## Related analyses

The analyses related to this chapter (mean comparisons) are covered next. Remember, they are presented primarily for later reference, so you may want to skip to the family of statistics covered in Chapter 12.

### F ratio

The *F* ratio is another approach to research questions that require comparisons between means. As with the *z* statistic or the *t* test, the researcher begins by selecting random samples from a population. The mean and standard deviation are then calculated for each.

It is assumed that the scores within each group will differ from each other in much the same way as do the scores in the whole population. Such variation should be about the same for every random sample drawn from the population with some chance, or random, fluctuations that are due to factors like unreliability in the tests and random differences in the samples. Any variation between groups, as reflected by differences in the means and standard deviations, should likewise be due only to chance factors. In other words, if such fluctuations within groups and between groups belong to the same distribution, they should be about the same. This issue can be investigated by comparing them in the form of a ratio:

$$F \text{ ratio} = \frac{\text{variance between groups}}{\text{variance within groups}}$$

If two such variances are about the same (say a variance between groups = 12.07 and a variance within groups = 11.68), you would expect the ratio to be about 1.0, or

$$F \text{ ratio} = \frac{\text{variance between groups}}{\text{variance within groups}} = \frac{12.07}{11.68} = 1.03$$

In such a case, the variance between groups and the variance within groups are said to be about the same, and any differences probably arise from chance alone.

Recall that variance between groups is reflected by the magnitude of the differences in the theoretical distribution of the means of the samples. As that difference becomes greater, the numerator of the $F$ ratio also increases. Thus, the $F$ ratio departs further and further from 1.0 as the difference between samples increases relative to the variation within the groups. If the variation between the groups becomes much larger than the variation within the groups, the $F$ ratio can lead to a decision to reject the null hypothesis of no significant difference between means, using much the same logic as that underlying the $z$ distribution and the $t$ test.

However, the $F$ family of distributions is different from the $z$ distribution and $t$ distributions, so, naturally, the critical value of $F$ that is necessary to reject the null hypothesis is different. As with the other two distributions, the researcher simply refers to tables that are readily available to ascertain any of the critical values that are necessary for statistical comparisons.

For an example of how the $F$ ratio works, let's return to the study shown in the abstract and in Table 11.2. At the outset, remember that

TABLE 11.5. SOURCE TABLE FOR THE *F* RATIO

| Source of variation | SS | df | MS | $F_{obs}$ |
|---|---|---|---|---|
| Between groups | 45,000 | $(k - 1) = 1$ | 45,000 | $\dfrac{MS_{BG}}{MS_{WG}} = 10.59^*$ |
| Within groups (error) | 841,500 | $(N - k) = 198$ | 4,250 | |
| Total | 886,500 | $(N - 1) = 199$ | | |

$^*p < .01$ ($F_{crit} = 6.76$).

each sample was randomly drawn from a population, so the mean of each is considered to be representative of the population mean. The mean of both groups combined would logically be a better, or at least the best available, estimate for that population mean. The researcher begins by calculating that mean, or what I will designate as the *grand mean* ($\overline{X}_G$), which turns out to be $\overline{X}_G = 515$ for Table 11.2.

The calculations for what follows tend to be laborious and do not necessarily contribute to the goals of this book. Therefore, I will skip over some details in favor of more important conceptual points. To begin with, the *sums of squares between groups* ($SS_{BG}$) are derived from the differences between each group mean and the grand mean. In the example, they are $SS_{BG} = 45,000$. Next, the *sums of squares within groups* ($SS_{WG}$) are calculated by subtracting the mean of each group from each score in that group, squaring those values, and summing them across all groups. For the individual groups, these would be the basic operations involved in calculating $\Sigma(X - \overline{X})^2$ that were part of the discussion of the standard deviation in Chapter 6. In the example, the sums of these operations are $SS_{WG} = 841,500$. Both sets of sums of squares and their total are recorded in a *source table*, as shown in Table 11.5.

Because the *F* ratio, like the *t* test, is actually a family of distributions, the next step is to determine which distribution. But first, it is necessary to know the degrees of freedom, which are for each of the sums of squares involved. For $SS_{BG}$, the degrees of freedom are based on the number of group means ($k$) being compared to the grand mean. So the degrees of freedom between groups will be the number of samples minus one, or $df_{BG} = k - 1 = 2 - 1 = 1$. For $SS_{WG}$, the *df* depend on the number of subjects in each group who are being compared to the group means. The *df* within groups will be the total of the number of subjects in each group minus one summed across groups. Or, more simply, you take the total number of subjects ($N$) and subtract the number of groups ($k$), or $df_{WG} = N - k$, which will be the same value. In the example,

$df_{wG} = N - k = 200 - 2 = 198$. The *df* are then recorded in a table, as shown in Table 11.5. Notice that the *df*, like the sums of squares, are totaled. Since the total *df* should be the total number of subjects minus one ($N - 1$), this provides the researcher and you with a check for the accuracy of these calculations. In Table 11.5, $N - 1 = 200 - 1 = 199$ and so does the sum of the *df* for $SS_{BG}$ and $SS_{wG}$, that is ($k - 1$) + ($N - k$) = ($2 - 1$) + ($200 - 2$) = $1 + 198 = 199$.

With all this information in hand, the researcher divides each of the sums of squares by the relevant degrees of freedom to obtain the *mean squares (MS)*. The *mean squares between groups ($MS_{BG}$)* is the average variance that is due to differences between the sample means and the grand mean. The *mean squares within groups ($MS_{wG}$)* is the average variance that is due to the differences of each subject from the appropriate sample means. Remember that theoretically all samples are drawn from the same population. However, sample means can vary within that population and subjects can differ from sample means by chance alone. Since all subjects within a particular sample performed under the same conditions, that variation ($MS_{wG}$) can be considered error, or owing to chance alone. The variation of sample means from the grand mean ($MS_{BG}$) is based on means that may be related systematically (e.g., one sample has been given a treatment while the other has not) but will also contain some error.

The *F* ratio is one way of using this information to determine the proportion of systematic variation (from the treatment effect) to unsystematic variation (from chance, or error) as follows:

$$F = \frac{MS_{BG}}{MS_{wG}} = \frac{\text{error variation} + \text{treatment effect variation}}{\text{error variation}}$$

Conceptually, then, the *F* ratio is the ratio of the error variation plus the treatment effect variation to the error variation alone. Since error variation divided by error variation would logically equal 1 (any quantity divided by that quantity equals 1, e.g., $5/5 = 1$), the degree to which the *F* ratio differs from 1 is an estimate of the relative strength of the variation because of the treatment effect. In Table 11.5, this observed *F* ratio is as follows:

$$F_{obs} = \frac{MS_{BG}}{MS_{wG}} = \frac{45,000}{4.250} = 10.59$$

As with procedures for the *z* statistic and the *t* test, the researcher then refers to readily available tables to find the $F_{crit}$ for a study with the degrees of freedom involved here and finds that $F_{crit}$ is 6.76 for degrees of freedom of 1 and 198 and $\alpha < .01$. If $F_{obs}$ exceeds $F_{crit}$, the relative strength of variation from the treatment effect is sufficient to indicate that the probability is less than 1 percent that the observed difference between means was due to chance alone. Hence, the null hypothesis $H_0$: $\overline{X}_E = \overline{X}_C$ can be rejected and the alternative hypothesis $H_1$: $\overline{X}_E > \overline{X}_C$ must be accepted. In Table 11.5, the $F_{obs}$ of 10.59 clearly exceeds the $F_{crit}$ of 6.76. Therefore, the researcher puts an asterisk after it, indicates that $p < .01$, and proceeds to interpret the hypotheses as discussed earlier: There is only a 1 percent probability that the observed 30-point difference in means (see Table 11.2) occurred by chance alone.

The assumptions underlying the use of the $F$ ratio are the same as those listed for the $t$ test. However, the design requirement of independence between the groups being compared is even more important because it is not a simple matter of adjusting the formulas. Different statistics must be used if the scores for groups being compared are correlated.

It is interesting that, like the $z$ statistic and the $t$ test, the $F$ ratio and $t$ test are related. When *two* independent means are being compared, the $F$ ratio will be equal to the squared value of $t$, or $F = t^2$. The $t_{obs}$ for the same set of sample data was 3.2537 (see Table 11.2). Its squared value is 10.59, which is what was obtained for the $F$ ratio. However, the $F$ ratio has much more flexibility because both the $z$ and the $t$ statistics are restricted to one comparison of two means. With the proper calculation of various combinations of sums of squares and the appropriate determination of degrees of freedom, the $F$ ratio can be used to compare three or more means. Thus, this statistic opens up an entire group of different types of multiple mean comparisons, called *ANalysis Of VAriance* (ANOVA). (See later sections on One-way Analysis of Variance and Two-way Analysis of Variance.)

## Friedman's two-way analysis of variance

Friedman's two-way analysis of variance is analogous in interpretation to the two-way analysis of variance discussed later. It differs, however, in that two nominal-scale independent variables can be analyzed on the basis of an ordinal-scale dependent variable. Multiple comparisons can only be made within the design after the overall Friedman test is found to be significant, that is, it rejects the overall null hypothesis of no difference between any of the ranks other than chance differences.

## Kruskal-Wallis test

The Kruskal-Wallis test is an extension of the Mann-Whitney $U$ *test* but is more easily applicable to the testing of more than two means. It is usually applied only to ordinal scales or in cases where the interval scales lack normal distribution. In other words, it can be used to make multiple comparisons in situations in which the more powerful statistics discussed in the body of the chapter cannot be applied. It assumes that all groups are random samples from their respective populations and independence among the samples. The logic involves first testing the null hypothesis of no difference among the various means. If the null hypothesis is rejected, then multiple comparisons can be made between the various pairs of means. Note, however, that it would be a tactical error to apply this statistic when the *t* test or some variation of ANOVA could be applied because it is a much weaker statistic, that is, it is less likely to find statistically significant differences even if they are present in the data.

### Mann-Whitney U test

The *U* test is analogous to the *t* test in that it is used to test the null hypothesis that two samples are the same in terms of means. It is sometimes used instead of the *t* test because it requires neither the assumption of normal distribution in each of the two samples nor that of equal variances and can be used with ordinal scale dependent variables. It does assume, however, that the scores in each of the two samples are independent and that the distributions of the two groups are similar except for central tendency. Otherwise the logic is similar to the logic for the *t* test. Like the Kruskal-Wallis test, it is a much weaker statistic than the *t* test and should be applied only when the *t* test is not appropriate.

### Median test

The median test is used to test the null hypothesis that the medians for two or more samples are the same. The scales can be ordinal or interval. The median test assumes that each sample is randomly drawn from its respective population and that the samples are independent of each other. The median test is a special application of the chi-square distribution to the problem of comparing medians.

### Multivariate analyses

Multivariate analyses are a complex group of statistical approaches that are used when two or more dependent variables are to be considered simultaneously within a given study. They may be applied with one independent nominal variable or more than one. It was this set of analyses that were applied to the study described in the abstract in Chapter 5 because there were three dependent variables: course grade, final examination, and cloze test. There was one nominal independent variable in that study: whether the students were placed or continuing. Multivariate analyses were called for because of the three dependent variables measured for the the same subjects in each group.

Often the results of multivariate analyses will be converted into familiar statistics like the $F$ ratio, so they will be easier for the reader to understand. Thus, statistics like the Mahalanobis $D^2$ and Wilks's lambda are converted and explained as approximate $F$ ratios that are then interpreted as was just described. The study in Chapter 5 did so first for overall differences between placed and continuing students on all three dependent measures with $D^2$. Then mean comparisons were made for each dependent variable using lambda.

A major pitfall found in language studies is that two or more dependent variables are analyzed separately as though they are independent of each other within a given study when they are in fact related. If you find this situation, there may be major problems with the results and with interpreting them.

## One-way analysis of variance

The one-way analysis of variance is used to make mean comparisons when there is one interval-scale dependent variable and one nominal-scale independent variable. Thus, the example explained under $F$ ratio is a one-way analysis of variance. In that case, however, the $z$ statistic and $t$ test were also applicable because there were only two levels (two means) of the independent variable and the samples were reasonably large. The striking advantage of the one-way analysis of variance is that it can be applied when there are more than two groups in the independent variable. So the means of three, four, or even more groups on a dependent variable can be tested simultaneously for significant differences.

Let's say that the study shown in Example 11.1 and Table 11.2 was modified to include a control group ($\overline{X}_C$), a treatment group receiving two extra hours per week of language laboratory time ($\overline{X}_{LL}$), and another group receiving two hours per week of a language study hall ($\overline{X}_{SH}$). The one-way analysis of variance would be used to determine if there were any overall significant differences among these three means. The null hypothesis would be $H_0$: $\overline{X}_C = \overline{X}_{LL} = \overline{X}_{SH}$. An $F_{obs}$ would normally be calculated and reported, as shown in Table 11.5. With the correct $df$ and $F_{crit}$ in hand, the $H_0$ could be rejected (or accepted), just as was explained under the $F$ ratio. Of course, if the $H_0$ was accepted, the analysis would stop because observed differences were probably due to chance alone.

If the $H_0$ can be rejected, it indicates that at least two of the individual means are significantly different from each other. But which ones? Follow-up analyses can be conducted, once an overall significant $F$ is found, to determine which individual pairs are different because of factors other than chance. Such comparisons take many forms, but the most common are orthogonal comparisons, Duncan's multiple range test, Newman-Keuls test, Tukey's test, Dunn's test, and Scheffe's test.

Within the scope of this book, the important things to look for are (1) that an overall $F$ ratio was calculated for the one-way analysis of variance and found to be significant and (2) that one of the procedures enumerated previously was used (and labeled as such) to make the individual mean comparisons, each testing $H_0: \overline{X}_1 = \overline{X}_2$. Use of the ordinary $t$ test is not appropriate for making multiple comparisons.

The assumptions underlying this type of ANOVA are the same as those given for the $t$ test in earlier in this chapter. The additional design requirement of independence is crucial here. Each mean in the design should be based on different subjects who were randomly selected into the groups. Otherwise, the analysis of variance described here is not the proper form of analysis. Multivariate analysis or other, more complex, statistics may be required if the groups are not independent. Even if independence has been properly built into the design of the study, the assumptions should be checked and multiple comparisons using the $t$ test should be avoided.

## Two-way analysis of variance

The basic reasoning behind the $t$ test, the $F$ ratio, and the one-way analysis of variance is applied in the two-way analysis of variance. However, it is applied correctly when there are two nominal-scale independent variables (each with two or more levels) and one interval-scale dependent variable. It should be noted that exactly the same logic can be extended to three-way and four-way designs, and so on.

This type of design can vary widely, depending on the types of samples and sampling procedures, but the basic logic should include at least the following five steps.

1. An overall $F$ ratio should be reported. If it is significant, the researcher knows that at least one pair of means somewhere within the design is significantly different. But there can be many such pairs in this complicated design.
2. A source table, like Table 4 in Example 11.2, should be set up.
3. To narrow the decision about which pairs of means are significantly different, the researcher should examine the $F$ ratio for each main effect (each independent variable).
4. When it is determined which main effects are significant, the researcher may make comparisons testing $H_0: \overline{X}_1 = \overline{X}_2$ between individual pairs of means (within those significant main effects) to determine which pairs are different because of factors other than

chance. Such comparisons most commonly are performed using orthogonal comparisons, Duncan's multiple range test, Newman-Keuls test, Tukey's test, Dunn's test, or Scheffe's test.

5. The researcher should report and examine an *F* ratio for interactions between the independent variables. If this *F* ratio is significant, the researcher must explain the interactions within the context of the study and its results.

Aside from violations of the assumptions (the same as those for the *t* test), inappropriate multiple comparisons is the single biggest pitfall found in language studies.

EXAMPLE 11.2

### 4. Construct validity

The sample means and marginals are shown in Figure 1 for the two-way ANOVA design used here to investigate the construct validity of the test. The results are reported in Table 4. Since the overall *F* value for this study was 91.31 (df = 3/112; p < .01), the main effects were examined and found to be significant (p < .01 for both major and nationality). The effect due to the interaction of these main effects was not significant. Therefore, the null hypotheses of no significant differences between means according to major and according to nationality were rejected. The test did indeed distinguish

|  |  | Engineer | TESL/TEFL |  |
|---|---|---|---|---|
| Nationality | American | $\bar{x}$ = 50.52<br>n = 29 | $\bar{x}$ = 44.79<br>n = 29 | $\bar{x}$ = 47.66<br>n = 58 |
|  | Chinese | $\bar{x}$ = 36.97<br>n = 29 | $\bar{x}$ = 27.38<br>n = 29 | $\bar{x}$ = 32.17<br>n = 58 |
|  |  | $\bar{x}$ = 43.74<br>n = 58 | $\bar{x}$ = 36.09<br>n = 58 | Grand mean = 39.91<br>N = 116 |

*Major*

*Figure 1.* ANOVA sample means and marginals

*Table 4*
Results of two-way ANOVA

| Source | SS | df | MS | F |
|---|---|---|---|---|
| Major | 1699.45 | 1 | 1699.45 | 35.88* |
| Nationality | 6951.76 | 1 | 6951.76 | 146.75* |
| Major x Nationality | 108.14 | 1 | 108.14 | 2.28 |
| Residual (error) | 5305.65 | 112 | 47.37 |  |
| Total | 14064.99 | 115 | 122.30 |  |

*p < .01

178

between engineers and non-engineers, as well as between native and non-native speakers of English. Note, however, that both groups of native speakers, even the TESL subjects, performed better than both groups of non-native speakers, even the engineers. This may indicate that overall knowledge of English is more important to success on such a test than knowledge of the special English of engineering.

*Table 5*
Omega squared analysis

| Source | Omega squared | Percent of variance |
|---|---|---|
| Major | .1171 | 11.71 |
| Nationality | .4893 | 48.93 |
| Major x Nationality | .0041 | .41 |
| Residual (error) | .3894 | 38.94 |
| Total | .9999 | 99.99 |

To explore this notion, omega squared analysis was performed (see Table 5). This analysis estimated that approximately 61 percent of the variance in the design was accounted for by the major and nationality variables. Nationality itself accounted for nearly 49 percent of the overall variance, while major accounted for only about 12 percent. The interaction of these two variables accounted for virtually no variance, but an important 38.9 percent was error variance and thus remained unaccounted for in the design.

Example 11.2 is an excerpt from an investigation (Brown 1984) of a test of the ability to read engineering materials. This test was administered to four groups of graduate students who were from the United States or the People's Republic of China and whose major field of study was engineering or TESL/TEFL. Thus, the two independent variables were nationality and major with two levels of each. Although there could have been more levels, two were all that were needed in this two-way analysis of variance. The dependent variable was scores on the engineering reading test.

Even though the explanation is clear in the example, I will point out a number of things. First, an overall $F$ of 91.31 ($df = 3/112$: $p < .01$) was reported, so the analysis proceded. Second, a source table was presented with variation from four sources: each independent variable (nationality and major), their interaction (major $\times$ nationality) and residual (error, or chance variation). Third, the $F$ ratios were significant for each main effect (independent variable). Fourth, no comparisons

179

were made between individual pairs of means (although they could have been) because the significant main effects were sufficient for rejecting the null hypotheses for each two-level independent variable. Fifth, the *F* ratio for interaction between main effects was not significant, so no further explanation was necessary for possible interactions.

Notice also that there was an additional follow-up analysis called *Omega squared*. This procedure is sometimes used to determine what percentage of the variation in scores on the dependent variable was due to each of the sources of variation. The last paragraph of the example describes the results of this procedure.

### Wilcoxon test

The Mann-Whitney *U* test and Wilcoxon test are equivalent forms of the same thing (see Mann-Whitney *U* test).

## Terms and symbols

| | |
|---|---|
| dependent | $t$ |
| experimental/control group design | $t$ test for correlated means |
| independent | $t$ test for independent means |
| levels (two levels, three levels, etc.) | $\overline{X}_C$ |
| naturally occurring group design | $\overline{X}_E$ |
| pretest-posttest design | $z$ |
| quasi-experimental design | $z$ distribution |
| sampling between distribution of | $z$ statistic |
| distributions between means | $\mu_C$ |
| standard error of the difference | $\mu_E$ |
| between means | |

## Review questions

1. What general types of problems are explored using the mean comparison family of statistics?
2. What type of analysis should be used to investigate mean comparisons for a study with more than one nominal-scale independent variable and one ordinal-scale dependent variable? (See Table 11.1.)
3. What types of scales, what sample sizes, and what number of independent and dependent variables are permissible if a researcher reports that a *z* statistic was used in a study? (See Table 11.1.)
4. Can you list the null hypothesis and the two possible alternative

hypotheses for the $z$ statistic in Question 3 (given an experimental/control group study)?

$H_0$:

$H_1$:

$H_2$:

5. In the same experimental/control group study ($\alpha < .05$, two tailed, $df = 26$) a $t_{obs} = 2.10$ was calculated. What would be the $t_{crit}$ for this study? (See Table 11.3.) Could $H_0$ be rejected under the conditions of this study? If so, which alternative hypothesis would logically be accepted?

6. Answer the same questions for an experimental/control group study in which $\alpha < .01$, one tailed, $df = 30$ and $t_{obs} = 2.40$ (don't forget to look at Table 11.3).

7. What are the two primary assumptions underlying the $t$ test?

8. What are the six steps that are necessary to test the hypothesis in a $t$ test?

9. What is the relationship between the $z$ statistic and the $t$ test? What are the similarities and the differences?

10. What is the most common pitfall in using the $t$ test? And why is it a problem?

## Application

Look back at the study in Chapter 5 (Examples 5.1–5.11). Why did I choose to use multivariate analysis rather than just $t$ tests – one for each dependent variable: grade, final examination, and cloze test? (Hint: see Table 11.1 and Potential Pitfalls.) If only the final examination had been used as the dependent variable and only one experiment was conducted (say Fall 1977), would it then have been appropriate to use the $t$ test? With groups of 133 and 31 for placed and continuing students, respectively, would I have been able to use the ordinary $t$ test? Which assumption should be checked, given these sample sizes? Do you think it is met?

# 12   Comparing frequencies

We are all familiar with the political polls that are conducted as the interest and tension build toward a national election. In the United States, they often take the form of surveys of a representative sample of citizens who are registered to vote and asking them if they intend to vote for the Democratic or Republican presidential candidate. The analysis of results is often broken down to look at different voting patterns according to sex, religion, economic status, and the like. The purpose of such polls is to shed some light on how people view the election. But these polls sometimes do not agree with the actual results of the election. There seems to be some error in conducting such studies and, in all fairness, pollsters do usually account for this problem in a footnote that gives the "margin of error." Unfortunately, many people forget about this footnote and condemn statistics in general and polls in particular because they are not always right.

Perhaps a more reasonable approach would be to realize that the family of analyses involved, comparing frequencies, is just a simple form of logic that can help you discern patterns in probabilistic terms. Let's see how this logic works for this particular family.

## Stage 1: focusing the study

### Identifying a problem

This family of analyses has two limitations in the types of problems it can address. First, it is limited to looking only at nominal scales. You may have noticed that all the variables that were mentioned – presidential choice, sex, religion, and economic status – are or can be converted to nominal scales. Recall that nominal scales are categorical in nature. This means that any given individual will fall into only one category within a given variable. For the variable sex, for instance, one is either male or female.

The second limitation is related to the first. If only nominal scales are analyzed, ordinal and interval scales are not involved. So what is actually counted in this type of analysis? Frequencies. Frequency and frequency distributions were introduced in Chapter 7. Expanding on that expla-

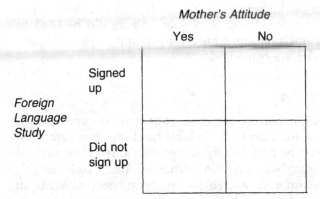

*Figure 12.1  Design for the study in Example 12.1*

nation, let's define *frequency* here as the number (or tally) of people (or ants or trees or even language students) who fall into a particular category.

Language researchers use this family to analyze any question that deals exclusively with frequencies. Example 12.1 shows one such possibility.

EXAMPLE 12.1. HYPOTHETICAL INVESTIGATION OF
PARENTAL ATTITUDES TOWARD HIGH SCHOOL
FOREIGN LANGUAGE STUDY

(1) Do you think it is important for your child to study a foreign language in high school? (2) This question was asked in August 1985 of every mother who would have at least one child entering Crescenta Valley High School, La Crescenta, California, in September 1985. (3) A study was conducted to determine whether there was any difference between students whose mothers answered yes and those who answered no in terms of whether the child actually signed up for a foreign language class. (4) A total of 150 mothers responded to the question (95 percent of those who were asked), and only the first entering child of each mother was then considered for the study. (5) Chi-square analysis was used to determine whether the observed differences were significant ($p < .01$). It was found that students whose mothers answered positively were far more prone to sign up for foreign language classes than the others ($\chi^2 = 90.31$, $df = 1$). (7) The need to change parental attitudes is discussed, along with some suggestions for how to do so.

Notice that in the abstract, the two types of nominal variables are involved, each with two levels, or categories: mothers' attitudes (yes or no answer) and foreign language study (whether students signed up or not). The design for such a study is shown in Figure 12.1. The researcher wants to know how many (the frequency) of the students fall in each box. For example, if 55 of the students whose mothers said yes finally did sign up, 55 would be the frequency placed in the upper-left box in the design. This family of analyses, then, can and should be used to address any research questions in which only nominal variables are included and frequencies are compared.

## Operationalizing variables

Since all variables are nominal in this case, your main concern should be with how clearly and logically each variable has been designated and categorized. You should be particularly wary when interval or ordinal data have been transformed into a nominal scale. For instance, a variable like economic status is often measured by family income, which is an interval scale. But this scale can be converted to a nominal scale as follows: \$0–\$11,999 = low, \$12,000–\$29,999 = middle, and \$30,000 or above = high. Aside from being arbitrary, these divisions might make sense in one setting but not in another, or at one point in history but not at another. So you should think carefully about any scale transformations that were made, while keeping in mind the context of the study and the generalizability that the researcher claimed. Transforming scales from interval to ordinal to nominal is statistically proper in a study, as you saw in Chapter 3. But statistically proper and theoretically logical are not necessarily the same thing.

## Research hypotheses

The central question underlying this family of statistics is whether the observed frequencies for the different categories within the variables are related or independent. To test this question, the researcher usually formulates research hypotheses similar to those formulated for the study described in Example 12.1:

$H_0$: The observed frequencies for mothers' attitudes and foreign language study are independent.

$H_1$: The observed frequencies for mothers' attitudes and foreign language study are related.

The focus here is on the null hypothesis; if it cannot be rejected, the researcher should conclude that mothers' answers (yes or no) have no relationship other than chance with whether their children choose to study a foreign language. If the $H_0$ is rejected and the $H_1$ is accepted, there probably is a relationship between the variables within a certain probability – 99 percent at the $\alpha < .01$ in the study described in the abstract.

*Chi-square* ($\chi^2$) is the most appropriate test for analyzing these data. It is usually viewed as a nondirectional (two-tailed) test. But only one alternative hypothesis need be given because if the variables are related, it does not matter which direction is involved, mathematically or logically.

## Stage 2: sampling

The overriding concern for data gathering within this family of analysis is that the categories should be truly discrete, with each subject appearing in only one category for each variable. To ensure that the categories are discrete requires careful operationalization of the variables and categories, as well as thoughtful planning in the design stage.

Another problem that often arises in data gathering has to do with the fact that such studies are often based on a *survey*, that is, the data are gathered through questionnaires, interviews, and so forth. Human nature being what it is, there is usually a certain amount of noncooperation. So you should always check to see what the *response rate* was in a given study, which will usually be stated as a percentage. For instance, the abstract (Sentence 4) says that "150 mothers responded to the question (95 percent of those asked)." In this case, the response rate was 95 percent, which is unusually high in my experience. However, studies in which questionnaires were mailed out (to be returned later by the respondent) often have appallingly low response rates. Of course, a low response rate could have a dramatic effect on the results of a study because those who do not respond are part of the population but are not represented in the sample. The thing to remember is that a low response rate may yield a nonrepresentative sample. This issue should be foremost in your mind when you read survey research – in terms of both the internal and external validity of a study.

## Stage 3: setting up statistical decisions

### Choosing the correct statistic

By now, Table 12.1 should be clear to you. It not, review the discussion of Tables 10.1 and 11.1. Briefly, though, notice that this family is made up of a limited set of analyses (see bold-face entries) that are commonly used in language studies. Note also that the phi and tetrachoric coefficients are included here as well as in Chapter 10 because they show the degree of relationship between two variables, as explained in Chapter 10, but do so for variables that are on nominal scales represented by frequencies.

The statistic chosen for the study in Example 12.1 was chi-square. What design conditions does this imply? Were those conditions met?

TABLE 12.1. COMMON ANALYSES FOR COMPARING FREQUENCIES

Type and Number of Independent Variables

| Dependent variable | | Interval — 1 variable | Interval — More than 1 | Ordinal — 1 variable | Ordinal — More than 1 | Nominal — 1 variable — 2 levels | Nominal — 1 variable — more | Nominal — More than 1 |
|---|---|---|---|---|---|---|---|---|
| Interval | 0 | | | | | | | |
| Interval | 1 | Simple regression and Pearson $r$ | Multiple regression and Multiple $R$ | Transform the ordinal variable into nominal and use C-1, or transform the interval variable into ordinal and use B-2, or transform both variables into nominal and use C-3. | | $z$ stat. (large sample), $t$-test (any sample) | One-way ANOVA | Two-way ANOVA, three-way ANOVA, etc. *(Row 1)* |
| Interval | More than 1 | | Multiple regression and Multiple $R$ | | | Multivariate analyses | | Multivariate analyses |
| Ordinal | 0 | Transform the ordinal variable into a nominal variable and use C-1, transform the interval variable into an ordinal variable and use B-2, or transform the interval variable into a nominal variable and use C-2. | | | Kendall's $W$ | Median test, $U$ test | | |
| Ordinal | 1 | | | Spearman rho Kendall's tau | | | Kruskal-Wallis test | Friedman's two-way ANOVA *(Row 2)* |
| Ordinal | More than 1 | | | | | | | |

| | Column A | Column B | Column C |
|---|---|---|---|
| | | | Chi-square |
| 0 | Biserial, Point-biserial correlation | | Phi coefficient, Tetrachoric corr., Fisher exact test Chi-square |
| 1 | (see C-1) | (see C-2) | |
| More than 1 | | (see C-2) | |
| *Nominal* | | | |

*Note:* Boldface indicates common analyses for comparing frequencies. *C-1* stands for Column C, Row 1.
*Source:* Adapted from Tuckman (1978: 255).

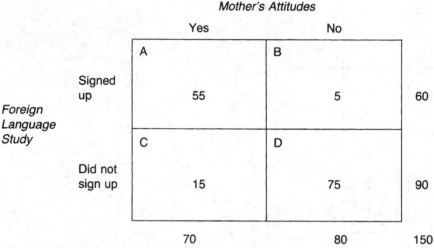

Figure 12.2 Descriptive results of the study in example 12.1

## Statistical hypotheses

At this point, you must shift your thinking to accommodate the new family of analyses. Here, we are concerned with two types of frequencies: observed frequencies and expected frequencies. *Observed frequencies* ($f_O$) are those frequencies that actually occur in each cell, or box, of a *contingency table* like the one in Figure 12.2. These observed frequencies are based on the samples involved. *Expected frequencies* ($f_E$) theoretically represent the population as a whole. They are not observable in sampling research but can be estimated. The best available population estimate in the sample is based on the *marginals* – those numbers to the right of and below the boxes in Figure 12.2. All these ideas will be made much more clear through demonstration in the section on Observed Statistics. For the moment, remember that $f_O$ represents the individual cell frequencies as observed in the sample and $f_E$ is the best estimate of what those frequencies would be in the population by chance alone.

The statistical hypotheses for the study presented in the abstract might be stated as follows:

$$H_0: f_O = f_E$$
$$H_1: f_O \neq f_E$$

$H_0$ means that the observed sample frequencies and expected population frequencies are equal. Thus, the pattern of observed frequencies that appears to indicate a relationship between the variables is actually only equal to what would be found in the population regardless of the var-

TABLE 12.2. CALCULATING $\chi^2$ FOR THE RESULTS IN FIGURE 12.2

| Cell | (1) $f_O$ | appropriate marginals | (2) $f_E$ | (3) $(f_O - f_E)$ | (4) $(f_O - f_E)^2$ | (5) $(f_O - f_E)^2/f_E$ |
|------|-----------|----------------------|-----------|-------------------|---------------------|--------------------------|
| A | 55 | $(70 \times 60)/150 = 28$ | | 27 | 729 | $729/28 = 26.04$ |
| B | 5 | $(80 \times 60)/150 = 32$ | | $-27$ | 729 | $729/32 = 22.78$ |
| C | 15 | $(70 \times 60)/150 = 42$ | | $-27$ | 729 | $729/42 = 17.36$ |
| D | 75 | $(80 \times 90)/150 = 48$ | | 27 | 729 | $729/48 = 15.19$ |

$$(6) \quad \chi^2 = \Sigma \frac{(f_O - f_E)^2}{f_E} = 81.37$$

iables involved. In such a case, the pattern is not strong enough to be due to anything other than chance.

$H_1$ means that the observed frequencies and expected frequencies are not equal. Hence, the pattern of observed frequencies in the individual cells deviates sufficiently from what would be expected by chance alone in the population to be statistically significant at a certain probability level ($p < .01$, in this case). The directionality is then interpreted in the direction of the observed frequencies.

### Alpha decision level

Alpha should be set at the beginning of the study at the conservative $\alpha < .01$ or at the more liberal $\alpha < .05$.

## Stage 4: necessary calculations

### Observed statistics

The chi-square test ($\chi^2$) is a researcher's delight because it is so easy to calculate. For this reason alone, I will inflict the actual calculations on you. But the calculations should also help you to understand how this statistical test works.

To begin with, recall that both observed frequencies ($f_O$) and expected frequencies ($f_E$) are necessary to test the statistical hypotheses. The observed frequencies for each of the four cells in Figure 12.2 (labeled A, B, C, or D in the upper-left corner of each) are shown in Column 1 of Table 12.2.

The expected frequencies are calculated by multiplying the appropriate column and row marginals for each cell and dividing the result by the grand total (row or column marginal totals, which are both the same). For Cell A, this would mean multiplying the marginal for the column in which Cell A is found (70) by the marginal for the row in which Cell

189

A is found (60) and dividing the result (70 × 60 = 4,200) by the grand total (150). This procedure will yield the expected frequency for Cell A: 70 × 60/150 = 4200/150 = 28. This process is repeated for each cell. The resulting expected frequencies are shown in Column 4 of Table 12.2.

With $f_O$ and $f_E$ in hand for each cell, the formula for $\chi^2_{observed}$ is fairly easy to apply:

$$\chi^2_{obs} = \Sigma \frac{(f_O - f_E)^2}{f_E}$$

where $\Sigma$ = sum, $f_O$ = observed frequency for each cell, and $f_E$ = expected frequency for each cell.

Referring to Table 12.2, let's see how this formula is applied. Having (1) lined up the observed frequencies, we (2) multiply the appropriate marginal and divide by the grand total to find the expected frequencies. (3) Then, we subtract the expected frequency for each cell from the observed frequency for that cell and (4) square the result. (5) Next, we divide this squared value for each cell by the expected frequency for that cell and (6) get the sum of these $\chi^2_{obs}$, which turns out to be 81.37.

This formula is designed to produce a numerical value that can be viewed as the degree to which observed sample frequencies differ from expected population frequencies. With $\chi^2_{obs}$ in hand, the researcher next needs to check the asuumptions underlying this statistical test.

## Assumptions

First, did you notice that nothing was said about assumptions in the study described in Example 12.1? You should have! The assumptions that should have been checked for this type of design are these:

1. Each observation is independent of all others.
2. Each observation falls in only one cell.
3. Observations are frequencies.
4. All the expected frequencies are higher than 10.

The first three assumptions should be clear to you. However, the fourth assumption warrants some explanation. The assumption as stated means that none of the values calculated in Step 2 for $f_E$ in Table 12.2 can be lower than 10. Since those values turned out to be 28, 32, 42, and 48, the assumption was met. Had this not been the case, it would have been necessary to apply *Yates's correction for continuity*. This formula must be applied when expected frequencies are too small in the sampling distribution to be consistent with the theoretical $\chi^2$ distribution.

The fourth assumption is for the type of design in Example 12.1. A more general way of stating this assumption so it applies to the other designs is this: All the expected frequencies are higher than 5 for studies in which $df > 2$ and higher than 10 for studies in which $df = 1$. An explanation of these $df$ comes next.

### Degrees of freedom

The degrees of freedom for $\chi^2$ analyses in general is calculated by multiplying the number of categories in each row minus one by the number of categories in each column minus one. Figure 12.1 indicates that there are two categories in the rows ($r$) of the study design described in the abstract (yes and no) and two in the columns ($c$) (signed up and did not sign up). So $df = (r - 1)(c - 1) = (2 - 1)(2 - 1) = (1)(1) = 1$. The $df$ for the example study, then, is 1.

### Critical values

To find $\chi^2_{crit}$, the researcher turns to a table like the one in Table 12.3. First, look across the top row for the appropriate alpha level. For Example 12.1, it is $\alpha < .01$ – the third column from the right. Then, move down that column until you come to the appropriate row for $df = 1$. (This $df$ is often labeled $v$ in statistical tables.) You do not have to move down far for $df = 1$; it is in the first row. So the appropriate value of $\chi^2_{crit}$ for a study with $\alpha < .01$ and $df = 1$ would be $\chi^2_{crit} = 6.63490$, or about 6.64. The $\chi^2_{crit}$ value will, of course, vary, depending on the conditions that differ from study to study.

## Stage 5: statistical decisions

### Hypothesis testing

With all the necessary calculations in hand, the researcher is now ready to make statistical decisions, starting, of course, with hypothesis testing. The six steps involved are shown in Table 12.4.

### Interpretation of results

The issue of distinguishing significance and meaningfulness in this family is no less important than with the other two families. The descriptive results of the study in Example 12.1, which are shown in Figure 12.2, seem to indicate that the significant findings are meaningful as well. That is, 55 children whose mothers answered yes did sign up for foreign language classes, while only 5 of those whose mothers answered no did so. At the same time, only 15 of the students whose mothers answered

TABLE 12.3. CRITICAL VALUES OF $\chi^2$

| $v$ \ $Q$ | 0.250 | 0.100 | 0.050 | 0.025 | 0.010 | 0.005 | 0.001 |
|---|---|---|---|---|---|---|---|
| 1 | 1.3233 | 2.7055 | 3.8415 | 5.0239 | 6.6349 | 7.8794 | 10.828 |
| 2 | 2.7726 | 4.6052 | 5.9915 | 7.3778 | 9.2103 | 10.5966 | 13.816 |
| 3 | 4.1084 | 6.2514 | 7.8147 | 9.3484 | 11.3449 | 12.8381 | 16.266 |
| 4 | 5.3853 | 7.7794 | 9.4877 | 11.1433 | 13.2767 | 14.8602 | 18.467 |
| 5 | 6.6257 | 9.2364 | 11.0705 | 12.8325 | 15.0863 | 16.7496 | 20.515 |
| 6 | 7.8408 | 10.6446 | 12.5916 | 14.4494 | 16.8119 | 18.5476 | 22.458 |
| 7 | 9.0372 | 12.0170 | 14.0671 | 16.0128 | 18.4753 | 20.2777 | 24.322 |
| 8 | 10.2188 | 13.3616 | 15.5073 | 17.5346 | 20.0902 | 21.9550 | 26.125 |
| 9 | 11.3887 | 14.6837 | 16.9190 | 19.0228 | 21.6660 | 23.5893 | 27.877 |
| 10 | 12.5489 | 15.9871 | 18.3070 | 20.4831 | 23.2093 | 25.1882 | 29.588 |
| 11 | 13.7007 | 17.2750 | 19.6751 | 21.9200 | 24.7250 | 26.7569 | 31.264 |
| 12 | 14.8454 | 18.5494 | 21.0261 | 23.3367 | 26.2170 | 28.2995 | 32.909 |
| 13 | 15.9839 | 19.8119 | 22.3621 | 24.7356 | 27.6883 | 29.8194 | 34.528 |
| 14 | 17.1170 | 21.0642 | 23.6848 | 26.1190 | 29.1413 | 31.3193 | 36.123 |
| 15 | 18.2451 | 22.3072 | 24.9958 | 27.4884 | 30.5779 | 32.8013 | 37.697 |
| 16 | 19.3688 | 23.5418 | 26.2962 | 28.8454 | 31.9999 | 34.2672 | 39.252 |
| 17 | 20.4887 | 24.7690 | 27.5871 | 30.1910 | 33.4087 | 35.7185 | 40.790 |
| 18 | 21.6049 | 25.9894 | 28.8693 | 31.5264 | 34.8053 | 37.1564 | 42.312 |
| 19 | 22.7178 | 27.2036 | 30.1435 | 32.8523 | 36.1908 | 38.5822 | 43.820 |
| 20 | 23.8277 | 28.4120 | 31.4104 | 34.1696 | 37.5662 | 39.9968 | 45.315 |
| 21 | 24.9348 | 29.6151 | 32.6705 | 35.4789 | 38.9321 | 41.4010 | 46.797 |
| 22 | 26.0393 | 30.8133 | 33.9244 | 36.7807 | 40.2894 | 42.7956 | 48.268 |
| 23 | 27.1413 | 32.0069 | 35.1725 | 38.0757 | 41.6384 | 44.1813 | 49.728 |
| 24 | 28.2412 | 33.1963 | 36.4151 | 39.3641 | 42.9798 | 45.5585 | 51.179 |
| 25 | 29.3389 | 34.3816 | 37.6525 | 40.6465 | 44.3141 | 46.9278 | 52.620 |
| 26 | 30.4345 | 35.5631 | 38.8852 | 41.9232 | 45.6417 | 48.2899 | 54.052 |
| 27 | 31.5284 | 36.7412 | 40.1133 | 43.1944 | 46.9630 | 49.6449 | 55.476 |
| 28 | 32.6205 | 37.9159 | 41.3372 | 44.4607 | 48.2782 | 50.9933 | 56.892 |
| 29 | 33.7109 | 39.0875 | 42.5569 | 45.7222 | 49.5879 | 52.3556 | 58.302 |
| 30 | 34.7998 | 40.2560 | 43.7729 | 46.9792 | 50.8922 | 53.6720 | 59.703 |
| 40 | 45.6160 | 51.8050 | 55.7585 | 59.3417 | 63.6907 | 66.7659 | 73.402 |
| 50 | 56.3336 | 63.1671 | 67.5048 | 71.4202 | 76.1539 | 79.4900 | 86.661 |
| 60 | 66.9814 | 74.3970 | 79.0819 | 83.2976 | 88.3794 | 91.9517 | 99.607 |
| 70 | 77.5766 | 85.5271 | 90.5312 | 95.0231 | 100.4250 | 104.2150 | 112.317 |
| 80 | 88.1303 | 96.5782 | 101.8790 | 106.6290 | 112.3290 | 116.3210 | 124.839 |
| 90 | 98.6499 | 107.5650 | 113.1450 | 118.1360 | 124.1160 | 128.2990 | 137.208 |
| 100 | 109.1410 | 118.4980 | 124.3420 | 129.5610 | 135.8070 | 140.1690 | 149.449 |
| $z_Q$ | +0.6745 | +1.2816 | +1.6449 | +1.9600 | +2.3263 | +2.5758 | +3.0902 |

*Source:* From Pearson and Hartley (1963).

TABLE 12.4. HYPOTHESIS TESTING ($\chi^2$)

| Steps | Example |
|---|---|
| 1. Look at the hypothesis. | $H_0$: $f_O = f_E$<br>$H_1$: $f_O \neq f_E$<br>Nondirectional decision (both directions expressed in "$\neq$" of $H_1$). |
| 2. Look at the $\alpha$ level. | $\alpha < .01$. |
| 3. Compare the observed and critical statistics | $\chi^2_{obs} = 81.37$;<br>$\chi^2_{crit} = 6.64$ when $\alpha < .01$,<br>$df = 1$. |
| 4. a. If the observed statistic is less than the critical statistic, accept the null hypothesis and stop. | Not so here. |
| b. If the observed statistic is greater than the critical statistic, reject the null hypothesis and continue. | $\chi^2_{obs} > \chi^2_{crit}$ (81.37 > 6.64), so reject $H_0$. |
| 5. Decide which alternative hypothesis is more logical. | There was only one alternative hypothesis: $H_1$: $f_O \neq f_E$. |
| 6. Interpret the results in terms of the $p$ level. | $H_0$ is rejected at $p < .01$. $H_1$ is accepted. So there is only a 1% probability that $\chi^2_{obs} = 81.37$ occurred by chance alone or a 99% probability that the observed relationship between frequencies was due to factors other than chance. |

yes failed to sign up, but 75 of those whose mothers answered no failed to do so. This appears to be a meaningful relationship with important policy implications: It seems like a good idea to figure out a way to change mothers' attitudes so more children will sign up for classes. But a researcher must be careful in making such an interpretation because, among other things, it implies a causal relationship – that mothers' attitudes cause children to sign up for foreign language classes. As you will see next, this interpretation may not be justified.

## Potential pitfalls

Two major pitfalls that are often found in this type of research are violations of the assumptions (especially the fourth assumption) and the sampling problem of low response rates. Equally important are design problems related to the operationalization of variables and categories within them. For instance, although the title of the study in Example

11.1 cites "Parental Attitudes," when this variable was finally operationalized, it turned out to be mothers' attitudes. As a reader of this study, I must wonder if the answer to a single question like that in the study is really a reliable and valid measure of the underlying construct "mothers' attitudes."

Even if the question were shown to be a reliable measure, might there not be some other variable that would more clearly explain what appears to be a causal relationship? Consider, for instance, the mothers' educational levels. Perhaps the number of years of schooling would turn out to be highly related to whether the children signed up for language classes. Or perhaps, whether the mothers had taken foreign language classes might show an even stronger relationship? Or how about foreign travel? All these potential variables might explain why mothers answered yes or no. An exploration of these variables might produce a much clearer picture of what is actually going on.

The point is that researchers may sometimes overgeneralize or imply causal relationships – all of which may be built on the weak foundation of an unreliable and invalid measure. Straightforward logic is all that the reader needs to detect this type of pitfall. Even without understanding all the statistical nuances, you are, therefore, in a position to catch such errors and incorporate that knowledge into your evaluation of such statistical studies.

## Related analyses

The analyses that appear in this section are all related to $\chi^2$ analysis. Unlike the Related Analyses in previous chapters, it would probably be useful to read the entries for one-way chi-square and two-way chi-square immediately so you will understand the difference. These entries will show you that the chi-square analysis that was covered in this chapter was a two-way chi-square.

### Fisher's exact test

Fisher's exact test refers to a two-way chi-square analysis in which the contingency table has two levels of a nominal variable in the rows and two levels in the columns. This was the case in Figure 12.1. Some researchers use this name for that analysis.

### One-way chi-square

One-way chi-square is used to analyze data in studies in which there is one nominal variable with two, three, or more levels. For example, a

| Australia | Canada | England | United States |
|---|---|---|---|
|  |  |  |  |
|  |  |  |  |

*Figure 12.3. Contingency table for the sample one-way chi-square analysis*

researcher might wish to study whether there is a significant difference in the frequency with which students from four countries – Australia, Canada, England, and the United States – study at least one foreign language in secondary school. A contingency table for such a study is shown in Figure 12.3.

After taking a random sample of 200 students each from secondary schools in all four countries, the researcher would tally in the contingency table the number in each category who studied a foreign language. Then the researcher would apply the same basic logic as was shown in the text of this chapter. The calculation of $\chi^2_{obs}$ would differ because there is only one row. But the logic for finding the *df* and $\chi^2_{crit}$, as well as for testing the hypothesis, would be the same. The assumptions and potential necessity for applying Yates's correction for continuity would also be the same. In addition, the researcher might wish to make individual comparisons between the frequencies for different pairs of nationalities by repeating individual $\chi^2$ analyses. This procedure would be permissible and logical as long as the overall $\chi^2_{obs}$ was first found to be significant and all the assumptions had been met.

## Two-way chi-square

The example used in the text of this chapter is a two-way chi-square analysis. This entry is included so I can point out that the same procedures and logic can be applied to larger designs. Recall that the nominal-scale independent and dependent variables in Chapter 12 only had two levels each (yes/no answers of mothers and sign up/did not sign up for foreign language classes). Similar studies may include three or more levels of each variable.

For example, if the same study had been conducted with samples of 150 students each at three other high schools, the researcher might wish to investigate whether there were significant differences in the frequency of students signing up and not signing up in the four different schools. A contingency table for such a study is shown in Figure 12.4. Once the data were collected and tallied into the contingency table, the same basic logic as was shown in the text of Chapter 12 would be applied. The

195

|  | High School | | | |
|---|---|---|---|---|
|  | Crescenta Valley | John Muir | Glendale | Pasadena |
| **Foreign Language Study** — Signed up |  |  |  |  |
| Did not sign up |  |  |  |  |

*Figure 12.4. Contingency table for the sample two-way chi-square analysis*

calculation of $\chi^2_{obs}$ would differ slightly, but the logic for finding the *df* and $\chi^2_{crit}$, as well as for testing the hypothesis, would be the same. The assumptions and potential necessity for applying Yates's correction for continuity would also be the same. The researcher might also wish to make individual comparisons between the frequencies for different pairs of high schools by repeating individual $\chi^2$ analyses. This procedure would be permissible and logical as long as the overall $\chi^2_{obs}$ was first found to be significant and all the assumptions had been met.

## Terms and symbols

| | |
|---|---|
| chi-square $(\chi^2)$ | response rate |
| column $(c)$ | row $(r)$ |
| contingency table | survey |
| expected frequency | Yates's correction for continuity |
| frequency | $f$ |
| marginals | $f_O$ |
| observed frequency | $f_E$ |

## Review questions

1. What types of problems are explored using chi-square analysis?
2. What types of scales and what number of dependent variables would you expect if the researcher stated that the Fisher exact test had been used in a study? (See Table 12.1.)

3. Can you list the null hypothesis and alternative hypotheses for a chi-square test like that shown in Question 4?

    $H_0$:

    $H_1$:

4. What would the $\chi^2_{obs}$ be for the frequencies in the following contingency table?

*A*

|   | $a_1$ | $a_2$ |
|---|-------|-------|
| $b_1$ | 100 | 5 |
| $b_2$ | 20 | 150 |

*B* is the row label spanning $b_1$ and $b_2$.

5. Would the researcher need to apply Yates's correction for continuity for these data?
6. What would $\chi^2_{crit}$ turn out to be if $\alpha < .05$?
7. What decision would you make in testing the hypotheses in Question 3 with regard to the information in Questions 4 and 6?
8. What are the four assumptions you would want to check?
9. What pitfalls would you watch out for?
10. Do you mind that I actually made you do statistics and, if you did not mind, are you considering the idea of learning to do statistics and conducting your own research?

*The Application follows on the next page.*

## Application

Consider the following three (admittedly sketchy) descriptions of language studies. Then answer the questions that follow.

*Study A.* This study investigated the degree of relationship between self-image scores (as measured on a well-established self-image inventory) and language achievement (as measured by the end-of-term school district examination for all students in second-year German).

*Study B.* This study compared the mean performances of two groups of students on the end-of-term school district examination for students of second-year German. The two groups were (1) students judged to have a high self-image (scores of 25 or higher out of 50 on the self-image inventory) and (2) those with a low self-image (scores of 24 or below).

*Study C.* From all students who took the districtwide second-year German examination, two groups were sorted out: high achievers – those in the top 50 percent on the test – and low achievers – those in the bottom 49 percent. These students were asked to fill out a questionnaire. The relative frequency of the two groups' answers (yes or no) to various questions was then compared statistically.

1. What family of analyses would be appropriate for each study? And what specific statistical procedures would you expect to find?
2. Can you state the statistical hypotheses that are appropriate for each study?
3. What assumptions should be checked for each study?
4. If significant results were found for each of these studies, what would their existence indicate? Would such results necessarily be meaningful?
5. What potential pitfalls would you look for in each study?
6. What further information would you need to replicate each study?

# 13 Hands-on critique and posttest

In this chapter, I will attempt to provide an "unbiased" critique of the study presented in Chapter 5. I say "attempt" because any one person's reading of a study is just that – one person's reading. You and I may approach a given statistical study in different ways, just as we would a poem. After all, different individuals have different backgrounds and different needs at a particular point in time. I say "unbiased" because no reading can really be unprejudiced – again, because of one's background and needs. But, obviously, I am much closer to the study than most people would be because I wrote it. This fact alone may make me more critical of it than most readers would be. The study was done in 1978, for the most part, and I have learned a great deal since then.

Part of what I have learned is that the logic underlying statistical studies – aside from being elegant, simple, and straightforward – must be taken as a whole pattern that makes a complete statement about the study involved. My major criticism of the study at this point in my development is that it is fragmented and lacks a certain wholeness of purpose and logical argument.

Now, to fly in the face of what I just argued about wholeness, let's look at the study piece by piece. In the process, I hope you will see how the headings and organizational pattern of a typical language study fit neatly with the statistical logic on which I have dwelt for the last four chapters. So let's turn to my naive early effort and see how I did. But, before doing so, perhaps you should reread the study and decide what you think.

## Abstract

The abstract presented in Example 5.1 seems reasonably good. The topic and purpose of the study seem clear, although a statement of the actual research hypotheses might have helped. The description of the subjects, materials, and procedures is adequate but brief. However, the explanation of statistical procedures could be better. The type of analysis involved is clear to those who know the purpose and rationale behind using multivariate analyses, and the alpha level seems to be implicit in the "$p < .05$" in the second-to-last sentence. But if I were to rewrite this abstract, I would mention that mean comparisons were the issue and that multivariate analysis was necessary because there were three dependent variables (grades, scores on the departmental examination, and cloze scores). A note about the assumptions being checked also might have been useful. Finally, I think that the brief summary of the results and implications is adequate for an abstract. All in all, I think the abstract gives enough information to let the reader know what the study is about and to help the reader decide whether to read the report.

## Introduction

The introduction (Example 5.2) begins with a statement about language testing in general; then moves to the purpose of the study, including the research question; and ends by giving a brief explanation of the significance of the problem to the field. It appears to be a good general-to-specific introduction that sets up the study and explains where it is headed. However, two things strike me.

First, the discussion of the "discrete-point" and "integrative" approaches to testing seems irrelevant to the study at hand, particularly because the concepts never come up again. It tells the reader that these concepts were on my mind, but so what? Second, the first two paragraphs strike me as a weak excuse for not having a formal review of the literature. Although it may seem as though this study is of the "breaking-new-ground" variety, which would have no literature to review, I later belie the idea by reviewing three related studies in the conclusions section of the study. It seems that I got things just a little bit backwards. What do you think?

The statement of purpose accomplishes pretty much what it should. It gives the reader an idea of where the study is heading by presenting the general research question. Today, I would probably reword this statement so that the null and alternative hypotheses were also clear. I would also insert a discussion of directionality and the alpha decision level at this point instead of under the Analyses as in this study.

## Method

In retrospect, I like the way I set up the method section (Example 5.3) by showing the way courses were organized at UCLA. I think it establishes the context or framework for how the study fit into the program. At the same time, this little section provides a transition into the description of subjects. Did you notice, however, that Table 1 is not a table at all? It would normally be considered a figure. Thus "Figure 1" would have been more appropriate.

### Subjects

The description of the participants (Example 5.4) in the study (in fact, the studies – there were three separate ones) is unusually thorough. Language background, sex, and academic status are all broken down into placed and and continuing groups and shown for each of the three studies (Fall 1977, Winter 1978, and Spring 1978). Although unusually thorough, such descriptions make me uneasy. The three variables (language background, sex, and academic status) might have made a difference in the results if they had been included as moderator variables. Unfortunately, as is typical of language studies, particularly in ESL, these variables remained uncontrolled. Does it seem right that the description of the subjects appears to have been used to explain away those variables? Did you notice the sample sizes and sampling procedures? How do they affect your thinking about the generalizability of the study? I believe that the sample sizes were adequate. But because the sample included only UCLA students, it really is only generalizable to that population, or at best, to universities with similar students.

### Materials and procedures

Materials and procedures might well have been two separate sections. However, I chose to lump them together into one section called Measures of Proficiency (Example 5.5). The description of the measures is adequate. There is a clear statement of why the cloze test was considered reliable and valid for this study. But the presence of this information makes me wonder why there was no equivalent argument for either of the other two measures. Do you believe that the grades and departmental examination are valid? You have no way of knowing from the study. So why should you or I accept results based on these two measures as reliable and valid?

The description of procedures is also vague in this study. How, when, and where were the tests given and under what conditions? This whole section could and should have been written more clearly and thoroughly.

### Analyses

The analyses section (Example 5.6) explains that only posttests were used and that mean comparisons were the issue. It also explains in technical terms the steps that were taken, the reasoning behind nondirectional decisions, the null hypotheses, and the alpha decision level

($\alpha < .05$). I now think that a number of other issues should have been discussed. The reasoning behind choosing multivariate analysis (more than one dependent variable, see Table 11.1; see also, Multivariate Analyses under Related Analyses in Chapter 11) should have been explained. It would also have been useful to discuss the assumptions underlying the analysis and how they were checked and met. As I already mentioned, I now believe that the alpha level and directionality issues should have been discussed, along with the null and alternative hypotheses, at the end of the statement of purpose rather than in this section. All in all, the whole section should have been made much clearer to the audience involved: TESOL members, who are primarily ESL teachers.

Nevertheless, on the basis of what you have read so far (particularly in Chapters 9 and 11), you should understand most of this explanation. What is your opinion about this section? Are you more comfortable with it than you would have been before reading this book?

## Results

My only criticism of the results section (Example 5.7) is that I fell into the ever present trap in the table of differentiating between the mean differences that were significant at $p < .01$ and and those that were significant at $p < .05$ – as though the mean differences that were significant at .01 were "more significant" than those that were significant at .05. Alpha is not a sliding scale; it is a decision point. So I should have interpreted all differences at $p < .05$ and been satisfied.

There are several things that I like about this section, however. First, I managed to explain what the results meant in terms of probability. Second, I clearly differentiated between "significant" and "meaningful."

## Discussion

I think that this section (Example 5.8) does exactly what it should. It brings the reader back to the original purpose of the study and gives direct answers to the research questions at hand. I am also satisfied with these answers and the way they are explained. Do you agree?

## Conclusions

If I were to rewrite this report, I think I would eliminate this heading (Example 5.9). I would simply end the discussion section with the first paragraph and with the discussion of further research (Example 5.10). The arguments that I present under Possible Causes seem speculative and not illuminating. I think the study would stand on its own without them. At the same time, however, remember that the three articles discussed here could be moved into the introduction as a literature review.

## References

The references (Example 5.11) appear to be adequate. All those found in the text of the article are included and I still know of none that were pertinent then that were left out. There is one error, however. One of my graduate students tried to find the Mosback (1977) reference and could not (see the References in this book for correct citation).

## Conclusion to Chapter 13

On the whole, the study criticized in this chapter seems a bit naive from my present perspective. However, given the nature and quality of the studies I have read in our field, I am not ashamed of my first effort. But I am not ashamed of what I have learned since then either. Much of it is reflected in this book. And my research has also improved. I hope that it will continue to improve. Like the field at large and other researchers, I am growing and learning.

I hope this book has succeeded in its original purpose, which was to give you a strong sense of how the organization and logic of statistical studies provide a framework for discovering patterns in probabilistic terms. By definition, studies are *never* absolute. They must instead be viewed in relative terms – relative to probability, relative to other studies, relative to theoretical frameworks, but, most of all, relative to you and your experiences in teaching language. To that end, I hope you have found this book as useful to read as I did to write.

I would like to leave you with one last thought taken from the well-known psychologist Abraham Maslow (1966: 129, 133):

There are some who will insist that "scientific" knowledge is and must be clear, unequivocally defined, unmistakable, demonstrable, repeatable, communicable, logical, rational, verbalizable, conscious. . . . But what shall we say, then, about the first stages of knowledge, the precursors of these final forms, the beginnings that each of us can easily enough experience himself. It is both useful and correct to consider as falling within that definition of knowledge all "protoknowledge," so long as its probability of being correct is greater than chance. Knowledge is then seen as more reliable or less reliable but still knowledge so long as its probability is greater than chance.

## Posttest

The following test is meant to show you how much you have learned by reading this book. No claims are made for its reliability and validity, but I think you will find the experience of taking the test worthwhile, illuminating, and maybe even enjoyable.

*Directions*: Read the following study and count the number of times that you chuckle or laugh. (Yes, I am serious!)

### An empirical analysis of psychological constructs underlying the desire to teach ESL/EFL: a satire*

**by James Dean Brown**

While it has been observed that many people go into the teaching of ESL/EFL (R. Manic, 1982), there has been insufficient empirical research into the nature of that which motivates perfectly sane people to go into such a field [at least nothing that I've read, which isn't much because I can't understand all those numbers and tables anyway].

One interesting series of case studies is now in progress in the People's Republic of China (Mei You, In typewriter), which has demonstrated with fair substantiation that there is a much higher than usual correlation ($r = 10.57$, $n = 3$) between teaching EFL and a lack of protein in the diet. The author concludes cautiously that we might all be better EFL teachers if we were to become vegetarians.

A related study (N. Vitro, Unpublishable ms.) indicated (though not explicitly stated) a strong relationship between ESL/EFL teaching and poverty [as measured by hourly wage (it was also noted that this field is one of the few "professions" dominated by an hourly wage)]. Investigating variables such as sex (or lack of same), educational background (where relevant) and years of experience,** the investigator used Kai-square analysis to invest his study with his own preconceived notion that ESL/EFL teachers are poor – in fact, significantly ($p < .000001$) poorer than national averages for welfare recipients.

While such studies point to physical and economic factors as underlying the depressing tendency to teach English as a second language, it is this author's firm, though totally unsubstantiated, belief that all second language teaching is motivated by (a) psychological construct(s). *The purpose of this paper*, then, is to ferret out these deeply embedded and clearly detrimental

---

* I would like to thank George English, Susan Scholz, Ann Graham, Peggy Hilferty, Fiona Walker and Dianne Connell for the chuckles and derision that made this study possible. Any errors are, of course, intentional.

** n.b., interestingly, he found that many teachers have only had one year of experience over, and over, and over again.

constructs [but mostly to make use of the computer (a HAL 2001) printout my friend helped me with].

The research questions in this study are as follows:

1. Do ESL/EFL teachers have psychological constructs?
2. If so, how can they be cured?
3. If they cannot be cured, should euthanasia be legalized?

The alpha level for all statistics is set at .98 (three tailed, multidirectional).

## Methods

### Subjects

It was felt that, due to the complexity of obtaining subjects (Ss) and keeping them alive, a minimal number should be used. Hence, a sample of six Ss was selected on the basis of characteristics sought by this researcher. All six were semi-literate ESL, EFL, TESL, TESOL, Peace Corps or TOEFL Prep teachers between the ages of 12 and 85, who had a minimum of zero years teaching experience and a maximum of "unknown" years experience. These six subjects were divided into six groups, all with equal sizes. Group A was the control group, while Groups B-F were out of control.

### Materials

Three measures were deemed appropriate for answering the research questions (above): 1) The Test of English as a Feudal Language (TOEFL), 2) The Test for English Speakers who Obviously Lisp (TESOL) and 3) the Farbeblind Examination of Constructs and Language (FECL).

Since the first of these measures (TOEFL) is already a widely used, respected, reliable and valid test of overall English language profligacy, the findings were based primarily on it. The other less well established measures, TESOL ($r_{xy} = .95$, $r_{xx} = .69$), and FECL ($r_{xy} = .01$, $r_{xx} = 1.53$), were used because it was felt desirable to include relevant sibilant and scatologically related variables. Thus, both ends of the spectrum of possible variables were covered.

### Procedures

The tests were administered as take home tests to most of the Ss. Some of them spilled coffee on the exam papers.

### Design

When the investigator went to the homes of various Ss to collect the tests, it was found that most were not home. As a result, the design chosen for this

TABLE 1. MEANS $(\bar{x})$, STANDARD DEVIATIONS $(s)^*$ AND NUMBER OF POSSIBLE POINTS (k)

| Group | TOEFL $\bar{x}$ | $s$ | $k$ | TESOL $\bar{x}$ | $s$ | $k$ | FECL $\bar{x}$ | $s$ | $k$ |
|---|---|---|---|---|---|---|---|---|---|
| A | 500 | 0.00 | 800 | 3 | 0 | 3 | 092 | .00 | 80 |
| B | 200 | 0.00 | 800 | 3 | 0 | 3 | 080 | .00 | 80 |
| C | 651 | 0.00 | 800 | 3 | 0 | 3 | 103 | .00 | 80 |
| D | 957 | 0.00 | 800 | 3 | 0 | 3 | 161 | .00 | 80 |
| E | 000** | 0.00 | 800 | 0** | 0 | 3 | 000** | .00 | 80 |
| F | 349 | 0.00 | 800 | 3 | 0 | 3 | 087 | .00 | 80 |

*n.b., the formula used here, $s = \sqrt{\dfrac{N - N}{\Sigma_x^2 - \dfrac{(\Sigma_x)^2}{N}}}$ turned out to be a useful

and easy to estimate shortcut because it always works out to be zero.
**n. very b., not collected because of distance of S's home from university.

TABLE 2. INTEREST CORRELATIONS

|  | TOEFL | TESOL | FECL |
|---|---|---|---|
| TOEFL | 1.00 | .64 | .94 |
| TESOL | .64 | 1.00 | .83 |
| FECL | .94 | .83 | 1.00 |

study was that of Group E, who seemed to have the best taste in three categories: drapes, furniture *and* landscaping. This was, of course, demonstrated by bivariate multinonparametric PREFAB analysis to be nonheteroscedastistic (p. < .98, df = 0).

## Results

Once the results were obtained, it was decided to change the research questions and raise the alpha level to .99. The means, standard deviations and number of possible points for the three tests and six groups are reported in Table 1.

A Right Person Produces Moments Correlation Coefficient was calculated with Groups A-F combined for each pair of tests above. These are reported in Table 2. Note the extremely high correlations ($r_{xy} = 1.00$) between each of the tests and itself. It is also interesting that the TOEFL-TESOL and TESOL-TOEFL correlations are exactly the same, as are the TOEFL-FECL and FECL-TOEFL, as well as the TESOL-FECL and FECL-TESOL correlations. Such patterns are often important in correlational analysis. In addition, it is noteworthy that TOEFL is more highly related to the FECL than to TESOL.

## Conclusions

Because the revised research questions (RQs) have little to do with the title of this paper, they will not be mentioned here. However, it *is* necessary to address these revised RQs, so that future research can be biased by them.

*RQ1*. The results showed that RQ1 was not only logically correct, but also statistically significant ($p < .99$). Therefore, we should probably limit our EFL teaching to areas of the world rich enough to treat us in the manner to which we would like to become accustomed.

*RQ2*. RQ2 was also significant ($p < .99$, $df > \infty$), which seems to indicate that we, as a field, should perhaps hold six annual conventions per year rather than one.

*RQ3*. Perhaps most interesting of all, RQ3 can be interpreted to mean that ESL/EFL teachers are significantly better people than all others tested in this experiment because they have learned through absolute necessity to laugh at themselves and poke fun at their own seriousness.

## References

Manic, R. 1982. *Masochism and the Teaching of Languages*. Rowley, Miss.: A. E. Newmanbury Press.

Mei You. In typewriter. The effects of a lack of protein on the brain cells of EFL teachers.

Vitro, N. Unpublished ms. Poverty: the baseline in ESL/EFL teaching. *Language Leering*, Vol. 4571, No. 657.

# References

American Psychological Association. 1983. *Publication manual* (3rd ed.). Washington, D.C.: American Psychological Association.

*Biomedical Computer Programs: P-series*. 1977. Berkeley: University of California Press.

Brown, J. A. C. 1954. *The social psychology of industry*. Middlesex, England: Penguin.

Brown, J. D. 1980. Newly placed students versus continuing students: Comparing proficiency. In J. C. Fisher, M. A. Clarke, and J. Schacter, eds. *On TESOL '80 building bridges: Research and practice in teaching English as a second language*, pp. 111–119. Washington, D.C.: TESOL.

Brown, J. D. 1982. An empirical analysis of psychological constructs underlying the desire to teach ESL/EFL: A satire. *TESOL Newsletter* 16 (3):9, 12.

Brown, J. D. 1983a. An exploration of morpheme-group interactions. In K. M. Bailey, M. Long, and S. Peck, eds. *Second language acquisition studies*, pp. 25–40. Rowley, Mass.: Newbury House.

Brown, J. D. 1983b. A cloze is a cloze is a cloze? In J. Handscombe, R. A. Orem, and B. P. Taylor, eds. *On TESOL '83: The question of control*, pp. 109–119. Washington, D.C.: TESOL.

Brown, J. D. 1984. A norm-referenced engineering reading test. In A. K. Pugh and J. M. Ulijn, eds. *Reading for professional purposes: Studies and practices in native and foreign languages*, pp. 213–222. London: Heinemann.

Campbell, D. T., and J. C. Stanley. 1963. Experimental and quasi-experimental designs for research on teaching. In N. L. Gage, ed. *Handbook of research on teaching*, pp. 171–246. Chicago: Rand-McNally.

Educational Testing Service. 1964. *A description of the MLA Foreign Language Proficiency Test for Teachers and Advanced Students*. Princeton, N.J.: Educational Testing Service.

Educational Testing Service. 1987. *Test of English as a Foreign Language*. Princeton, N.J.: Educational Testing Service.

Farhady, Hossein. 1982. Measures of language proficiency from the learner's perspective. *TESOL Quarterly* 16 (1):43–59.

Fisher, R. A., and F. Yates. 1963. *Statistical tables for biological, agricultural and medical research*. London: Longman.

Guilford, J. P., and Benjamin Fruchter. 1973. *Fundamental statistics in psychology and education* (5th ed.). New York: McGraw-Hill.

Huff, Darrell, and Irving Geis. 1954. *How to lie with statistics*. New York: Norton.

Krashen, Stephen D. 1977. Some issues related to the monitor model. In H. D. Brown, C. A. Yorio, and R. Crymes, eds. *On TESOL '77 teaching and*

## References

learning English as a second language: Trends in research and practice, pp. 144–158. Washington, D.C.: TESOL.

Lado, Robert. 1961. *Language testing*. New York: McGraw-Hill.

Leopold, Werner F. 1978. A child's learning of two languages. In E. M. Hatch, ed. *Second language acquisition: A book of readings*. Rowley, Mass.: Newbury House.

Maslow, Abraham H. 1966. *The psychology of science*. New York: Harper & Row.

Mosback, G. F. 1977. Service courses in ESL at the university level – How effective are they? *English Language Teaching Journal*, 31 (4): 313–318.

Pearson, E. S., and H. O. Hartley. 1963. *Biometrika Tables for Statisticians*, Vol. 1 (2nd ed.). Cambridge: Cambridge University Press.

Rosenthal, R. 1966. *Experimenter effects in behavioral research*. New York: Appleton-Century-Crofts.

Nie, N. H., C. H. Hull, J. G. Jenkins, K. Steinbrenner, and D. H. Bent. 1975. *SPSS: Statistical package for the social sciences* (2nd ed.). New York: McGraw-Hill.

Tuckman, Bruce W. 1978. *Conducting educational research* (2nd ed.). New York: Harcourt Brace Jovanovich.

# Index

A page number followed by a *t* refers to the table on that page; *f* refers to a figure.